Memoirs By The Right Honorable Sir Robert Peel, Part One: The Roman Catholic Question, 1828-29

Robert Peel

Printing Statement:

Due to the very old age and scarcity of this book,
many of the pages may be hard to read due to the
blurring of the original text, possible missing pages,
missing text, dark backgrounds and other issues
beyond our control.

Because this is such an important and rare work, we
believe it is best to reproduce this book regardless of
its original condition.

Thank you for your understanding.

MEMOIRS

BY

THE RIGHT HONOURABLE

SIR ROBERT PEEL,

BART., M.P., &c.

PUBLISHED BY THE TRUSTEES OF HIS PAPERS,

LORD MAHON (NOW EARL STANHOPE),

AND

THE RIGHT HON. EDWARD CARDWELL, M.P.

PART I,

THE ROMAN CATHOLIC QUESTION.

1828–9.

FOURTH THOUSAND.

LONDON:

JOHN MURRAY, ALBEMARLE STREET.

1857.

LONDON: PRINTED BY W. CLOWES AND SONS, STAMFORD STREET,
AND CHARING CROSS.

PREFACE.

In sending forth this volume to the public, the Editors think it proper in the first place to print the authority under which they act. It will be found appended to this Preface.

Among the numerous MSS. thus committed to their charge, those which engaged the earliest and most especial attention of the Editors were two Narratives or Memoirs drawn up by Sir Robert Peel, in his own handwriting, and placed together; the first on the Roman Catholic Question, the second on the Corn Laws. A short account of both has been given by Sir Robert himself at the beginning of the former, as contained in the present volume. But, besides these two, there is a third, to which Sir Robert does not there advert, and which in the order of time stands between them—a Memoir, drawn up probably at a much earlier period, and though of no great length, yet of high interest and value. It relates the circumstances that attended the formation of his first Ministry in 1834 and 1835, and comprises the letters that were despatched to him at Rome.

These three Memoirs it is the intention of the Editors

to publish. The first, as already stated, will be found in the present volume, and after a certain interval the other two will follow in their chronological series.

The Editors have not thought it requisite to add, in elucidation of this Memoir, any letters beyond those which it already comprised. Nor have they omitted anything from it beyond three or four names of no political importance, which, for reasons that will be obvious, they have left in blank ; and for similar reasons, more especially as applying to some persons now alive, a very few sentences or short passages which (as the Editors hereby pledge themselves) did not add in any degree to the arguments or main facts adduced on any side.

Considering the perfect order and arrangement in which these and nearly all the other MSS. were found, it would have been easy for the Editors to send them to press forthwith. That was not, however, their own opinion of their duty. Where the claims to an enduring renown are only few, or slight, it may be necessary to catch the popular favour as it flies. But, in the case of a truly great statesman, his fame has everything to gain, and nothing to lose, by well-considered delay in the publication of his papers. Such delay affords a proof that there are no party or personal motives to subserve ; it allows the party spirit in all other quarters to subside ; it both induces and enables every reader to contemplate every question in a calm, historic point of view.

According to the judgment of the present Editors, there are many things in the Peel Papers that ought not to be published as yet, and many things as affecting other persons that ought not to be published at all. In whatever they may send forth to the world, it will be their earnest desire to do full justice to the dead, without any injury to the welfare or offence to the feelings of those who still survive. Thus, as they hope, will they show themselves ever mindful of Sir Robert Peel's own and emphatic injunction, " so to exercise the discretion given to them that no honourable confidence shall be betrayed—no private feelings unnecessarily wounded—and no public interests injuriously affected."

S.
E. C.

LONDON, *April*, 1856.

CODICIL

OF THE

RIGHT HONOURABLE SIR ROBERT PEEL, BART.

DATED 24TH MARCH, 1849.

I, THE RIGHT HONOURABLE SIR ROBERT PEEL, BARONET, declare this Testamentary Disposition to be a Codicil to my last Will and Testament; and I desire that it shall remain in full force as a Codicil, or as a Testamentary Paper, notwithstanding the revocation of my existing or any future Will, except only in the case and to the extent that I shall specifically revoke or vary this Disposition. I give and bequeath to the Honourable Philip Henry Stanhope, commonly called Lord Viscount Mahon, and Edward Cardwell of Whitehall, Esquire, M.P., their Executors, Administrators, and Assigns, all the unpublished letters, papers, and documents, whether of a private or of a public nature, whether in print or in manuscript, of which I shall, at the time of my decease, be possessed, upon the trusts hereinafter declared of and concerning the same.

Considering that the collection of letters and papers referred to in this Codicil includes the whole of my confidential correspondence for a period extending from the year 1812 to the time of my decease—that during a considerable portion of that period I was employed in the service of the Crown—and that, when not so employed, I took an active part in Parliamentary business— it is highly probable that much of that correspondence will be interesting, and calculated to throw light upon the conduct and character of public men, and upon the political events of the time. I give to my Trustees full discretion with respect to the selection for publication of any portion of that correspondence. I leave it to them to decide on the period and on the mode of publication, in the full assurance that they will so exercise the discretion given to them that no honourable confidence shall be betrayed—no private feelings be unnecessarily wounded—and no public interests injuriously affected, in consequence of premature or indiscreet publication.

I am especially anxious that no portion of my correspondence with Her Majesty Queen Victoria, or with His Royal Highness Prince Albert, should be made public use of during the life of either without previous communication with parties who may be enabled to ascertain that there is no objection whatever on the part of either to the use proposed to be made of such correspondence.

I authorize my Trustees to sell or dispose of the copyright of any of the said documents if the case in which publication should be determined on by the Trustees should be one in which pecuniary compensation for such copyright could be fairly and equitably made; not meaning, however, in any way to fetter their discretion in respect to the giving of gratuitous access to the documents whenever they think such access advisable. In the case that any monies should arise from the publication of any of the said letters, papers, and documents, I authorize the said Trustees to apply the said monies in paying the costs and charges of such publication so far as the Trustees may be justly liable for such costs and charges, or other the expenses attending the execution of the trusts hereby reposed in them, and to apply the residue to the assistance or relief of deserving persons being in need of such assistance or relief engaged, or who have been engaged, in pursuits of art, literature, or science, or to apply such residue, or any part of it, in aid of institutions established for the relief or benefit of artists, or literary and scientific persons; and my said Trustees shall not be accountable to any persons whomsoever for the application of any such monies.

With these views it is my desire that the Trustees shall, with all convenient speed after my decease, collect together all the said letters, papers, and documents, and subject the same to such examination as they, in their uncontrolled discretion, shall think fit. I give them the fullest power to destroy such parts thereof as they shall think proper, and to provide for the immediate care and custody and ultimate disposition of all or any part of the said letters, papers, and documents. My Trustees will probably find it convenient to cause the said letters, papers, and documents to be brought, in the first instance, to London; and I authorize them to select and to rent, or otherwise procure, a convenient place for the deposit of the said letters, papers, and documents, during such period as they shall think fit, and to cause proper catalogues to be prepared of the same, and to employ such persons as they shall think fit, under their direction, for the purposes aforesaid, and for transcribing or editing the same, or otherwise, in relation thereto.

I authorize the Trustees to give all or any of the said letters, papers, and documents to the State Paper Office, the Trustees of the British Museum, or any other institution of the like nature, upon such arrangements as to the permanent preservation thereof as shall be satisfactory to such Trustees or Trustee. And with regard to the more permanent disposal of such of the said letters, papers, and documents as shall not have been otherwise dealt with, I recommend the Trustees, so far as shall be consistent with a due execution of the trusts hereby declared, to deposit the same at my mansion-house of Drayton Manor; and I request that the member of my family for the time being entitled to the occupation thereof will afford suitable rooms for the deposit and custody of the said letters, papers, and documents, and will concur with my Trustees in such arrangements as the latter shall think necessary for insuring the safety of the same, and for preserving to the said Trustees free access thereto, with full power for the said Trustees from time to time to regulate and prescribe the circumstances under which others shall be allowed access thereto, and to remove the same, wholly or partially, and from time to time, as they or he shall think fit. But I hereby expressly declare that these recommendations and requests shall not in any way be construed to create any trust in favour of any occupier of my said mansion-house, or to give any such occupier, or any member of my family, any estate or interest in the said letters, papers, and documents, or any of them, or in any way to abridge or restrict the discretion of the Trustees as to the custody or place of deposit of the said letters, papers, and documents, or otherwise in or as to the execution of the trusts hereby declared.

And I give to the said Viscount Mahon and Edward Cardwell, or the Trustees or Trustee for the time being, acting in the execution of this Codicil, the sum of 1000*l.* upon trust, to invest the same in their or his names or name in the public funds, or at interest on Government or real securities; and from time to time, when and as they or he shall think fit, to alter, vary, and transfer the securities in or upon which the same shall be invested into or for other securities of the same or a like nature, and to apply the dividends, interest, and annual produce of the said sum, or of the securities on which the same shall for the time being be invested, or if necessary the said principal sum, or any part thereof, in providing for the costs, charges, and expenses to be incurred in the execution of the trusts hereby declared. And I direct that the surplus of the interest, dividends, and annual proceeds of the said fund not required for the purposes of the said trusts which shall arise from time to time during the period of twenty-one years next after my decease shall be accumulated by such Trustees, and held by them, upon the trusts hereby declared of the said principal sum of 1000*l.*, and that any such surplus which may arise from time to time after the expiration of that period shall be paid from time to time to the Executors of my Will as part of my residuary estate; and that immediately on the expiration of the period hereinafter limited for the continuance and duration of the trusts hereinbefore declared of and concerning the said letters, papers, and documents, the residue, if any, of the said principal sum of 1000*l.*, and the accumulations thereof, and the securities on which the same shall be invested, and the dividends, interest, and annual produce thereof, shall be held, and go, and be disposed of, upon, and for, and subject and according to the trusts, powers, and provisoes in and by my last Will declared and contained of and concerning my residuary personal estate. And I declare that a certificate or certificates under the hands or hand of the Trustees, setting forth the sum or sums for the time being payable to my Executors on account of the surplus income of the said fund, or setting forth the balance for the time being remaining of the said sum of 1000*l*., or of the interest, dividends, and annual produce thereof, or stating that there is no balance thereof, shall be final and conclusive to all intents and purposes, and that no person entitled to any share or interest in my estate shall be entitled to call for any other account of the expenditure of the said Trustees, or to call in question any such certificate.

And I hereby direct and declare, that immediately on the expiration of the period of twenty-one years next after the time of the decease of the last survivor of my children, grandchildren, or more remote issue who shall be living at the time of my decease, or in case there shall not be any of my children, grandchildren, or more remote issue living at the time of my decease, then immediately on the expiration of the period of twenty-one years next after the time of my decease, all and singular the trusts hereinbefore declared of and concerning the said letters, papers, and documents shall absolutely cease and determine; and the Trustees shall thereupon forthwith deliver up to, or hold in trust for, the person or persons who shall then be my heir-at-law all and singular the said letters, papers, and documents, or such and so many of them as shall not have been theretofore burnt, destroyed, given away, or otherwise disposed of by the Trustees. And I hereby declare and direct that the receipt and receipts in writing of the Trustees for any sum or sums of money payable or to become payable to them or him under or by virtue of this Codicil, or in the execution of the trusts hereof, shall be a good and effectual discharge and good and effectual discharges for the money therein respectively acknowledged to be received, and shall, to all intents and purposes, discharge the person or persons taking such receipt or receipts, his, her, or their heirs, Executors, or Administrators, from seeing to the application or being accountable for the misapplication or nonapplication of the same, or any part thereof. Provided always, and I declare, that the expression Trustees herein contained shall apply to the Trustees or Trustee for the time being acting in the execution of this Codicil, whether under the above appointment or any appointment made in pursuance of the provisions for that purpose herein contained.

And I hereby direct and declare that it shall be lawful for the Trustees or Trustee of this Codicil for the time being, or for the surviving or continuing Trustees, or for the Executors or Administrators of the last surviving or continuing Trustee for the time being, as the case may be, at any time or times hereafter, and from time to time, to appoint any other person or persons to be a Trustee or Trustees of this my Codicil, either in addition to and in conjunction with the existing Trustees or in the stead of any Trustee or Trustees who shall die, or be absent from this kingdom for more than twelve months at one time, or shall desire to be discharged, or refuse, decline, or become incapable to act in the trusts aforesaid; and that upon every such appointment the premises for the time being subject to the trusts of this Codicil shall by delivery and by all other necessary assurances, if any, be assigned and transferred in such manner and so that the same may become vested in the persons who after such appointment respectively will constitute the Trustees of this Codicil; and every such new Trustee, and any and every new Trustee who may at any time be appointed by any order or decree of the Court of Chancery, shall, either before or after the said trust premises shall have become vested in him or them, have the same powers as if he or they had been originally named a Trustee or Trustees in this Codicil.

Provided also, and I hereby further declare, that the Trustees shall not be answerable the one for the other of them, and by no means for involuntary losses, nor for any loss or damage occasioned by fire, or by or through the negligence or inattention of any person or persons who may be appointed by any such Trustees under the powers and authorities hereinbefore contained to have the care and custody of the said letters, papers, and documents, or to aid in the examination, transcription, cataloguing, or publication thereof, or by or through any act which may be done or committed, or neglected or omitted to be done, by any such person or persons, nor for any loss or damage which may happen in the execution of the aforesaid trusts, or in relation thereto, except the same shall happen by or through their or his own wilful default; and also that it shall be lawful for the said Trustees to reimburse themselves or himself out of any monies which may come to their or his hands by virtue of the trusts aforesaid, or to require from the Executors of my said Will, or other the person or persons for the time being having the administration thereof, payment of all costs, charges, and expenses which may be incurred in or about the execution of the trusts hereby created and declared, or any of them, or in anywise in relation thereto. I give to each of them, the said Viscount Mahon and Edward Cardwell, the sum of 500*l.* for his own use and benefit. In witness whereof I, the said Sir Robert Peel, have to this Codicil to my last Will and Testament set my hand the 24th day of March, in the year of our Lord 1849.

Signed and declared by the said Sir Robert Peel, the Testator, as and for a Codicil to his last Will and Testament, in the presence of us (both of us being present at the same time), who in his presence, at his request, and in the presence of each other, have hereunto subscribed our names as Witnesses, } ROBERT PEEL.

JAS. W. FRESHFIELD, Jun., New Bank Buildings.
JOHN WISEMAN, same place.

MEMOIRS BY SIR R. PEEL.

PART I.

THE ROMAN CATHOLIC RELIEF BILL.

WHEN this packet shall be opened the time will probably have arrived when, without inflicting any wound on private feelings, or injury on public interests, the whole of the confidential documents and correspondence incorporated in the Memoir can be presented to the public eye.

They relate to two of the most important events in my political career, the removal of Roman Catholic Disabilities in 1829, and the repeal of the Corn Laws in 1846.

Those of the documents which I have selected for publication as part of this Memoir appear to me to be not only the most important, but to be all that are necessary or useful for the complete elucidation of the events to which they refer. My only motive for selection was the fear of encumbering the narrative with documents irrelevant or superfluous. The separate packets marked X and Y contain, however, every other letter and paper in my possession having the

B

slightest reference to the events of 1829 and 1846 respectively; and if those who may superintend the publication of this Memoir shall consider that the addition of any of the reserved papers would throw more light on the transactions referred to, or would render more complete justice to others who took a part with me in those transactions, it is my express injunction that such papers also may be introduced as part of this Memoir or appended to it.

I propose to connect the documents by a brief narrative of events, and I shall probably be impelled, by feelings which it is difficult for me to restrain, to comment upon those events and upon their consequences; but it is upon the documents themselves, and not upon the narrative or comments, that I rely for the explanation of my motives and the vindication of my conduct.

It is my firm conviction that not one of these documents was written with a view to subsequent publication. They relate and observe upon occurrences as they took place from day to day, and they faithfully reflect the feelings and impressions to which such occurrences gave rise.

I propose to keep the two transactions—that of 1829 and that of 1846 (separated as they are as well by the character of the subjects to which they refer as by a long interval of time) entirely distinct, and for the present to speak exclusively of the former of these transactions—the removal of the Roman Catholic Disabilities.

To that removal I had offered, from my entrance into Parliament, an unvarying and decided opposition,

an opposition which certainly did not originate in any
views of personal political advantage. When in the
year 1812 I voted against the Resolution in favour of
concession—moved by Mr. Canning after the death of
Mr. Perceval, and carried by a majority of 235 to 106—
I could not expect that by that vote I was contributing
to my political advancement.

The grounds on which my opposition was rested are
fully developed in a speech delivered by me in the year
1817.

It appeared to me that the question of Catholic
Emancipation was one much more complicated and
extensive in its bearings than it was considered to be
by the greater part of the very able and distinguished
men who supported the claims of the Roman Catholics.

Adverting to the past history of Ireland—her geo-
graphical position—her social state in respect to the
tenure of property, and the number and religious denominations of her people—I thought it would be extremely difficult to reconcile the perfect equality of civil
privilege, or rather the *bonâ fide* practical application
of that principle, with those objects on the inviolable
maintenance of which the friends and the opponents
of Catholic Emancipation were completely agreed—
namely, the Legislative Union, and the Established
Church in Ireland as guaranteed by the Act of Union.

The Relief Bill of Mr. Grattan, introduced in 1813,
declared in its preamble that the Protestant Episcopal
Church of England and Ireland was established permanently and inviolably, and that it would tend to
promote the interest of the same, and to strengthen the

free constitution of which it is an essential part, if the disqualifications under which the Roman Catholics laboured were removed.

It assumed that such removal would put an end to all religious jealousies between His Majesty's subjects, and bury in oblivion all animosities between Great Britain and Ireland.

I did not participate in the opinions or anticipations thus expressed.

I was not indeed insensible to the manifest evil of subjecting to incapacity and disqualification a class of His Majesty's subjects rapidly increasing in wealth, numbers, and importance, and constituting the vast majority of the population of one part of the United Kingdom. I was fully aware also that that evil had been aggravated by the inconsiderate arrangement made in 1793, when the elective franchise was lavishly conferred on the pauper tenantry of Ireland. But there were on the other hand many considerations which appeared to me not sufficiently weighed by the advocates of concession.

There was the danger of abolishing tests which had been established for the express purpose of giving to the Legislature a Protestant character—tests which had been established not upon vague constitutional theories, but after practical experience of the evils which had been inflicted and the dangers which had been incurred by the struggles for ascendancy, at periods not remote from the present.

There was the danger that the removal of civil disabilities might materially alter the relations in which the Roman Catholic religion stood to the State. I saw indeed no satisfactory solution of the difficulties with which those relations were encompassed under the existing state of the law, but I apprehended that they might be materially increased by the total removal of political incapacities from the professors of the Roman Catholic religion.

The connection of that religion with the most important events in the domestic history of this country— the forcible transfer of its temporal possessions to the reformed Church—the recognition of an external spiritual authority—the natural sympathies (in religious matters at least) with foreign nations acknowledging the same authority—the peremptory refusal by the Irish Roman Catholics to submit to those restrictions to which in all other countries, Protestant or Catholic, the ecclesiastical appointments in the Church of Rome and the intercourse with the Papal See were subject— the impossibility of imposing such restrictions by the mere will of the Legislature—these and other similar considerations presented to my mind matter for grave reflection—for serious misgiving, whether there could be that identity of interest and feeling which would permit the practical application of the principle of perfect civil equality in the administration of Irish affairs, and whether, if the equality were nominal and not practical, there would be satisfaction and contentment on the part of the Roman Catholics.

The Roman Catholic Church, with its historical associations—its system of complete organization and discipline—its peculiar tenets and ministrations, calculated and intended to exercise a control not merely spiritual over those who profess its faith, is an institution wholly differing in its political bearings and influence from other forms of religious belief not in accordance with the Established Church.

Whatever course might be pursued with regard to an institution so powerful and so anomalous in its relations to the government of this country—whether after the establishment of civil equality that institution should be left perfectly independent of and unrecognized by the State—whether it should receive a limited and qualified endowment—whether (as some proposed) it should be placed, in Ireland at least, on a footing of equality with the Established Church, there was in my opinion little hope of a final and satisfactory arrangement on that head—little hope of establishing religious harmony, or of excluding the influences of religious discord from the civil relations of society.

It appeared to me that admissions were made from time to time by the most able and eminent of the advocates of concession, little calculated to banish the apprehensions of its opponents.

Shortly before his decease Mr. Pitt had declared his opinion, " that in no possible case previous to the Union could the privileges demanded by the Roman Catholics be given consistently with a due regard to the Protestant interest in Ireland—to the internal tranquillity of that kingdom, the frame and structure of our constitution, or the probability of the permanent connection of Ireland with this country." *

* In the debate, 14th May, 1805.

Nearly twenty years afterwards Mr. Plunket* avowed his opinion, " that speaking of the Protestant Established Church in a political point of view, he had no hesitation to state that the existence of it was the great bond of union between the two countries; and that if ever that unfortunate moment should arrive when they would rashly lay their hands on the property of the Church to rob it of its rights, they would seal the doom and terminate the connection between the two countries."

These and many similar declarations of opinion that might be cited justified the apprehension that, notwithstanding the removal of political disabilities, adverse interests and conflicting views of public policy would prevent the harmonious co-operation of Protestant and Roman Catholic in the government of Ireland.

The Legislative Union no doubt materially affected the position of the Roman Catholics in this respect, that the influence over legislation which might have been predominant in an Irish parliament, became comparatively powerless in the Parliament of the United Kingdom. But the Legislative Union did not affect in the same degree the position of the Roman Catholics in respect to their influence on the administration of the executive government in Ireland. The establishment of the theoretical equality of civil privileges appeared to imply an equal claim for the practical enjoyment of the confidence and favour of the Crown, not merely as to subordinate, but as to the highest

* Debate, 6th May, 1824.

public trusts. I did not think it probable that that claim could be safely admitted. I thought the Government of Ireland, however desirous impartially to exercise its functions and administer its patronage, must remain in its general character essentially Protestant, if it were to act in harmony with the Government here, and to maintain inviolate the Act of Union, and that institution which Mr. Plunket considered essential to the connection between the two countries— the Established Church in Ireland.

If it were necessary for such purposes that the Government of Ireland should retain its Protestant character, it was a matter for serious consideration whether it were not better that that character should be impressed upon it by the law rather than by the discretionary exercise of prerogative controlling the assumption of the law, that there being an identity of interest between Protestant and Catholic, there ought to be an equal capacity for privilege.

It was upon the general grounds above indicated that I had uniformly offered my opposition to the general repeal of the disabling laws. But that opposition was limited, and it was uniformly declared by me to be limited, to the walls of Parliament. I never attempted to control the free discretion of Parliament on a question demanding the exercise of the calmest judgment, by external appeals to passions and prejudices easily excited on religious subjects, and especially on that subject.

I entered into no cabals against those from whom I differed on the Catholic question. I contracted no political engagements with those with whom I concurred, except that sort of tacit and implied engagement which is the natural consequence of a prominent part taken in debate for a long period of time. Whatever may be the obligations which such an engagement implies, no temptation of private interest or personal ambition should have induced me to disregard the lightest of them ; but I did not permit such obligations for one moment to countervail that higher obligation which I had contracted when I entered into the service of the Crown, and which I had ratified by the solemn oath " that I would, in all matters to be treated and debated in Council, faithfully, openly, and truly declare my mind and opinion, according to my heart and conscience."

I make the full admission that, from the part I had uniformly taken on the Catholic question—from the confidence reposed in me on that account—from my position in the Government—from my position in Parliament as the representative of the University of Oxford—that interest which I will call by the comprehensive name of the Protestant interest had an especial claim upon my devotion and my faithful service. And if the duty which that acknowledged claim imposed upon me were this—that in a crisis of extreme difficulty I should calmly contemplate and compare the dangers with which the Protestant interest was threatened from different quarters—that I should advise the course which I believed to be the least unsafe—that having advised and adopted I should resolutely adhere to it—that I should disregard every selfish consideration—that I should prefer obloquy and reproach to the aggravation of existing evils, by concealing my real opinion, and by maintaining the false show of personal consistency—if this were the duty imposed upon me, I fearlessly assert that it was most faithfully and scrupulously discharged.

It will be for those who dispassionately review the documentary evidence incorporated into this Memoir, to determine whether the assertion thus confidently made be fully borne out or not. It will be for them to determine whether that evidence does not throw light upon much that has hitherto remained obscure—whether it does not account for the apparent abruptness of the change of counsel, and for the maintenance of that reserve which was apparently unnecessary after the course to be taken had been actually resolved upon.

It will be seen from that evidence whether there was any disposition on my part to truckle to or to coquet with agitation, or to shrink from the responsibility of using any legal power which could be rendered available for the repression of disorder in Ireland, or for the control of that dangerous influence which it was sought to establish by means of political confederacies, and of an organized excitement of the public mind.

A review of the events which took place in Ireland in the course of the year 1828, and of the discussions in Parliament during the Session of that year, is indispensable to a correct understanding of the motives and conduct of those who resolved to recommend the adjustment of the Catholic question at the commencement of the following Session.

In the month of January, 1828, I received the following letter from the Duke of Wellington, inviting me to assist him in the formation of a new Government, rendered necessary by the voluntary abdication of Lord Ripon and his colleagues, shortly before the intended meeting of Parliament.

Duke of WELLINGTON to Mr. PEEL.

"London, Jan. 9, 1828.

"MY DEAR PEEL,

"I enclose a letter which I received from Lord Lyndhurst this morning, in consequence of which, having received him shortly after eight o'clock, he told me that, the Government being dissolved, the King wished to speak to me along with him.

"I went to Windsor with him immediately; and His Majesty told me that he wished me to form a Government of which I should be the head. I told His Majesty that I was so situated professionally that I could not say that I would form a Government of which I should be the head without consulting with others. That I could not say I could form a Government at all without such previous consultation; but that, if he would give me a little time, and leave to go to town to consult with others, I would inquire and see what could be done, and report to him the result.

"I then inquired what he wished—whether he had any wishes for any particular persons, or any objections to any. He said that he thought the Government must be composed of persons of both opinions with respect to

the Roman Catholic question; that he approved of all
his late and former servants; and that he had no objection to anybody excepting to Lord Grey. He afterwards expressed a wish to retain the Duke of Devon-
shire and Lord Carlisle in his service; and he spoke
highly of Lord Lansdowne and Lord Dudley; but upon
the whole he left me *carte blanche*, with the single
exception above mentioned; and he repeatedly desired
that I would form for him a strong Government. The
Chancellor was present.

" Now, my dear Peel, I entreat you to come to town,
in order that I may consult with you and have the
benefit of your co-operation in the execution of this
interesting commission. You will see that the whole
case is before you for discussion. I have declined to
make myself the head of the Government unless upon
discussion with my friends it should appear desirable;
and excepting Lord Lyndhurst, who it must be understood is in office, everything else is open to all mankind
excepting one person.

" I have sent for nobody else, nor shall I see anybody till you come, which I hope you will early in the
morning. I send to your house to desire that a room
may be prepared for you in case you should come this
night.

" Believe me,

" Ever yours most sincerely,

" WELLINGTON.

" The King said that it was to be understood that
the Roman Catholic question was not to be made a

Cabinet question; that there was to be a Protestant Lord Chancellor, a Protestant Lord Lieutenant, and a Protestant Lord Chancellor in Ireland."

I obeyed, though not without great reluctance, the summons thus received.

I had no desire whatever to resume office, and I foresaw great difficulty in the conduct of public affairs, on account of the state of parties and the position of public men in reference to the state of Ireland and the Catholic question.

It appeared to me on the one hand that the attempt to form an united Government on the principle of resistance to the claims of the Roman Catholics was perfectly hopeless. In the preceding year the measure of concession had been negatived in the House of Commons by a majority of four votes only in a very full House, the numbers being 276 to 272.

On the other hand it was very doubtful whether, after the events which had succeeded the retirement of Lord Liverpool—the schism among the members of his administration—the adherence of some to Mr. Canning—the separation of others—they could now be reunited in office. It was with my cordial concurrence that the endeavour to effect this reunion was made. It was so far successful that Mr. Huskisson, Lord Palmerston, and Mr. Charles Grant became members of the Duke of Wellington's Cabinet. Lord Dudley, Mr. William Lamb, and other friends of Mr. Canning who had not been connected with Lord Liverpool's

Government, consented also to lend their assistance to the Duke of Wellington.

The following is a Memorandum communicated by me to the Duke (I forget whether before or after my first interview with him), in which I explained my views as to the basis on which the new Government should be constituted :—

Mr. PEEL'S MEMORANDUM, Jan. 1828.

" I do not think that an efficient Government can be formed on the principle rigidly adhered to of replacing the seceding members of Lord Liverpool's administration.

" If it be thought that that principle ought to be adhered to, I most cheerfully acquiesce to this extent : I will decline all offers of office for myself; I will be governed by the principle so far as exclusion from office is concerned.

" If I am to take office, or called upon for an opinion respecting the formation of a Government, I must, with the utmost pain to myself, disregard many considerations of private esteem and friendship, which nothing but a sincere and overpowering sense of public duty would induce me to disregard.

" I see no alternative but an attempt to reunite the most efficient members of Lord Liverpool's administration, calling to their aid the abilities of others who are willing cordially to co-operate with them in an administration of which the Duke of Wellington shall be the head, in the usual station and with the full power of Prime Minister.

" The Government ought, in my opinion, to be

strengthened in the House of Lords by the addition of one or two Peers qualified to take a part in debate. If Lord Aberdeen and Lord Ellenborough could be included, it would tend greatly, in my opinion, to the advantage of the Government and of the public service. With neither one nor the other have I the slightest political connection. Both differ from me on the Catholic question. My motives therefore for suggesting them are entirely disinterested.

" Mr. Goulburn has, in my opinion, a full claim for efficient Cabinet office ; and I earnestly hope that there may be no insuperable difficulty, on account of recent differences, to admit Mr. Herries into the Cabinet also. 1 have had no communication with him, direct or indirect. I suggest his name merely on the principle on which I suggest those of Lord Ellenborough and Lord Aberdeen."

I find two letters addressed by me immediately after the formation of the Government to my friend Mr. Gregory, Under Secretary to the Lord Lieutenant of Ireland, written without the reserve of formal communications, and perhaps more faithfully on that account expressing the feelings and opinions of the writer.

Mr. PEEL to Mr. GREGORY.

(Most private.)

" Whitehall Gardens, Jan. 18, 1828.

" MY DEAR GREGORY,

" I hope that the basis of the Government is settled—that that arrangement is made which appears

to me to present the only satisfactory method of meeting the difficulties of the country—namely, the reunion
in an administration of former colleagues—the recon-
struction of a Government on the principle of Lord
Liverpool's Government.

" I will say at once that, looking at the present state
of this country in its various relations, domestic and
foreign—looking at the conflicting and nicely-balanced
interests at home—political, commercial, religious—the
menacing attitude of foreign powers towards each other
—I never could have consented to form part of an
administration proceeding upon an exclusive basis, till
every honest and sincere effort had been exhausted to
unite in the public service men of principles correspond-
ing to those which were entertained by the administration of Lord Liverpool.

" I care not for the dissatisfaction of ultra-Tories.
This country ought not, and cannot, be governed upon
any other principles than those of firmness no doubt,
but of firmness combined with moderation.

" If reasonable and honourable offers had been rejected—if personal animosities, felt only on one side,
had precluded union—it would have been no common
difficulty that should prevent me from fighting to the
last; but then I must fight with a safe conscience and
an honest conviction that the utmost has been done on
the side of moderation and temper.

" I must be quite sure that such men as Lamb have
rejected *fair* offers before I can make a common cause
with inferior men, and commit the public service to
their hands.

" My last week has been spent in unceasing efforts
to promote the reunion of the old party. Some sacrifices—not of principle, but of personal feeling towards
individuals—are unavoidable. God knows they are
most painful.

" Ever affectionately yours,

" R. PEEL."

Mr. PEEL to Mr. GREGORY.

" Whitehall, Feb. 1, 1828.

" MY DEAR GREGORY,

" Look at the date of the enclosed.

" I had begun it and nearly finished it almost a
fortnight since, but I have been so overwhelmed, and
I might say distracted, by business—the unavoidable
consequence of being called on to take an active part
in public affairs a fortnight before the meeting of Parliament—that everything but the immediate object of
consideration was driven out of my head.

" My scrap, however, will show you that in the midst
of my turmoil you were not absent from my thoughts.

" Ever affectionately yours,

" ROBERT PEEL."

(Most private.)

" What must have been the inevitable fate of a
Government composed of Goulburn, Sir John Beckett,
Wetherell, and myself? Supported by very warm
friends no doubt, but those warm friends being pros-
perous country gentlemen, foxhunters, &c. &c., most
excellent men, who will attend one night, but who will
not leave their favourite pursuits to sit up till two or

three o'clock fighting questions of detail, on which, however, a Government must have a majority, we could not have stood creditably a fortnight.

" I say this as a *raison de plus*. I for one, on other grounds, could not be a party."

Mr. GREGORY to Mr. PEEL.

(Confidential.)

" Phœnix Park, Feb. 3, 1828.

" MY DEAR PEEL,

" I feel more than thankful, for I feel gratified beyond measure at the receipt of your letter: that you should in the midst of your difficulties and incessant labours think of an absent friend, and open yourself without reserve, is more than I could have expected. I wish I had kept a copy of a letter I wrote to Lord Talbot about ten days since, that I might send it to you, and you would read how fully aware I was of the arduous situation in which you are placed, the personal sacrifices to be made, and the impracticability of forming an administration purely Protestant. That the Duke of Wellington and you have done all that honestly and conscientiously could be effected, none of your friends ought to doubt, and having done so they should be satisfied. I think your Government will settle well, and that the angry ultra-Tory feeling will subside, and, the anger removed, support follow. There was no middle course to be pursued. You must either have formed the mixed Government of which you are now composed, or have thrown up the reins to the Whigs, and have given to them full dominion. I have heard some ultra-Tories declare they would have preferred the latter. It is not necessary to inquire whether reason or common sense were consulted in such declarations. I am very glad that Lamb has consented to remain; he is an honourable man, with an excellent understanding; he has kept some very bad company in Ireland, and profited by so doing; when he returns I make no doubt he will shake them off. I have no acquaintance with Lord Anglesey; he was not long since strongly prejudiced against me, and perhaps still continues to be; if so, he has his remedy in his own hands.

" God bless you, my dear Peel, and may He prosper and reward your honest and arduous undertaking.

" Always affectionately yours,

" H. GREGORY.

" I am glad you marked your letter 'most secret,' as it precludes my showing it to any one. There is a community of information and gossip in this town, that makes it impossible to communicate anything without its becoming a topic of general conversation."

Lord Anglesey undertook the duties of Lord Lieutenant of Ireland; Mr. William Lamb (afterwards Lord Melbourne) those of Chief Secretary.

Lord Anglesey replaced Lord Wellesley in the appointment of Lord Lieutenant.

The following letters passed between Lord Wellesley and me on the occasion of my resumption of office, and

the almost simultaneous relinquishment of it by Lord
Wellesley.

They will show the friendly relation in which we
had stood to each other during our former official connection in the administration of Lord Liverpool.

Mr. PEEL to Lord WELLESLEY.

(Private.)

" Whitehall, Jan. 29, 1828.

" MY DEAR LORD,

" It was not until this day that I have been
enabled to take possession of the office to which His
Majesty has been pleased to re-appoint me.

" I cannot transmit to you the accompanying formal
notification of my appointment without expressing my
sincere regret that, in pursuance of arrangements made
in the interval of my retirement from office, the relation in which I stood to your Excellency for many
years, and in which I again stand at the present
moment, is so soon to be terminated.

" The confidential intercourse which grew out of
that relation has left upon my mind a deep impression,
which I characterize by too cold a phrase when I term
it an impression of sincere respect and esteem.

" I am suffering from indisposition upon which I had
no right to calculate—the hooping-cough ; but it shall
not deprive me of the satisfaction of calling upon you
at any time that may be convenient to your Excellency,
provided you have no fear of infection—of which I

apprehend there is no risk whatever to those who have once been affected by the cough.

" I have, &c.,

" ROBERT PEEL."

Lord WELLESLEY to Mr. PEEL.

(Private.)

" Hyde Park, Jan. 30, 1828.

" MY DEAR SIR,

" It was a painful addition to my regret, on the occasion of your retirement from office, that no opportunity was afforded to me of expressing my sense of the uninterrupted and honourable confidence and assistance which I experienced from you for so many years in the arduous duties of the Government of Ireland. Your most acceptable letter of the 29th instant enables me to offer to you now those assurances of gratitude, respect, and esteem, which, to my sincere concern, have been so long delayed. Although these sentiments have not before reached you in the manner which would have been most suitable to the subject, I trust that you have not been unacquainted with the real impressions which your kindness and high character have fixed in my mind, and which it is always a matter of the most genuine satisfaction to me to declare.

" I am very anxious to communicate with you in the same unreserved confidence so long subsisting between us on the state of Ireland; and I shall be happy to wait on you for that purpose, or to receive you here at any time which you may appoint.

" I am concerned to hear that you are afflicted by so troublesome a complaint as the hooping-cough; I am under no alarm respecting it, having been severely visited by it early in life.

" I apprehend that it may be necessary for you to be cautious at this season, and I therefore hope you will permit me to have the pleasure of seeing you at your house.

" I have, &c.

" WELLESLEY."

Of questions relating to Ireland, requiring immediate consideration and decision, the most important one was as to the policy of continuing the Act passed in the year 1825, 6 George IV. chapter 4, relating to unlawful societies in Ireland.

The main object of this Act was the suppression of the Roman Catholic Association, and the prevention of similar confederacies in Ireland.

The duration of this Act was limited, and, unless continued, it would expire at the end of the Session of 1828.

After personal communication on this subject with Mr. Lamb, I received from him the accompanying note, with an extract from a letter from Lord Anglesey, and the memorandum dated the 29th March prepared by himself.

The documents that follow, or portions of them, so immediately relate to this particular subject, that it will be convenient to insert them here consecutively, and, though other matters may be occasionally adverted to, it is better to insert the letters and papers *in extenso* than to make extracts from them.

A clearer view will thus be had of the opinions expressed with regard to the policy of continuing the Act of 1825.

Mr. LAMB to Mr. PEEL.

" Having had yesterday some conversation with the Duke of Wellington upon the question of the renewal of the Act for the Suppression of Unlawful Societies in Ireland, and he having expressed a wish that we should have a meeting upon the subject before I go to Ireland for the Easter recess, I send you an extract of a letter from Lord Anglesey dated the 20th instant, in order to put you in possession of the opinion which he is inclined to form upon the question.

" Yours faithfully,
" WM. LAMB."

Lord ANGLESEY to Mr. LAMB.

(Extract.)

" Do keep matters quiet in Parliament, if possible. The less that is said of Catholic and Protestant the better. It would be presumptuous to form an opinion, or even a sanguine hope, in so short a time, yet I cannot but think that there is much and reciprocal inclination to get rid of the bugbear and to soften down asperities.

" Amongst the more moderate I am certain this is

the case, and I am by no means sure that even the most violent would not be glad to have an excuse for being less violent.

" Even at the Association they are at a loss to keep up the extreme irritation they had accomplished, and if they find that they are not violently opposed, and that there is no disposition on the part of the Government to coercion, I do believe that they will dwindle into moderation.

" If, however, we have a mind to have a *good blaze* again, we may at once command it by re-enacting the expiring Bill, and when we have even improved it and rendered it perfect, we shall find that it will not be acted upon. In short, I will back Messrs. O'Connell's and Sheil's and others' evasions against the Crown lawyers' laws. I am calling for opinions upon this most momentous subject from the several authorities, and am getting all the information I can from sensible and dispassionate people, and my conviction is, that the great bulk of opinion will be in favour of allowing the Bill to go out without notice or observation."

Mr. LAMB to Mr. PEEL.

" Whitehall, March 29, 1828.

" I am entirely of opinion that if a law could be framed which should have the effect of preventing perpetual debates in Dublin upon Roman Catholic affairs, it would be a result highly to be desired, would be highly advantageous to the political objects of the Roman Catholics, and would, however it might be op-

posed and contemned in public, be secretly approved
by all the more moderate and rational amongst themselves and their supporters. It is, however, perfectly
clear that this Act of the 6th George IV. chap. 4, has
not answered this purpose, and should it be re-enacted,
it will hardly be thought prudent now to carry the provisions of it into stricter execution than before. As it
stands, it seems rather to facilitate by, as it were, permitting and legalising the proceedings of the Association to the extent to which they are carried, than to
prevent or impede them. Having failed in fulfilling
its main object, can it be said to have fulfilled any
other advantageous purpose? It has not prevented the
collection of the Rent, nor do I believe that it has
much obstructed any other measure which they had
either the power or the inclination to adopt.

" With respect to the third section of the Act, which
was directed to the suppression of the Orange lodges, it
must be observed, that when the formation of secret
societies has become such an inveterate habit as it has
in Ireland, it is very difficult indeed to prevent them
by law, and I should very much doubt, whatever may
be held forth and professed, whether this law has in
reality been effectual for this purpose. Secret societies,
bound together by secret oaths, sound very formidable,
but it appears to me that more real mischief is to be
apprehended, in the present state of Ireland, from open
demonstrations of party feeling, such as processions
upon particular days, &c. &c., as by them the public
peace is hazarded and the danger of conflict and bloodshed incurred. Now, against such processions, &c. &c.,

this law provides no security, it having been judicially
laid down by one of the judges, and no doubt rightly,
that, in order to bring such a procession within the prohibition of the Act, you must prove that the individuals
walk in it as an illegal society, which of course it is
very difficult to do. At the same time I am willing to
admit that a general opinion has prevailed amongst the
Protestants that such processions are forbidden by this
Act, and I believe that they have been discontinued to
a great degree in consequence of it, and I should not
be surprised, on the contrary I should rather expect,
that they would be resumed upon its expiration.

"Having now considered shortly the actual effect of
the law, I proceed to that which is no less important,
namely, the general impression which will be produced
upon the public mind either by renewing it or suffering
it to expire. I pass over the obvious topic of the irritation, &c., of the Roman Catholic body, but it appears
to me certain that the mere re-enacting of this law,
with the understanding that the Government is satisfied
with the operation which it has already had, will be in
no degree satisfactory to the Protestants, the more eager
of whom demand a measure of strength enough to suppress the Roman Catholic Association, and will reject
and despise any enactments that fall short of this degree of vigour. Such a course would be exasperating
to the Roman Catholics without being conciliatory to
the other party, and would wear towards both the worst
character of a measure, viz., that of weakness.

"It must also be remembered that you would take a
debate, as upon the former occasion of this Bill, upon

the whole state of Ireland in the most unfavourable form, because you bring it on yourselves by proposing the renewal of a coercive law, and thereby relieve your opponents of all appearance of unnecessarily starting contentions and irritating topics, an appearance which always, to a certain degree, belongs to a motion originated by themselves. You also expose your own supporters to all the odium and unpopularity consequent upon their votes, which, in my opinion, never should be done without very good and sufficient cause.

"There are also circumstances at present supposed to exist in the state of the Roman Catholic body which deserve to be taken into consideration; there is evidently a coolness growing up between the Roman Catholic Association and the supporters of the Roman Catholic question. There is also said to prevail, in those who have hitherto been the leaders of the Association, a considerable jealousy of another party, which is said to be obtaining influence in that assembly, and it is confidently asserted that great alarm is excited in the minds of the Roman Catholic prelates by the power which the Association assumes and exercises over the parochial clergy. I know how fallacious rumours, and even appearances, of this nature are apt to be, and therefore I do not wish them to be relied upon or taken for more than they are worth; but it is evident that if any differences of this nature are taking place, you will at once put an end to them and reconcile and reunite all parties by bringing forward this measure.

"Now what are the inconveniences of suffering the Act to expire, and leaving the Roman Catholic Association, the Orange Lodges, &c. &c., to the ordinary course of the law? No serious danger is to be apprehended, and if either party or both break out into acts of violence, or adopt dangerous courses, we shall be fully justified in enforcing the law against them both, or if the law should be insufficient, we shall apply to Parliament for extraordinary measures with a clearer case and a more general concurrence.

" WM. LAMB."

Mr. PEEL to Mr. LAMB.

" Whitehall, March 31, 1828.

" MY DEAR SIR,

" I enclose a Memorandum on the Act relating to the Association. You quite understand the view with which I prepared it, and that it is entirely a confidential paper.

" Ever most truly yours,
" ROBERT PEEL."

Mr. PEEL'S MEMORANDUM.

(Secret and confidential.)

" Before it is determined whether the Act 6 George IV. chap. 4, the Act directed against the Roman Catholic Association and against the Orange Societies, ought to be renewed, modified, or permitted to expire, it will be very convenient to the Government to have precise information upon the present state of the facts to which it is material to advert.

"That information will be conveyed in answers to the following queries.

"What is the exact constitution of that body, whatever be its name (Committee, Association, Assembly, &c. &c.), which now meets from time to time in Dublin for the management of the affairs of the Roman Catholics?

"Was there not, independent of that body, another body which called itself the Fourteen Days Association; and which met about the time of the meeting of Parliament, professedly for the purpose of preparing petitions to the Legislature relating to the interests of the Roman Catholic body? How was this latter body constituted?

"If the body first referred to meets from time to time, and adjourns its meetings to some time beyond fourteen days from its first meeting, does it not sit in contravention of the first clause of the Act, and would not this violation of the law be capable of distinct and easy proof in a court of justice?

"In the newspapers there constantly appears an account of the weekly receipts of what is called the Catholic Rent. The first clause of the Act provides that every assembly, the members of which shall appoint any person to receive any money or contributions from His Majesty's subjects, shall be deemed an unlawful combination, and the meetings thereof shall be unlawful assemblies.

"Now in what mode and under what regulations is the Catholic Rent received?

"Are there not persons employed by some society or body of persons to collect this rent, or to receive it?

" Would there be any difficulty in the proof of the collection or receipt of this rent in such a manner as manifestly to subject the parties concerned in the collection or receipt to the provisions of the Statute?

" It is not pretended, I believe, that the rent is collected or received by individuals acting merely as individuals, and not being authorised to act by any society or body of persons. If this be so, might not the collections or receipts of the rent be at once evidence of the illegality of a body which authorised it? or could it be argued successfully that the present Catholic Association and the collection of rent were covered by the exceptions contained in the 8th and 9th clauses of the Act?

" The information suggested in the above queries appears to be material before the Government finally determines on the course to be pursued with respect to the continuance or abandonment of the Act.

" We ought very maturely to consider the grounds on which either renewal or abandonment is to be rested in Parliament—not only with reference to our own course in Parliament, but with reference to public impression in Ireland.

" I do not disguise from myself the difficulty of renewing an Act which has not effected its purpose— either through tacit acquiescence in its enactments, or by the practical enforcement of them by the Government. We cannot deny that the law has been on the Statute Book three years, and that the Catholic Association exists apparently in defiance of it, without any abatement of violence, and without the discontinuance of any proceeding that was before deemed dangerous, except perhaps that there has been less of interference in the prosecution or defence of criminal cases.

" But why has the law not been enforced?

" This question we must consider, because we must be prepared to answer it.

" If there had been attempts to enforce the law, and they had failed—if the proof of illegality was so difficult to be procured, that no honest jury could convict— or if, the proof of guilt being clear, juries had acquitted, we should have good ground either for abandoning the law as impracticable, or for asking for its amendment.

" But what is the distinct ground which we shall now allege for permitting the law to expire?

" May not Parliament fairly say to the Executive Government, ' We gave you at your own request the powers which you thought necessary for the control of a certain evil. That evil exists in an undiminished degree. Why do you part with the power you took, in order that you might be enabled to suppress it? Why have you never once tried the powers which you asked for? The Act declares that the continuance of meetings beyond fourteen days shall be illegal; that the collection of money by the members of such meetings shall be illegal. Every Irish newspaper affords a strong presumption at least that the Act is violated —and violated in a manner of which a court of justice would take cognizance. Why decline the appeal to a court of justice? If you do not make the appeal, and if you at the same time admit the evil to be undiminished, you, the Government, have no right to say to Parlia-

ment that it has passed an useless and inoperative law.'
The Parliament have a much better right to say to you,
' We gave you the powers you demanded, and you have
been afraid even to try their efficacy.'

" It certainly does appear to me that the position of
the Government in abandoning the law without having
made a trial of it, is a very embarrassing one.   Whatever course we may pursue, we ought to look at the full
extent of the difficulties which may attend it.

" When I left this office in April of last year, directions had been given for the prosecution of Mr. Sheil—
one of the most active members of the Association—for
seditious language uttered by him at some public
meeting.

" I believe the prosecution was afterwards abandoned, but I do not know under what circumstances ;
the prosecution was not under the Act 6th George IV.;
but I mention the intention to prosecute, and subsequent abandonment of it, because I think the worst
part of the case of the Executive Government is, that
it has remained a quiet spectator of an increasing evil,
and that it has been too much afraid of the possible
failure of an attempt to enforce the law.   It is now,
perhaps, too late to enforce the particular statute 6th
George IV., because as it stands limited at present, it
would expire before any conviction could be had under it.

" I have written this paper, not so much with the
intention of expressing any strong opinion of my own
as to the particular course to be pursued, as with that
of bringing the whole case under the view of the Irish
Government, and of submitting to its consideration the

difficulties of allowing the law to expire, as well as those of continuing it in operation.

" Those provisions of the law which affect Orange Societies and secret societies of all kinds deserve attention also—not merely with reference to the express enactments which they contain, but with reference to the impression which may arise from their repeal, and the effects of that impression upon the tranquillity of the country.

" ROBERT PEEL.

" Whitehall, March 31, 1828."

Lord ANGLESEY to Mr. PEEL.

" Dublin Castle, March 31, 1828.

" MY DEAR MR. PEEL,

" As I have kept up a communication with Mr. Lamb, and have not had anything very particular to relate, I have refrained from taking up your time at a moment when you must be sufficiently occupied by much and most important business.

" I do not know precisely to what extent you would like me to carry my communications,—whether it is desirable that I should enter into periodical and minute details, or confine myself to subjects of importance only as they may arise.

" I have just closed the examination of the Police and Constabulary reports of the two last months, and I have also received several from the Judges on circuit.

" I should say that neither are unfavourable. I do not collect that much mischief is abroad either of a political or of a religious character.

c 3

" Tipperary is, as I am told it ever has been, the grand focus of disturbance ; and Leitrim stands next on the list for disorder and outrage.

" In these counties the Rockite system prevails to a distressing extent.

" In a few others there are apprehensions that Ribbonism is extending, but the reports do not satisfy me that this is so.

" I send herewith a general, but mere skeleton statement ; and if you wish for anything more in detail, I will furnish you with it.

" Monthly reports from the Inspectors-General of Provinces will be sent in by the 6th of each month, and intermediately I shall have notices of all extraordinary occurrences.

" I propose to forward to you a mere summary of these, unless you have any other plan of proceeding to suggest.

" We hear very little of the Catholic Association at this moment. There appears to be a sort of calm, not however, I fear, much to be depended upon. In order that we may not be enabled to sleep at our posts, Sir Harcourt Lees is putting himself in full activity. About the 10th of May he commences his operations. He has announced himself at several towns to the northward, and invites all good Orangemen to meet him.

" I shall be enabled to write to you within the next week upon the grand question.

" Believe me, my dear Mr. Peel,

" Very truly yours,

" ANGLESEY."

Irish Police Reports, Jan. and Feb. 1828.

Sligo.—Generally quiet ; 1 murder ; 7 outrages.

Mayo.—Perfectly quiet ; 1 murder ; 1 outrage.

Roscommon.—Rockites rather busy ; apprehensive of their extending their operations ; 2 murders ; 11 outrages.

Clare.—Quiet ; apprehensive of Ribbon spirit extending ; 9 outrages.

Leitrim.—Much disturbed ; the sway of the Rockites formidable ; magistrates supposed to be deficient in energy ; 36 outrages.

Galway.—Perfectly quiet ; 1 murder ; 6 outrages.

Antrim.—Disturbed ; robberies of fire-arms ; not insurrectionary ; 3 murders ; 7 outrages.

Armagh.—Quiet ; 1 outrage.

Cavan.—Strong political feeling ready to develop itself ; 9 outrages.

Donegal.—Not tranquil ; 2 murders ; 4 outrages.

Down.—Quiet ; 2 outrages.

Fermanagh.—Tranquil ; 6 outrages.

Londonderry.—Generally quiet ; 1 murder ; 4 outrages.

Monaghan.—Disturbed ; party violence runs high ; 1 murder ; 6 outrages.

Ulster may be considered tolerably tranquil, with the exception of some baronies in the counties of Donegal and Monaghan.

Tipperary.—Whiteboy system prevails very generally ; no organized insurrectionary system founded upon political feeling ; 4 murders ; 75 outrages.

Cork.—Generally quiet ; 1 murder ; 4 outrages.

Waterford.—Quiet ; 3 outrages.

Kerry.—Quiet ; 3 outrages.

Roscrea.—Dissatisfied spirit excited by inflammatory speeches.

Limerick.—Satisfactory state ; 9 outrages.

Wicklow.—Western division disturbed ; considered necessary to increase the constabulary force by ordering three men to Dunlavin, and three more to another disturbed point ; Talbotstown the most disturbed ; 3 outrages.

Kildare.—Nothing to notice.

Mr. PEEL to Lord ANGLESEY.

(Private.)

" Whitehall, April 7, 1828.

" MY DEAR LORD ANGLESEY,

" I shall always be most happy to hear from you upon Irish matters.

" The official returns from police inspectors you can order to be sent officially in the usual course ; but I think it will be advantageous that we should keep up a regular correspondence on all points relating to the tranquillity and general interests of Ireland that may occur out of the regular beaten routine of business.

" It is not at all necessary that our communications should be in the shape of formal despatches. Every purpose will be answered, and perhaps more effectually, by a private correspondence such as we have now commenced.

" I am glad to see that two of the murderers of Mara have been convicted at the last assizes in Tipperary. The Solicitor-General seems to have done his business well. The details of the trial give a terrible picture of the interior of Tipperary society.

" I was told a few days since that the Association had not only appointed in each parish of Ireland certain office-bearers, called Roman Catholic Churchwardens, but that at least in some parishes, and in those as part of a general system, twelve persons were nominated, standing in some relation or other to the Association.

" What that relation was, was not very accurately defined ; but the nomination was considered by my informant as connected with some scheme of general organisation of the Roman Catholic population.

" I have learnt by long experience the necessity of distrusting Irish information, and at the same time of not neglecting statements which one is inclined to disbelieve.

" Probably you can find out what has actually been done with respect to the nomination of persons calling themselves Roman Catholic Churchwardens, and whether there be any truth whatever in the statement respecting the nomination of twelve persons in certain parishes by the directions of the Roman Catholic Association.

" Lamb will show you a paper which I gave him before his departure respecting the Association, and will explain to you my object in writing it. It was much less to express an opinion than to suggest matters for inquiry and consideration.

" To my queries I ought to have added the following. What is the amount remaining of the Rent collected before the Bill for the suppression of the Association passed into a law ?

" What is the amount collected since that period— and if there have been any payments, to what purposes have they been applied ?—So much for Irish affairs.

" We are still without any positive intelligence of the intentions of Russia, though every thing seems to announce the probability of active operations on her part against Turkey.

"It is true that the Porte has not only offered an unconditional armistice of three months to the Greeks, but has sent orders to her military and naval commanders to abstain from all hostile movements whatever for that period.

"The reason very probably may be that hostile movements are inconvenient to herself; but if her object be to be enabled to resume them when the armistice expires with greater effect, she will totally fail. Her armistice, whether accepted or not, will not interrupt the blockade of the ports of the Morea.—I think that we have no other news worth sending to you.

"I am, my dear Lord Anglesey,

"Very faithfully yours,

"ROBERT PEEL."

Lord ANGLESEY to Mr. PEEL.

"Dublin Castle, April 9, 1828.

"MY DEAR MR. PEEL,

"I have received your letter of the 7th. I will make inquiry about the Rent, and write more fully in a few days.

"Tipperary is not in so desperate a state as you seem to imagine. The prosecutions are going on in the most satisfactory manner, under the very able management of the Solicitor-General.

"The two principals in the murder of Mara have been hanged. Two of the accessories, and in fact the planners of the murder, will be hanged on Saturday. Another is under trial with every prospect of conviction.

Several have already pleaded guilty upon a promise of transportation for life, and it is expected that many of the others will follow the example.

" I remain very truly yours,

" ANGLESEY.

" The utmost consternation prevails throughout the gangs of the country."

Lord ANGLESEY to Mr. PEEL.

" Dublin Castle, April 13, 1828.

" MY DEAR MR. PEEL,

"I have put together and send you my ideas upon the subject of the Catholic Association, &c., and of the difficulties attendant either upon its positive existence, or its forcible suppression.

" Mr. Lamb is prepared to answer the several questions upon the points of law you put in your paper sent to him.

" In respect to those you added in your letter to me, I have to state that I have caused inquiry to be made; but I have not obtained accurate information, and I do not believe it will be possible to discover what is the actual amount of rent received.

" Some assert that it is extremely exaggerated, whilst others contend that a vast deal more is collected than the Association acknowledge the receipt of.

" I shall pursue the inquiry.

" Believe me, my dear Mr. Peel,

" Very truly yours,

" ANGLESEY."

Lord Anglesey's Memorandum, April 12, 1828.

" The time is arrived when it becomes necessary for
His Majesty's Government to determine upon the course
to be pursued in reference to the Catholic Association
of this kingdom.

" Conscious of the immense importance of the subject, and aware that it would be expected of me
to state an opinion upon the case, I have not ceased
to avail myself of every opportunity of forming a
judgment, by frequent discussions with those persons
who, from their acknowledged ability, their habits of
business, their great legal knowledge, might be considered the best calculated to give a firm and unbiassed
opinion upon this momentous question.

" But I have not confined myself in my inquiries to
persons of this class only—I have pursued them amongst
the best informed of every profession—amongst the
moderate as well as amongst the most intolerant of the
parties that divide this distracted country.

" There is no one, I feel persuaded, except the most
violent of the Roman Catholic agitators, whose consequence mainly depends upon the degree of excitement
and of agitation they are enabled to keep up in the
public mind by the meetings of this body, who does not
deprecate and deplore its existence, and who would not
joyfully get rid of the acknowledged evil.

" It appears to me, that in order to determine upon
the method of meeting the difficulties that present
themselves at every step, it is necessary to ascertain—
First, if any law *can* be framed that shall effectually

suppress the meeting. Secondly, if it is determined to attempt to draw *such* a Bill, is there reasonable ground of hope that the Legislature will pass it? Thirdly, what effect will the re-agitation of the question have upon the Roman Catholics, and indeed upon the whole population?

" It will be more convenient to begin with the second question. I believe it to be very generally the opinion of the best lawyers, that a Bill so framed as to be certain of effectually crushing the evil must necessarily trench materially upon the right of assembling and of petitioning, and it may be presumed that such a measure would be vehemently opposed, and it might possibly be universally reprobated, in Parliament.

" Of this the King's Government is to judge.

" It must now be considered if there is a possibility of framing a Bill to attain the object sought without the objections before stated.

" Experience shows that the Bill now about to expire has been of no avail ; and with whatever judgment and ability any new measure may be prepared, it is certain that not less ability and ingenuity will be immediately put in action to counteract and to nullify it.

" Unless then you are certain that a law can be framed, which, without being impoliticly coercive, shall nevertheless effect that object which the Bill now in existence has failed to produce, the question will be this—Is it not better to allow the Bill to expire without notice, rather than to re-enact it, or to attempt to introduce one which, if it was calculated to *insure* success, might be considered of too arbitrary a character, or which, as in the present case, you might be unable to act upon ?

" To me it appears that nothing tends more to fix upon any Government the character of weakness than the passing of strong laws which it has not the vigour to enforce.

" It is next most important to consider what effect the re-agitation of the question will produce upon the Association and its supporters.

" My information leads me to believe that it is not in so united and flourishing a state as its advocates would have it thought to be.

" The higher orders of the Roman Catholic clergy have long felt a great jealousy of the ascendant that the leaders of the Association have assumed over the lower priesthood.

" Many of the most respectable of the Catholic landlords are irritated that their tenantry, in direct opposition to their injunctions, continue to pay the Catholic rent.

" In regard to the rent itself, it is reasonable to suppose that sooner or later the poorer contributors must consider it as onerous, arbitrary, and oppressive. It is surprising that they should so long have submitted to the imposition ; but if the expected event has not yet been produced by it, it inevitably will take place. It is the last feather that breaks the camel's back.

" Here then are seeds of dissolution sown, quite strong enough to grow into discord, and finally to lead to dissolution ; but I fear that the necessary consequence of any coercive attempt to put down the Association, which may be approaching its end, will be to reunite and to strengthen in a firmer bond the several interests that are now more or less at variance.

"However, it must not be disguised, that inconvenience may arise from allowing the law of 1825 to expire, and that not merely from the possible increased action of the Association, but also from another party in the State.

"The meetings and the processions of the Orangemen have certainly been suppressed by the present Bill, but it is reasonable to conclude that they would not be backward in resuming their meetings if they found that the Catholic Association was in active operation.

"However, it seems to be generally admitted, that in the case of any treasonable, or seditious, or libellous offence committed at any meeting, or generally of any disturbance of the public peace, either in assemblies or in processions, it would be found more easy to convict under the common law than under either the Convention Act, or that of 1825, or any other Act which could be framed. A jury, it is said, would be more easily induced to give a verdict of conviction, and the law officers would prefer to conduct a prosecution, under the old rather than under the new laws; for any new law, in order to be effectual for the suppression of the Association, must to a certain extent abridge the liberty of the subject, and would be proportionably unpopular; besides I am informed that, being a penal statute, there would be very great technical difficulty in bringing it into operation.

"It is with extreme reluctance that I venture an opinion upon this important subject; but my situation requires that I should give one. I ground it upon the information I have assiduously and impartially collected from the best sources.

"I think the Bill should be allowed to expire without notice—if possible, without allusion to the possibility of its re-enactment.

"Should this course be adopted, the vigilance of Government must be exercised in speedily applying the strong arm of the common law to suppress every violation of the public tranquillity and good order.

"Supported by the powerful aid of that excellent establishment, the Constabulary force, already working the greatest benefit, and capable of still further improvement, and protected, as this force is, by an efficient army, ably commanded, I feel perfect confidence that no material mischief would arise during the short period of seven months, when the Parliament would probably re-assemble.

"During that interval the intentions of the Association will have been developed.

"The forbearance and the temperate disposition of the Government will have been manifested.

"If during this time measures should be resorted to by the Association that might seem to be dangerous or insulting to the State, any law of energy and coercion that it might then be deemed necessary to propose would be met by the Parliament and by the public with a far different feeling from that which such a course would probably encounter at this moment.

" ANGLESEY.

" Dublin Castle, April 12, 1828."

Mr. LAMB to Mr. PEEL.

(Confidential.)

" April 22, 1828.

" I send you the answer of the Attorney-General to
the queries contained in the paper which you communicated to me before my departure for Ireland, together
with the copy of a letter giving information upon the
subject of the Churchwardens and the amount of the
old Catholic rent. You will perceive by its date that I
only received it the day · before I quitted Dublin, and
therefore had not time to make any of those further
inquiries which might appear to be suggested by it. It
is not satisfactory with respect to the mode of appointing the Churchwardens, who, however, I believe, are
elected by the parishioners at large, upon notice previously given. Their duties are sufficiently explained
by the reports, which have been made by them, read at
the meetings, and afterwards published in the newspapers. They are general reports upon the state of
the parish, upon the characters and conduct of the
clergymen and larger landholders, upon the manner in
which the rents and tithes are collected, upon the
schools, and more particularly upon any proceedings
against the forty-shilling freeholders on account of their
votes, or for the purpose of clearing the estates, and
upon any attempts to make converts from the Roman
Catholic to the Protestant faith.

" I add also a printed account of the receipt and
expenditure of the Roman Catholic rent for the last

year. These accounts are, I believe, quite public, and
to be obtained by everybody.

                    " Yours faithfully,

                              " WM. LAMB."

                Mr. JOY to Mr. LAMB.

                              " April 18, 1828.

" MY DEAR SIR,

          " I was out of town yesterday, which prevented
my getting the papers you wished for. Some of the
old ones—I mean of a date prior to 1827—can only be
had by a reference to the newspapers, which is a very
tedious mode. If you wish to have any forwarded to
you in London, it can be done. The Churchwardens
were instituted in January, 1828, and are not, I fancy,
very generally appointed as yet. Their duties are to
collect the rent, and to report as to the new reforma-
tion, ejecting of peasantry, &c. in their respective
parishes. The amount of the old rent altogether collected I have not been able exactly to ascertain; but
the balance remaining on hand when the Association
was suppressed was 14,000*l.* Of this sum 3000*l.* has
been voted to establish a model school in Dublin, and
for purposes of education. The interest of the old rent
has been applied, I understand, to pay the salary of
the agent in England, the rent of the house, servants'
wages, &c. The collection of the old rent is not coeval
with the Association, the latter having been formed in
1823; the former commenced in the end of 1824, I
think. The new Association was formed in July, 1825.
It never petitions, and meets only on Saturdays. The

other meetings, which you see taking place, are distinct, and got up by a requisition to the secretary. All the documents, &c. are open to the public, and 'we pride ourselves upon having no secrets.'

        "Believe me to be, &c. &c.

                    "HENRY JOY."

Mr. JOY'S OPINION, April 12, 1828.

"When the 6th George IV., chapter 4, was in preparation I distinctly declared (as Mr. Goulburn will recollect), that unless the Act was framed to meet what I suggested was an obvious way of evading it, viz. by calling distinct and repeated aggregate meetings (as they were named), it would not answer the purpose. The course that I said the Roman Catholic leaders would probably adopt would be to dissolve the old Association, and without forming a new one, to summon every week a distinct aggregate or other meeting, at which there would be as much sedition spoken, and as much violence exhibited, and by which almost as much mischief would be done, as if the old Association had continued. Something like this was actually done; with this difference, that they formed a new Association. The course they adopted was this: they established a permanent Association, which professed not to discuss the question of Catholic emancipation, but to be formed for the purposes of education and other charitable purposes; and they every week convened what they called a 'separate meeting,' which professed to be distinct from the Association, and unconnected with it, and to terminate on the day on which it met;

and at this meeting all the sedition and all the viru-
lence of party spirit were to be exhibited. These separate meetings, they contended, were not affected by
the Act; which only applied to 'societies constituted'
for the purposes in the Act mentioned; and only
declared such 'societies' unlawful assemblies; thus
having recourse to the evasion which I predicted. And
in fact, when the Act is accurately considered, it affords
an opening to this evasion; for though it makes a
renewal of meetings by the society, or any members
thereof, a test or a cause of illegality in the SOCIETY
whose members so renew their meetings, and consequently makes the society an unlawful combination and
confederacy, it does not make the INDIVIDUAL MEET-
INGS themselves unlawful assemblies. So that were
the Catholic Association to be now dissolved, and no
new Association formed, there is nothing in the Act to
prevent them from holding a separate meeting—a distinct individual meeting of Catholics—every week, such
meeting terminating with the day on which it was convened. Besides this door which the Act left open to
evasion, another mode of evading it was not only practicable, but was even suggested by the Act itself; or
rather the Act, by an exception or saving in it, legal-
ized it; that was by permitting meetings for fourteen
days. It is obvious that fourteen days are not necessary for the purpose of preparing a petition to Parliament. The Roman Catholic leaders quickly availed
themselves of this. They convened 'fourteen days'
meetings,' and it was amusing to read the notice for
calling those meetings, which always ran thus—'A

fourteen days' meeting will be held pursuant to Act of Parliament;' as if the Act had enjoined and required such meetings. When I came to inquire why this fourteen days' meeting was permitted, I was told it was difficult to get the period for which they were allowed to meet reduced to fourteen days, as the House of Commons was for extending the period to twenty-one days, and that the permission to sit for fourteen days was a compromise. In addition to these meetings there were held occasionally 'Aggregate Meetings.' The permanent body called the 'New Catholic Association' they thought to exempt from the operation of the Act by virtue of the saving in the eighth section, as a society formed for a charitable purpose; professing that they met for the purpose of education of the poor, and for extending relief to such as were oppressed by their landlords. Notwithstanding all their efforts at evasion, they contravened the Act in many particulars. The separate meetings were manifestly in point of fact meetings of 'the Association.' The very same members attended them, and the requisition by which they were convened was always signed at a meeting of the Association by the members then present. Committees too were constituted to have permanent duration; the rent was collected and paid in to the Association; causes were defended and prosecuted out of the rent. No doubt therefore existed that the Association was an unlawful assembly. Its suppression was a question of expediency, which it is not my province to enter into. In some respects the Association has latterly gone greater lengths than before. The collection of the

D

rent is reduced to a system. Churchwardens, as they are called, are appointed in each parish by the direction of the Association, whose business it is to collect at the chapels (now called churches) the rent, and to remit it to the Association. They also make a report upon the state of the parish—whether there is any persecution carried on by the landlords against their tenants, and also how many persons have been converted to the ' *ancient faith.*' I have also been informed that it is their business to read to the people the inflammatory speeches of the members of the Association, in order to keep up a proper degree of zeal in the cause, and to increase in them that attachment to British connection, that love of order, that respect for and amenability to the law, for which the lower classes are so distinguished. This, however, I have only *ex relatione.* In addition to the appointment of Churchwardens, they have attempted their long-threatened simultaneous meetings of parishes; and though this measure failed of producing a great effect, and caused a considerable degree of disappoint-ment to those who originated it, yet it is impossible not to concur with Mr. Sheil that they thereby furnished a fatal precedent of a people 'gathered into a solid and perilous confederacy.' With respect to the application of the Catholic rent, that is (except in cases where it is applied to relieve tenants from the distresses of their landlords) veiled in secrecy. To give their proceedings with respect to it the appearance of charity, many con-tributors paid it in ' for the relief of the forty-shilling freeholders;' Mr. O'Connell pays his contribution in ' for all purposes allowable by law.' But there is no doubt that they have contravened the Act in this particular, notwithstanding the terms under which they endeavour to cloak it.

" With respect to the prosecution of Mr. Sheil, it was commenced by Lord Plunket when Attorney-General, after consulting the then Cabinet. The indictment was found, but Mr. Sheil traversed over to the next Commission, which the judges held he had a right to do. That brought it within a week of Term, and the Counsel for the prosecution thought it advisable to remove the proceedings into the King's Bench by *Certiorari*, in order to obtain, what could not otherwise be had, a special jury. Before that time Lord Liverpool's illness took place, and the consequent change of the Ministry. Lord Plunket's promotion to the peerage soon followed, when the office of Attorney-General became vacant, and continued so for a considerable time; and it was not till near the close of the second Term (Trinity) that my appointment took place. Mr. Sheil had not pleaded, and a trial could not have been had until last Christmas vacation. In the mean time things in the political world became involved in uncertainty and confusion. It had been deemed necessary to have the authority of the Cabinet for the commencement of the prosecution; and a similar authority ought equally to be required and obtained for its continuance. None such, that I heard of, was ever had. The transaction became stale; some things occurred which turned the tide of popular feeling, which had set pretty strongly against Sheil, in his favour, and rendered his conviction perhaps more than doubtful. Under these circum-

D 2

stances I did not think myself justified in volunteering
without authority to go on with a prosecution which
had only just commenced.

"I have thus, I believe, as far as I am able, answered
the queries put by Mr. Peel. There are two added by
Mr. Lamb:—1. As to the state of the law independent
of the 6th George IV., and the means it affords of suppressing such associations as the Roman Catholic Association and the Orange Lodges:—to bring a society
within the reach of the law, it must either be an unlawful assembly at common law; that is, it must either
be an assembly associated for the purpose of doing
some illegal act, or of doing a lawful act in an unlawful
manner; or else it must be brought within the Act of
1793, against unlawful societies, by being invested with
or having assumed a representative character. With
respect to the Association, the purpose for which they
assemble does not appear to me to be illegal by the
common law. A lawful purpose being admitted, an
assembly of people to accomplish it can only be rendered unlawful by its endeavouring to achieve its purpose by force and violence, and by an assembly of men
which by their numbers, their threats, or by a show of
arms, can cause terror to His Majesty's subjects. This
cannot be said either of the Catholic Association, or of
the Orange Lodges, meeting in their private rooms.

"With respect to Orange processions, I will consider
them hereafter.

"If, then, the Catholic Association is not illegal by
the common law, does it fall within the 33rd George III.
chap. 29? As to Orange lodges, it is clear they do

not, for they neither have, nor assume to have, a representative character, at least as far as I have been able
to learn the nature of the institution.

" As to the Catholic Association, it professes not to
represent the Catholic people, though it influences and
controls them. It would be difficult to bring it within
the Act, and the opinions of Sir John Copley and Sir
C. Wetherell, taken in December, 1824, were that it
did not fall within the Act.

" With respect to Orange processions, it is much to
be lamented that they should continue to take place ;
but, *as processions*, the Act does not touch them, and it
is only as members of a society which the Act makes
illegal (and which must be proved) that those who
engage in such processions can be brought within the
Act. A question was proposed by the Irish Government to the law officers, whether such processions were
or not illegal at common law. On that question Lord
Plunket and I differed, he holding that they were calculated to inspire terror, not from their own nature,
considered abstractedly, but because, being offensive to
the Roman Catholics, it was to be apprehended that the
latter would attack them and cause tumult and danger.
I, on the other hand, held, that to constitute an unlawful assembly it must be calculated *per se* to inspire
terror, and that its legality or illegality cannot depend
on the conduct of third persons, over whom they have
no control. I have to observe that Lord Plunket, when
he came to write his opinion, shortly before he quitted
office, so qualified it as to make it approach very closely
to that which I had expressed, and which I still enter-

tain. It will, in my opinion, require the interference of the Legislature to render such processions punishable by law.

" H. Joy.

" Temple Street, 12th April, 1828."

Mr. Peel to Lord Anglesey.

" Whitehall, May 1, 1828.

" My dear Lord Anglesey,

" I regret to hear that you have been suffering severely from indisposition, but as I see by the Irish papers that you have been able to ride on horseback, I trust that you are much better.

" I received a letter some days since, of which the enclosed is a copy; I have heard nothing more of the writer of it.

" I think it very probable that the chief motive for the communication is the payment of the expenses of the writer. However, the best rule in these cases is to act, so far as inquiry is concerned, as if a very improbable story might be true.

" Of course, the more cautiously any such inquiry is made the better, because ridicule attaches to it if the whole story be, as it may be, a fabrication.

" The names of parties are given in the enclosed letter with precision enough, but the object of their confederacy is most imperfectly explained. Perhaps you can learn something with respect to the character of the persons mentioned in the enclosed, who are or were residents in Dublin.

"I received your Memorandum on the subject of the law relating to the suppression of dangerous associations in Ireland and the policy of its renewal.

"This Memorandum, together with other documents material to the consideration of the subject, have been communicated by me to my colleagues, and I propose to summon a Cabinet very shortly for the purpose of finally ascertaining the opinions of the Government.

"I entirely concur with you in opinion that if the temporary and extraordinary powers given by the Act of 1825 be relinquished, and that Act permitted to expire, the ordinary powers of the law ought to be called into action against those who manifest a disposition to create irritation and discontent whenever they transgress the law. I doubt whether too much importance has not frequently been attached to the consequences of failure in prosecutions instituted by the Government. There are many cases in which, if there is a reasonable ground to expect a verdict from an honest jury, it is much better to incur the risk of failure than the imputation of indifference to proceedings that are at the same time violating the law and are dangerous to the public peace.

"I am, my dear Lord Anglesey,

"Ever very faithfully yours,

"ROBERT PEEL."

Note on the MS. by Sir R. P.—I do not find the enclosure in this letter. It was a letter from a person of the name of Quin, proposing to come to London for the purpose of giving information about a conspiracy.

Mr. Peel to Mr. Lamb.

(Private and confidential.)

" Whitehall, May 2, 1828.

" Dear Lamb,

" Pray refer to the Report, a copy of which you sent me the other day, respecting the appointment of Churchwardens under the direction of the Roman Catholic Association.

" The object of this appointment is evident enough. It is to organise a system of communication between an authority established in Dublin and agents in each parish of Ireland.

" I know not whether this can be done consistently with law, but I think we should put the question to the law officers of the Crown in Ireland.

" I am sure that it will be necessary to watch with increased vigilance all assumptions of authority or violations of the ordinary law by the Roman Catholic Association if we are to part with the temporary enactments which are intended to be a check upon them.

" Any attempt at a system of organisation, if contrary to law, should be met at the outset.

" This, like many others, may be so contrived as to be within the law; still the question of its legality might be put confidentially without the least embarrassment to the law officers.

" Ever yours,

" Robert Peel."

Mr. LAMB to Mr. PEEL.

(Confidential.)

"Irish Office, May 3, 1828.

" DEAR PEEL,

"I will immediately submit the Report in question to the Attorney and Solicitor-General. I agree with you that the measures of the Roman Catholic Association must be watched with the utmost strictness. Their object is to establish a system of concert, communication, and co-operation throughout all Ireland, and this object they unfortunately possess great means of accomplishing, provided they all, clergy and laity, act cordially together, which I rather doubt their doing, unless something should arise to unite them. When I read the Report respecting the Churchwardens first, it struck me as going very near the wind, but I apprehend any question which may arise upon it will resolve itself into the question of the legality of the new Association formed under the 8th section of the Act; because if an Association or any other body be legal in itself and formed for legal purposes, there is, I apprehend, nothing either in the common or statute law which prevents such a body from taking measures to procure information from all parts of the kingdom, nor from appointing persons to recommend and to receive voluntary contributions for the furtherance of such legal purposes.

" Yours faithfully,
" WM. LAMB."

The result of these communications with the Irish Government was a decision on the part of the Cabinet not to seek from Parliament a continuance of the Act of 1825.

In the Memorandum above inserted, prepared by Mr. Joy, then Attorney-General of Ireland, reference is made to the defects of the Act of 1825, and to the facility of evading it.

But the truth is, that without the absolute suppression of all liberty of speech, or at least of the power of holding public meetings of any description, it was no easy matter to frame enactments which should preclude evasion by the able and astute men who directed the proceedings of the Roman Catholic Associations that existed from time to time under various denominations and professed various purposes.

This Act of 1825 was passed with the approbation and sanction of an administration, the chief members of which were divided in opinion on the Catholic question, an administration which (speaking of the Irish as well as the British Government) included Lord Eldon, Lord Liverpool, Mr. Goulburn, and Mr. Peel, and Lord Wellesley, Lord Castlereagh, Mr. Canning, and Mr. Plunket.

Imperfect as the Act may have been, it was not passed without considerable difficulty. If it ought to have been much more stringent in its provisions, and if legal astuteness could have readily devised the means of making those provisions more effectual for their purpose, that very fact establishes the decisive proof of the evil which resulted from the necessity of uniting in the same Government public men opposed to each other in opinion on the main question—the removal of Roman Catholic disabilities.

It inevitably led to an unwillingness to entertain collateral questions affected by the decision on the main question, and if they were forced upon consideration, to a system of compromise in the practical treatment of them.

Such a system of compromise may be condemned by those who think that a Government could have been formed on the basis of united and decisive opposition to concession, and at the same time capable of conducting with vigour and success the general administration of public affairs, foreign and domestic.

A review of the eminent men who must have been thus excluded from the service of the Crown at very critical periods of public affairs, and ranged in opposition to a Government formed on such a basis, will probably be sufficient to convince a dispassionate judge that the attempt to constitute that Government would have been fruitless, and might have been followed by greater evils than the signal failure of the attempt itself. I refer especially to the period of time that elapsed between the years 1812 and 1829.

Subsequently to the year 1812, when the Regency had been established, the special reasons for postponing the consideration of the Catholic claims, founded on the conscientious scruples of George III., had lost their force.

The members of the administration formed under the Duke of Portland in 1807, though differing on the principle of concession, had concurred, some on the

ground of principle, others for reasons temporary in
their application, in meeting with united opposition the
proposals for taking into consideration the claims of
the Roman Catholics.

Lord Castlereagh and Mr. Canning joined with Mr.
Perceval in the year 1808 in resisting a motion to that
effect brought forward by Mr. Grattan.

But in the year 1812 that obstacle to concession
which was opposed by the decisive veto of George III.
was removed in consequence of his incapacity for the
exercise of the royal functions and the appointment of
a Regent without restrictions.

In 1812 Mr. Canning supported the Roman Catholic
claims, and in his speech on the question thus accounted
for the change in the course which he had theretofore
pursued.

Speaking in the House of Commons on the 24th of
April, 1812, Mr. Canning said :—

" Such are the opinions which I have held upon this
subject ever since I have been capable of forming an
opinion upon it.   I take no shame to myself for that
up to this period I have not found an opportunity of
declaring and acting upon them.   I take no shame to
myself for having on other occasions resisted the inquiry which I now recommend.   I did so on a view, a
just view, I think, I am sure an honest and well-inten-
tioned view of public duty.   While there existed in the
breast of the Sovereign an insurmountable obstacle to
the entertainment of this question—an obstacle not of
opinion but of conscience—the only alternative left to
a public man who held the opinions which I profess to

have holden on the question, was either to push those opinions into action, at all the hazard to which such a course would be liable—at the hazard of one calamity too dreadful to be contemplated without awe and terror (a calamity under the affliction of which we are now actually suffering, and to which therefore I may now without impropriety allude)—or manfully to interpose between the conscience of the Sovereign and the agitation of this question, at whatever risk of unpopularity or misconstruction. This latter was the course which I thought it my duty to adopt."

In the year 1813, and on all subsequent occasions, both Mr. Canning and Lord Castlereagh, and their immediate political friends, supported the Catholic claims.

If in the interval between the close of the year 1812 and the commencement of 1829, when the Roman Catholic Relief Bill was proposed to Parliament, the principle of united resistance to concession had been insisted on as the basis of an administration, the following persons, who in the course of that interval were employed in the official service of the Crown, must have been excluded—must, many of them at least, have been driven into opposition to a Government formed on the basis of unqualified resistance to concession.

Lord CASTLEREAGH.	Mr. HUSKISSON.
Mr. CANNING.	Mr. CHARLES WYNN.
Lord ABERDEEN.	Mr. CHARLES GRANT.
Lord WELLESLEY.	Lord DUDLEY.
Lord HARROWBY.	Mr. VESEY FITZGERALD.
Lord MELVILLE.	Mr. WILLIAM LAMB.
Lord RIPON.	Lord ANGLESEY.
Lord PALMERSTON.	Sir GEORGE MURRAY.

To this list the names might be added of other public
men, eminently qualified by character and talents to
render public service, and concurring generally on all
other public questions with those servants of the Crown
from whom they differed on the Catholic question.
Difference on that question was no doubt a great evil;
but in the position of public affairs and public men
I believe it to have been an evil which (for a very long
period at least) did not admit of a remedy.   It was an
evil submitted to by the Government of which Mr. Fox,
Lord Grenville, and Lord Grey were members, in the
years 1806 and 1807, as well as by the Governments
of Mr. Perceval, Lord Liverpool, and the Duke of
Wellington.   It may be asked why, considering the
number of distinguished men concurring in opinion on
the Catholic question, was not an united Government
formed on the principle of concession?   The answer,
I presume, is, because the want of mutual confidence
among statesmen of different parties concurring on the
particular question, or actual disagreement on other
questions of scarcely inferior importance, precluded the
hope of engaging them to act in cordial concert and
co-operation in the general direction of public affairs.
The fact is that shortly after the death of Mr. Perceval
an attempt was made, apparently under favourable circumstances, to form a Government united on the principle of a conciliatory adjustment of the claims of the
Roman Catholics.

I speak of the proposals made by Lord Wellesley on
the 1st of June, 1812, to Lord Grey and Lord Grenville.   That attempt was not successful.   Whatever

were the causes of its failure, they are not, I apprehend, imputable in the slightest degree to those who had taken a part hostile to concession. I have, however, no other information on this subject than that which is derived from the letters and minutes of conversation published at the time.*

I have made this digression—not one, however, irrelevant to the subject—because there is, I think, a tendency to underrate the difficulties which for many years stood in the way of the formation of a Government united on the principle either of concession or of resistance, and because that tendency will probably increase with the lapse of time.

I return to the immediate subject from which I have digressed—the events of 1828, and their bearing on the Roman Catholic Relief Bill of the following year.

No material correspondence passed with Ireland (excepting that which has been already given) before the discussion on the Catholic question in the House of Commons. Previously to that discussion a motion was made by Lord John Russell for the repeal of the Test and Corporation Acts. That motion, although it was opposed with all the influence and authority of the Government recently appointed, was carried by a majority of 44, the numbers being—

In favour of the motion   237
Against it   193

It was not my original intention to enter into any

---

* They will be found in the last volume of Parliamentary Debates for the year 1812.—(R. P.)

detail with regard to this motion, or to the course that
was subsequently taken by the Government in consequence of the adoption of the motion by so considerable
a majority.   But as the subject is one of considerable
importance, as the repeal of the Test and Corporation
Acts was not without its influence on the removal of
Roman Catholic disabilities, and as there is correspondence in my possession which throws light upon the proceedings that took place, I shall probably be pardoned
for giving such parts of that correspondence as are
likely to have any public interest.

The correspondence to which I especially refer passed
between the Bishop of Oxford (Dr. Lloyd) and myself.
The Bishop had been my private tutor at Christ Church.
There existed between us the most cordial attachment,
and the habits of perfectly unreserved intercourse formed
at college were continued without the slightest interruption until the period when the death of the Bishop
deprived me of a beloved and faithful friend.

The following letters passed between us previously to
the debate on the Test and Corporation Acts :—

Bishop of OXFORD to Mr. PEEL.

" Feb. 10, 1828.

" MY DEAR PEEL,

" I send you my lucubrations, which may perhaps be of no use, but still may possibly lead you to
attend to some points.

" In the present loose state of religious opinion, it is
more than probable that the debate will turn much on

the total independence of civil affairs on religious opinion ; and though the argument is perfectly absurd in any state where there is a church established by law, controlled by law, with her formularies authorised and unchangeable by law, still the licentious opinion is so much more popular in a democratic assembly, and so much within the grasp of all men, that it is very likely that it will only be argued on those grounds. However, put down any difficulties which may strike you in the form of questions, and I will answer them as I can.

" I have not yet been able to meet with Lord Mansfield's judgment. We have not the debates in our library; but the judgment was published by Mr. Furneaux in a pamphlet addressed to Blackstone.

" There is one judgment of Lord Mansfield which has, I believe, no application at present, because a man now is not punishable if he refuses to serve, being a Dissenter. Lord Mansfield talked then of the bed of Procrustes fairly enough.

" But have you quite made up your mind to oppose? My idea is that you must do so this Session at least; but at all events do not concede to the Dissenters without consulting some of the heads of the Church, and hearing their reasons—such as the Archbishop of Canterbury, the Bishops of London and Durham—because in either case it may be of great importance for you to be able to say afterwards that you acted with their sanction.

" I have now fourteen volumes lying before me on the subject of the Corporation and Test Acts, written in the years 1789 and 1790.

" The best tracts are Sherlock and Hoadley's, re-published in a very short form in 1787 ; and among the Dissenters, ' The Rights of Protestant Dissenters, by a Layman,' 1789.

" Always yours,

" C. O."

Mr. PEEL to the Bishop of OXFORD.

(Most private.)

" Feb. 19, 1828.

" MY DEAR LLOYD,

" All your letters are opened by me, and read exclusively by me.

" The Test Act, &c., is put off till this day week. There is therefore time to breathe.

" The argument against repeal, for a popular assembly like the House of Commons, is threadbare in the extreme. The distinction between the Sacrament as an actual qualification for office, and the proof it incidentally affords of qualification, is too refined for the House.

" It might do very well when people took the Sacrament once a month ; but now people take the Sacrament (when it is required in the case of office) not for the sake of religion, but for the sake of the office.

" The best argument—mind, I am speaking always of House of Commons' arguments—of arguments for people who know very little of the matter—care not much about it—half of whom have dined or are going to dine—and are only forcibly struck by that which they instantly comprehend without trouble—the best argument is this:—

" Under the existing system a kindly feeling has grown up between Dissenters and the Church of England. When was there a period when there has been less of religious acrimony—less of religious polemics mixed up with civil controversies—than there has been within the last forty years?

" Religious disputes were revived for a short time at the commencement of the French Revolution; but such an event as that was out of all common rule, and was sufficient to stir up every passion and every bitter feeling that might have been otherwise dormant.

" May not this state of comparative peace be connected with a state of law which gives practically to the Dissenter the enjoyment of civil rights, but recognises the predominance of the Established Church?

" The Dissenter is satisfied with practical possession; the Established Church with the admission—the annually renewed admission—by the Legislature of the legal claim to superior protection.

" Why bring principles into conflict, when for thirty years both parties have been satisfied?

" Why tell the Dissenter he may encroach with impunity, and force the Establishment into a feverish watchfulness against his encroachments?

" Now what I should like to show is, that at periods preceding the last forty years there was ill-blood and animosity between Protestant Dissenters and the Church of England, and then to trace the gradual abatement of religious animosities under the existing laws.

" I was very forcibly struck the other night by the
impression that this line of argument was the best
from this circumstance :—Alderman Wood adduced,
as a conclusive proof that the Test Laws should be
repealed, this fact :—' Thirty years since,' said he,
' there were only two or three persons in the corporation
of the city of London favourable to the repeal : the
other day, when the corporation met to petition for
the repeal, only two hands were held up against the
petition !'

" Can I have a more signal proof than this that,
coincidently at least with the present system of law,
there has been a very rapid approximation of parties—
an increase of kindly feeling—an abatement of religious jealousies?

" Will not the laws be executed with forbearance in
corporations which act in such a spirit of moderation
and generosity when the question is the repeal of those
laws?   Think of this.

" Ever affectionately yours,

" R. P."

On the 26th of February the House of Commons (as
I have before observed) declared in favour of the repeal
of the Acts in question by a majority of 237 to 193.
Notwithstanding this decision, adverse to the views of
the administration, it appeared to the advisers of the
Crown that, considering the state of parties, and all
that had passed since the death of Mr. Canning, the
abdication of one Government and the very recent constitution of another, we should not be justified in aban-

doning the service of the Crown, and exposing the King to all the embarrassment which must be the result of our resignation at such a period and under such circumstances.

Considering, on the other hand, the amount of the majority in the Commons in favour of the repeal of the Test and Corporation Acts, and that that majority included many attached friends of the Established Church (Lord Sandon, Sir Thomas Acland, and others generally concurring with them on religious matters), it appeared to me that it would be very unwise hastily to commit the House of Lords to a conflict with the House of Commons on a question of this nature.

I expressed this opinion to my colleagues, requesting only in the first instance that no decision on the course to be pursued by the Government should be taken without previous communication with the highest authorities in the Church, and an earnest effort to act in friendly concert with them, in order that, if the ultimate decision should be in favour of concession, the Church might have the credit of voluntary and cheerful acquiescence in measures which, without requiring any compromise of principle, were calculated to conciliate the good will of those who dissented from the doctrines of the Church. I thought that, after the declared opinion of the House of Commons, an eager yet unavailing opposition, or even a sullen neutrality or grudging and extorted consent, would deprive concession of all its grace, and increase whatever might be the amount of danger.

With the consent and at the request of my colleagues I undertook to enter into communication with the Archbishop of Canterbury and other prelates.

It terminated, as I earnestly desired that it should terminate, in the conciliatory adjustment of the question at issue with general concurrence in both Houses of Parliament. Had any other course been taken by the Government, the final result of Parliamentary discussion would probably have been the same—namely, the repeal of the Test and Corporation Acts. Whether it would have taken place under circumstances more favourable to the true interests of the Church, or more conducive to the maintenance of harmony and good will among the professors of different religious creeds, may fairly be questioned.

The following correspondence with the Bishop of Oxford, although of a purely private and confidential character, contains probably a fuller account of the progress and result of the intercourse which, as the organ of the Government, I had with the leading prelates, than can be found elsewhere.

I give without reserve all the letters which passed between the introduction and final passing of the measure.

Mr. PEEL to the Bishop of OXFORD.

(Private and immediate.)

" Whitehall, Saturday, March 1, 1828.
" MY DEAR LLOYD,

" You see the state of the House of Commons, and how little it is to be depended upon in Church matters.

" I have not time to write fully, but tell me immediately what is the feeling at Oxford with respect to

the course which should now be taken as to the repeal
of the Test Acts—the suspension of them—or the sub-
stitution of oath or declaration.

" The Commons will pass repeal. Is it advisable for
the Church that repeal should be rejected by the Lords?
When I say the Commons will pass repeal, I mean their
own opinion is decisive for repeal.

" How far they would accept a compromise, with a
view to procure the willing assent of the Lords to a
substitute, I cannot say at present.

" Ever affectionately yours,

" ROBERT PEEL."

Bishop of OXFORD to Mr. PEEL.

" Christ Church, March 4, 1828.

" MY DEAR PEEL,

" I send you a letter from Van Mildert,* which
I received this morning. I think it sensible and moderate. You may see him till the day he names by sending to Hanover Square.

" Always yours,

" C. O."

Bishop of DURHAM to the Bishop of OXFORD.

" Mongewell, March 3, 1828.

" MY DEAR LORD,

" I am unexpectedly called to town for a day
or two, and therefore have no time to do more than
thank you for your letter and its enclosure, which I

---

* The Bishop of Durham.

return to you.   Perhaps it might have been as well not
to have made it a Government question.   Yet I think
the disposition on the part of Government to uphold
the Church may .be at this moment beneficial to us,
especially in the House of Lords.   I do not feel anxious
to retain the sacramental test, if any other, equally
efficacious, or, if not efficacious, seemly and respectful,
as indicating an acknowledgment of the ascendancy of
the Church, can be devised.   Suspension, I hardly think,
will be borne, if repeal can be carried—else I see no
objection to it.   But it is only removing the practical
grievance, not obviating the main objection of the
Dissenters—the degradation it implies, and the pro-
fanation of a sacred ordinance, which they impute to
the very principle of the Acts.   It appears to me that,
at all events, the Bill of repeal should be rejected by
the Lords for this year at least, were it only to give
time for devising some measure to be brought forward
in a future Session by Government, with the concurrence
of the Bishops—to mediate between both parties, and
set the matter at rest.   All I am anxious for is to have
some demonstration of affection and respect for the
Church in the Upper House, and on the part of the
Government, as a counterpoise or a check to the increasing spirit of disaffection to it in the Commons;
and I cannot help thinking that some firm and temperate measure, originating in our House, and from the
friends of the Church, might avert the evil, and be
received thankfully by the country at large.   But of
course I write more as I wish and feel than as I have
any good reason to hope or expect.   While I am in

town I may possibly learn something of the views and
sentiments of others whose opinions are likely to have
more weight than mine. Should anything more occur
to you, I shall be thankful for your communications
whilst I am in town. I shall certainly not come away
till Thursday or Friday, and not till after the post
arrives.

" Yours, my dear Lord, most truly,

" W. Dunelm."

Mr. Peel to the Bishop of Oxford.

(Most private.)

" Whitehall, March 4, 1828.

" My dear Lloyd,

 " I have had opportunities of ascertaining the
opinions of the Archbishop, Bishops of Durham, London, and Chester, on the present state of the question
regarding the Corporation and Test Acts.

" Though they may not be in precise conformity,
my impression is that they all incline to a permanent
settlement of the question now. As might be expected,
Kaye, Copleston, and Law are at least as favourable
to such a course as they are.

" I enclose a letter received this morning from the
Bishop of Chester. He brought it to me, not being
certain of finding me at home.

" I think Declaration in lieu of Sacramental test—
the latter being repealed—will be the measure ; but we
must not say so now.

E

" The Declaration proposed by the Bishop of Chester is, I apprehend, too strong.

" Think of a Declaration—see Acts of Union, the present oath of an Irish Catholic and of an English one.

" Ever yours,

" ROBERT PEEL."

Mr. PEEL to the Bishop of OXFORD.

(Most private.)

" Whitehall, March 15, 1828.

" MY DEAR LLOYD,

" I have been all morning at Lambeth with the two Archbishops, Llandaff, Durham, London, and Chester. We settled a Declaration which I think will go down in the House of Commons, which we can carry against the Dissenting interest there, and will, in my opinion, or at least ought, under all circumstances, to be satisfactory to the Church.

" Ever affectionately yours,

" R. P."

Bishop of OXFORD to Mr. PEEL.

(Date probably March 17.—R. P.)

" MY DEAR PEEL,

" I thank you for your letter, and am glad that you have succeeded in forming a Declaration to which you think the Commons will agree.

" And now, in regard to the debate of to-morrow, I wish to suggest a few words, which you may utter or

not, as it shall seem fit to you. I have reason to know
that some disappointment was felt here at the former
speech on these Acts, which was not thought sufficiently
decided in favour of the Church of England. I should
not report this to you if it had been said only by men
for whose principles or judgment I have no respect;
but it was said by others of a different character.

"Now, if I am right in my opinion that you expect
to be joined in your Declaration by Acland and all
those whose objections were founded on the particular
point of a Sacramental test, might it not be possible to-
morrow to say something of this kind?

"That, on a former occasion, knowing, as you did,
the objections of many gentlemen to a Sacramental test,
who were still unfavourable to the total repeal, you
were hampered between your anxious wish to defend
the rights and privileges of the Established Church and
your respect for the pious scruples of your friends. That
for these scruples you felt all possible respect, although
the abstract argument on which the Sacramental test
was founded was perfectly unanswerable and true. But,
practically speaking, it could not be denied that many
persons who would not otherwise receive the Communion,
and who were not fit for it, did in fact receive it for the
express purpose of *qualifying*, as it is called. Feeling
this difficulty, and knowing how many of your friends
had taken this view of the question, it was not possible
on a former occasion to argue the matter with that confidence and comfort with which you were now enabled
to do it.

"That those of your friends who had entertained

these scruples must have felt a similar difficulty with yourself, because while they felt an insuperable aversion to a Sacramental test, they were equally unwilling with yourself to surrender the interests of the Established Church, and equally unprepared to admit the doctrine of Lord John Russell, that 'no test was necessary,' and that all persons, of whatever religious sect or party, were equally admissible to civil office. That the Declaration now proposed was equally satisfactory to yourself and to your friends: to yourself, because you were not now obliged to oppose scruples that you respected; to them, because they might now support the Church of England without what appeared to them the violation of a religious principle. That none could now vote with Lord John Russell who did not agree with him in the abstract principle of equal admissibility; that this principle, whether true or false in the abstract, was not the principle of the English Constitution; that it was not the principle which had been admitted in the Unions either of Scotland or Ireland; that the contrary principle pervaded the Statute-Book from beginning to end; that such a principle could not be acted on so long as the Constitution remained what it now was; that to talk of an Established Church and at the same time to assert the equal right of all religious sects was a contradiction in terms; that an established religion necessarily implied superiority of privilege; and that if Lord John Russell wished to affirm the equal right of all sects, the more manly way of doing it would be to move at once that there should be no Established Church. And then explain the Declaration, &c.

"I write all this, knowing that you will take in good part anything that I write.

"Always most sincerely yours,

"C. O."

Mr. PEEL to the Bishop of OXFORD.

"Whitehall, March 20, 1828.

"MY DEAR LLOYD,

"I not only take your letter, as I take all your letters, in good part, but I am very much obliged to you, and always shall be, for the most unreserved communication on matters on which it is of great importance to me to be well informed.

"The mode in which it is most prudent to discuss any question in the House of Commons must be determined by a variety of considerations, of which it is not easy for persons at a distance to judge.

"One of those circumstances, and a most material one, is the prospect of being victorious or being beaten.

"If you are to be beaten, the higher the tone you take, the more creditable it may be to the individual member who takes it; but, let me add, the more complete is the triumph over the party on whose behalf it is taken.

"It might have been right to say, 'the Test Act is essential to the security of the Church; it recognises the great principle that conformity to the Church should be the qualification for civil trust; it is the barrier and bulwark, and so forth. Remove it and the Church is

gone; the Dissenters will be triumphant; I disclaim all
responsibility for such an issue, and throw it upon the
House of Commons.'

"This is a high line and a good line, the best possible if it succeeds and is supported by a large majority.

"But if it fails.

"Of course the Minister taking it resigns, which is a
very subordinate part of the consideration. But what
is the position of the Church? and what is the position
of the Dissenter, admitted by the Minister to have had
a complete triumph?

"Now a word as to the substance of the argument
you advised me to hold.

"Is it possible to maintain, 'That to talk of an Established Church and at the same time to assert the equal
right of all religious sects is a contradiction in terms—
that an established religion necessarily implies superiority of privilege, and that if Lord John Russell
wished to affirm the equal right of all, the more manly
way would be to move at once that there should be no
Established Church?'

"Supposing I had said this in the House of Commons, first, what would Scotland reply to me?

"That she had as much an Established Church as
England had, a Church declared permanent and inviolable in terms as solemn and binding as any that are
applied to the Episcopal Church of England.

"She would scout my doctrine that the true test of
an establishment was exclusive civil privilege of any
kind for its members. There is no distinguishing test
in Scotland, none of any kind; there is equal right of

all sects so far as civil and corporate offices are concerned.

"There 'may be an exception in some cases as to Roman Catholics. If there is, it stands on special grounds. The general rule in Scotland is equal civil privilege for all, but an Established Church.

"Secondly, what would Ireland say to me?

"She has an Established Church; but with respect to every sect (except the Roman Catholics), Presbyterian, Seceder, Unitarian, Infidel, Atheist, she puts them on *a better footing* with respect to civil privilege than the members of the Church of England.

"She has released every Dissenter, by a permanent law, from the Sacramental test, but leaves it to be taken by the members of the Church of England.

"In the case of every sect except the Roman Catholic, there is, I apprehend, in Ireland at this moment equality of civil privilege, and yet there is an Established Church.

"Well then, in England, the moment you do that which the House of Commons resolved to do; repeal the Sacramental test, even if you impose a Declaration to be taken in common by all—whether they be members of the Church or Dissenters, provided that Declaration can be taken without scruple by a Dissenter, you do establish, I apprehend, practically, equality of civil privilege.

"You have established it and acted upon it with respect to Parliament for a century, so far as every Dissenter (except the Roman Catholic) is concerned.

"Take the case of France. Surely the Roman Catholic religion is an established religion in France; but there is a complete equality of civil privilege.

"The Church may have been materially injured by the events of the Revolution. Its property may have been confiscated, and its authority impaired; but it still is the Established Church of France, though co-existent with the equality of civil privilege.

"I do not think, therefore, that it is possible to contend for the abstract position that the true test, or one of the essential tests, of an Established Church is the superior privilege as to civil rights of its members.

"In these times it is not very prudent to lay down general doctrines with respect to the essential attributes of the Church, unless we are quite sure that they are safe doctrines for all parts of our empire.

"It is safe to say, *That* is the Established Church of England to which the King must conform—whose chief ministers have a right to seats in the House of Lords—which has an unalienable claim to ecclesiastical property.

"But I should be sorry for the sake of the Church to argue that she ceased to be the Established Church if you once admitted equality of civil privilege.

"I do not say that there ought to be equality of civil privilege: all I say is, that I should be sorry to rest the question of an Establishment or not upon that issue.

" Ever affectionately yours,

" ROBERT PEEL."

Bishop of OXFORD to Mr. PEEL.

" Christ Church, March 21, 1828.

" MY DEAR PEEL,

"Whenever you write me a long letter, I argue that you are in good spirits, and are not at the moment worked to death. I am very glad also to have your letter, because I had some distrust whether, amidst all your labours, and all the troubles you had taken, and are taking, for the Church and University, it was worth while disturbing you with the remarks of any set of men. But it has happened to me more than once to think, 'that if I had told him what the sentiments of people were, as far as I could learn them, so and so would not have happened,' and I have determined therefore at all hazards to let you know them whenever I judged them of importance; then you might decide for yourself whether they were worth any attention or not. And on this occasion I am not sorry, because, notwithstanding the supposed or real difference between us on the abstract principle, there was quite sufficient in the second speech to reassure those who had been partially offended by the first.

"Now for the argument. First, I did not *recommend* you to use any argument. I said, if I recollect rightly, 'Would it not be possible?' not presuming to recommend, nor thinking it safe to do so. I am as well aware as any man can be, that none but those who have constant opportunity of witnessing and of measuring the feelings of the House of Commons can pretend to decide on the line of conduct or argument which may

E 3

safely be pursued ; and on that ground I had already
answered the objectors, and had told them that you
were the best judge how far you could go safely ; and
in the same feeling I had asked whether it would be
possible to say so and so—meaning that if it was possible, the desires of the grumblers would be satisfied.

" But, secondly, in regard to the extract which you
have sent me from my letter, you have affixed a signifi-
cation to it which I had no intention it should bear.
My words are, '.that to talk of an Established Church,
and at the same time to assert the equal right of all
religious sects, is a contradiction in terms ; that an
established religion necessarily implies a superiority of
privilege ; and that if Lord John Russell wished to
affirm the equal right of all, the more manly way would
be to move at once that there should be no Established
Church.'

" Now, in all this, there is no mention whatever of
civil privilege, or *civil* rights ; nor did I intend of necessity civil privilege when I said privilege. I consider
Lord John Russell, Brougham, and all of them, whenever they talk of an equality of right, when they say
that there ought to be no distinctions of religion, and
use other expressions of the same kind, to say ' that the
State ought not to acknowledge or patronise, in any
way, one religion above another :' and I hold that
whenever such an assertion is made, it may be answered, first, by stating that it is too late to consider
such an argument in England, because there is already
an Established Church ; and secondly, by saying that an
established religion necessarily implies superiority, and

therefore that the State cannot, without first overthrow-
ing the established religion, admit the assertion that all
religions are to be considered equal.

"But whether this superiority be a superiority of spiritual or civil privilege I care not, nor does it matter to
my argument—providing that such superiority, be it
what it may, be acknowledged by the State. But how
stands the fact? The Church of England as far as
regards the exercise of spiritual power is infinitely inferior to the Dissenters: not that the Legislature has
directly done anything to assist or encourage the spiritual power of that body, but that it has placed the
Church of England under so severe a cognizance, has
passed such severe laws in relation to her exertion of
such power, has so impeded and controlled the action
even of the Ecclesiastical Courts, that the spiritual power
of the Church of England is not only virtually but positively taken away by direct acts of the Legislature.
For how stands the law? The Church of England
cannot meet now in any assembly for the purpose of
discussing points of doctrine, of denouncing schism, of
making rules of discipline, or for any other purpose of
the same kind. You abolished all this when you did
in fact abolish Convocation. Nor can her ministers
expel a noxious member, excommunicate, or any thing
of the same kind. You force them at the same time,
without any reference to right or conscience, to baptize,
bury, marry Dissenters. Now, in regard to Dissenters,
they meet, with the full allowance of the Legislature,
in annual conferences; they expel their members; they
refuse them the Sacraments, and so keep up their dis-

cipline by means of which the use is not permitted to
the Church of England. What therefore does the
Church of England derive from being the established
religion of the country, in this point of view? Nothing
whatever; but she loses much; and, if it were not for
civil privileges, it would be impossible for the Church
to cope at all with Dissent, in consequence of the restrictions which the Legislature has imposed upon her
discipline.

"There was a trial the other day in the King's
Bench. A woman is expelled from a Methodist meeting for some alleged moral offence. She brings an
action against the expellers for libel; the Court would
not hear of it; they said any society had a right to
expel its own members, and would not interfere. Can
the Church of England do this? If not, which has the
superiority?

"The Legislature, in fact, say to the Church of
England, ' So long as we guarantee you your property,
we will take to ourselves the right of controlling your
discipline, and of preventing you from exercising any
spiritual power over your own members.' It is a villain-
ous argument, and as oppressive as it is mean.

"Well then, all the spiritual power of the Church
being taken away by law, where can her superiority,
where can her establishment be found, if there be on
all points a perfect equality of civil rights between her
and the Dissenters? Surely nowhere. And if I take
for my essential characteristics of the Church of England those which you point out—namely, the necessity
of the King's conformity, the seats of the chief mi-

nisters in the Legislature, and the property—I see
nothing here but certain civil privileges, which, according to this definition of the Establishment, are necessary
to its existence. Take then away these civil privileges,
and where will be the Establishment?

"As for France, Scotland, and Ireland, I consider
my argument sufficient to overthrow these instances.
In regard to any Roman Catholic country in which the
spiritual power of the priesthood is uncontrolled and
undiminished, I have no fear of the Church losing that
superiority which belongs to an Establishment; and in
the Presbyterian Church of Scotland the uninterrupted
exercise of the same spiritual power by the Moderator
and in her assemblies is a sufficient proof of her
ascendency. In Ireland the surrender of the Test Act
was a wise measure, as being an important instrument
of union between the Church and the Dissenters against
the Roman Catholics. But I am not concerned with
Test Acts. I might be for the repeal of the Test Acts,
and still maintain my proposition 'that an Established
Church of necessity implies superiority.'

"So far I had written when in comes the enclosed
note from the Warden of Wadham, and at the same
time the Bishop of Durham comes from Mongewell in
alarm about the form of the Declaration. Dr. Tournay's note will give you the objections of both: both
were particularly violent against any dispensing power
being left to the Crown.

"I read the latter part of your speech in the newspaper, and conceived that it was wrongly reported; but
what is the meaning of giving the Crown the power of

saying who shall take the oath, and who not? Did you propose this?

"But the Bishop of Durham told me that he had written to the Archbishop on the subject, and I think it probable that before this time you have seen his letter.

"I am myself quite satisfied that the Church will be content with a Declaration, if that Declaration appear sufficient to them. I am satisfied of this, both from the sentiments of the University (though they are not on occasions of this kind a perfectly adequate representative of the opinions of the Church, the Church being in general, as a body, higher in its opinions and more opposed to change than the University), and also from what Van Mildert and others report to me of the opinions of all the clergy whom they have had an opportunity of seeing. But I should think that you may now venture on any Declaration you please. The Sacramental test being removed, I am convinced you will have a majority with you; and it is really of extreme importance to give what satisfaction you can to the high party, both in the country and the House of Lords.

"Van Mildert is manifestly alarmed lest the Bishops should be accused of truckling. He told me that two or three members of the House of Lords had said to him, 'So I hear you have deserted us;' and had added, 'I am sorry you should have left us to fight the battle without you.'

"I have just seen this morning's papers, which give your clauses, and I observe that all persons in corporations or magistracies must make the Declaration, and that the King's power extends merely to *other* civil offices. Is not this so ? If it be, it may perhaps satisfy Tournay and the Bishop of Durham, but it should be very clearly explained.

"Always, my dear Peel, most sincerely yours,

"C. O."

Dr. TOURNAY to the Bishop of OXFORD.

"March 21, 1828.

"MY DEAR LORD,

"My fears on certain points may be morbid, and my information may be very incorrect, being merely derived from newspapers. Certain it is, however, that I am frightened by what appears to be the plan for substituting a Declaration for the Test and Corporation Acts. Most gladly should I part with the Sacramental test, but what we have in exchange should be sufficient in itself, and enforced without any dispensation or interruption whatever. But as matters now stand, the Dissenter is not to declare generally that he will not destroy the Church, but merely that he will not destroy her by means of his official power and opportunities.

"What is still worse, when the Declaration is made what it ought to be, it is only to be made when the Crown thinks fit. So that when Lord Lansdowne is Prime Minister it will never be made at all.

"Can this be so ? If so, the Church will surrender all and gain nothing.

"Yours always,

"W. T."

Mr. Peel to the Bishop of Oxford.

" Whitehall, Saturday, March 22, 1828.

" My dear Lloyd,

" The discussion in the House of Commons has turned exclusively on the question of civil rights.

" I do not know what the private sentiments of Brougham and Lord John Russell may be, but they have never avowed that they wish to see the Church of England severed from the State; and they have always voted for that Declaration which asserted her establishment as permanent and inviolable.

" Any argument from me, therefore, would have been considered—reference being had to the nature of the question under discussion, and the avowed opinions of my opponents—as an argument about civil rights, and about them exclusively.

" As the Bishop of Durham was present at the meeting at Lambeth, and as I understood him distinctly to be an assenting party to what was there agreed to, I am not a little surprised at *his* alarm. However, I most certainly shall refer, without hesitation, to all that passed at Lambeth, as the vindication of the course I have pursued, in case it should be necessary. I have the Declaration which I took down in the presence of the Bishops at Lambeth, and which only differs from the one I moved in being somewhat less strong.

" Dr. Tournay's proposal is this:—Let every man who was formerly subject to the test be now compelled to take the Declaration previously to his admission to

office; that is, let every man who receives the King's
wages—who holds any office or any commission, be
required to make a Declaration about the Church of
England. The annual Indemnity Act of course is not
to apply to this Declaration—it must really be made
and subscribed. Now it certainly would be very edi-
fying to administer to midshipmen, young ensigns in
the Guards, state-trumpeters, all the King's household
servants, all gaugers and tide-waiters, a solemn Declaration that they would not use their influence to the
injury of the Protestant Church.

"But it may be said, 'Specify who are to take this
Declaration, or make all take it as the general rule, and
then specify the exceptions.'

"Just let Dr. Tournay try his hand at a clause spe-
cifying *nominatim* the offices to which the Declaration
is to apply, or the exceptions. It appears to me that
either course would involve the Declaration in ridicule,
or would just confine it to a very few enumerated
offices, at the risk of omitting many which ought to be
included.

"Be it enacted that all Privy Councillors, Sheriffs,
Magistrates, are to take the Declaration : very good.
But what am I to do with officers of the Ordnance ?—
the Surveyor-General of the Ordnance for instance ?—
the Commissioners of Customs—an Indian Judge—is he
to make the Declaration, that whereas all his influence
being confined to the island of Ceylon, he will not use
it in injuring the Church of England ? Really to
attempt in an Act of Parliament to nominate either the
offices or the exceptions, would in my opinion cover the

Declaration with ridicule, even if the attempt were not a hopeless one.

" The taking of the Declaration is essential in the case of all corporate offices—there is no power of dispensation there.

" May we not trust the King—being the head of the Church of England—if we are prepared to entrust him with the power of appointing a Dissenter to the highest civil office, may we not trust him with the power of naming the offices to which the Declaration shall apply?

" Ever yours,

" R. P."

Bishop of OXFORD to Mr. PEEL.

" Christ Church, March 23, 1828.

" MY DEAR PEEL,

" If the Bishop of Durham was aware that your Declaration was the same with that drawn up at Lambeth, or at least not weaker than that—if mention was made at Lambeth of any dispensing power given to the King; and if it was understood by the Bishops there assembled, that the words ' by virtue of my office' were to be introduced, then I have no doubt that he will agree instantly to the Declaration in the present form. I conceive the truth to be this—that the words ' by virtue of my office' were admitted by the Bishops, but that the dispensing power was not mentioned to them. I have no reason, however, for saying this, except that, putting all things together, I suppose it to have been the case.

" But in regard to ' the dispensing power,' though

I agree with you entirely on the impossibility of making a catalogue, either of declarers or of exceptions, and in the ridicule which either catalogue might cast upon the whole measure, yet I do not see the necessity of making this catalogue, or of getting rid of it by allowing the King or his Minister to exercise an individual judgment in this matter; not that I think it of any importance in itself, but the Church is ready to be alarmed: it thinks enough has been done; and though, from the objection of very many of her members to a Sacramental test, she is glad that this test is taken away, yet the difference between a Declaration and a test is so enormous, that she will not be satisfied unless all persons who were before liable to the test are made liable to the Declaration. I should propose, therefore, instead of any catalogue, or of a clause admitting a dispensing power in the King, that a clause to this effect be introduced—that 'all who by the Corporation and Test Acts are required to take the oath of allegiance, shall also at the same time make the Declaration.'

"I can see no objection to this; and all the argument derived *ab absurdo et ridiculo* is immediately done away; for the gauger and tide-waiter are just as likely to subvert the Church as the Crown; and as they must (if they must) take the oath of allegiance, there would be no difficulty or inconvenience in their making the Declaration at the same time, and before the same person. And if the said gauger or tide-waiter are *not* required to take the oath of allegiance, then neither let them be required to make the Declaration.

"But the new Act will, as I conceive, only repeal
that part of the old Corporation and Test Acts which
relates to the Sacramental test; and therefore *all* who
were before obliged to take the oath of allegiance must
still do it; then why not *all* make the Declaration?
It seems to me that the matter is without difficulty, and
would pass without objection, unless indeed you are
already so far committed to the House of Commons or
the Committee that you cannot retrace your steps.

"Now, supposing such to be the case, and that you
could not, without much difficulty and much inconvenient explanation, now alter the Declaration, would
there be any objection to the Bishop of Durham moving
an amendment to that effect? If the Bill were to be
sent down to you so amended, do you think it would
run the risk of being thrown out in the House of
Commons? I confess to you I think not.

"Pray consider this and let me know.

"Of one point you may be quite certain. A very
large majority of the Church and the University are
against a Sacramental test; and this is a great point.
Still they would like the security without the Sacrament,
and they feel the difference between a Declaration and
a test to be enormous. Satisfied as I am that not one
out of a hundred persons was aware, before this discussion, that any persons except the members of Corporations were obliged to qualify, they might now be
satisfied, when they see that all whom they supposed
liable to test are now called upon to make the Declaration; but having now discovered that there were other
persons liable before, they think it hard that they

should be obliged not only to surrender the test in regard to all, but even the Declaration in regard to some.

" I am, my dear Peel, most sincerely yours,

" CHARLES OXFORD."

Mr. PEEL to the Bishop of OXFORD.

" Tuesday, March 25, 1828.

" MY DEAR LLOYD,

" (A.) I took the course I did take with respect to the Declaration at the earnest desire of some of the Bishops who were at Lambeth, particularly of the Archbishop of Canterbury. I wished to be merely an acquiescing party in the Declaration proposed by Sir Thomas Acland. Their wish was that I should propose the Declaration myself, or at any rate take a very prominent part in advising its acceptance.

" Their observation was—That which comes from you will be considered in a totally different light from that which comes from a private individual.

" I reluctantly promised to accede to their wishes, and either to propose or very actively to support the Declaration.

" (B.) I quite understand the Bishop of Durham. The lay Peers who have spoken to him, and accused him of deserting them and leaving them to fight the battle of the Church, terrify him. For the sake of the Church, let him trust to his own judgment, and not to that of Lord Redesdale, Lord Winchilsea, and the Duke of Newcastle.

" (C.) I will not be a party to any amendment that the Bishop of Durham may move in the House of Lords.

" I cannot now say what course I will pursue in respect to that or any other amendment; but I will not pledge myself, beforehand, to accept an amendment from the Lords which I am not myself prepared to move in the House of Commons.

" (D.) You propose that the Declaration shall be put on the same footing exactly as the oath of allegiance; that is — unless I am very much mistaken — you do away with the Declaration altogether practically.

" Whereas I insist upon it as a *sine quâ non* with respect to every corporate office, and enable the King to insist upon it in the case of every civil office.

" (E.) I do not believe that as the law stands at present, the oath of allegiance is required in the army or navy, or in half the civil offices in the country.

" The not taking it is, I apprehend, on just the same footing with the not taking the oath of supremacy.

" The omission is covered by the annual Indemnity Act.

" If it will satisfy the Church to put the Declaration I have proposed on the same footing; that is, to make it a dead letter by only requiring it to be made *after* the acceptance of office, and then covering the omission by the annual Indemnity Act—this course will satisfy me; but it is a mere nothing compared with what I have proposed, namely, that a corporate office shall be actually void unless the Declaration in favour of the Church be made *before* the entry into office.

" The difference between a Declaration and a test like the present is certainly enormous, if you will *bonâ fide* act upon your test; but eighty-five years' relaxation of it, and the notorious inability to enforce the test without absolute confusion, change the nature of the difference, and, in my opinion, all in favour of the Declaration.

" Ever most sincerely yours,

" R. P.

"I much doubt whether half of the Cabinet Ministers have taken the oath of allegiance as a necessary qualification for the offices which they hold."

Bishop of OXFORD to Mr. PEEL.

" Christ Church, March 26, 1828.

" MY DEAR PEEL,

" I return you your letter* for the purpose of reference, which I think will enable you more easily to understand my remarks.

" (A.) I think the Bishops were wrong in persuading you to be the *proposer* of the Declaration. I should have agreed with you entirely that you should have been the acquiescing party, consenting to it as a *pis aller* when you could not gain a majority against simple repeal. I see nothing but cowardice in the advice of the Bishops.

" (B.) Van Mildert did not tell me who the lay Peers were who spoke to him on the subject. He said

---

* Mine of the 25th of March.—R. P.

he should oppose the Bill, if any dispensing or discretionary power was left to the Crown; and I have not seen or written to him since.

" (C.) Van Mildert did not know that I said anything to you about an amendment, or about his proposing anything; and I only meant to ask you whether, if the amendment I proposed was substituted for your Clause C., you thought such a change would throw out the Bill in the House of Commons. Of course I could not ask you to be a party or a pledge to anything of the kind.

" (D.) No. I do not propose that the Declaration shall be on the same footing as the oath of allegiance, except so far as regards Clause C. I took for granted that in regard to all Corporate offices the Declaration was to be made by all, and of course, as the Corporation Act directs, made upon admission to office.

" (E.) I dare say not, because the Indemnity Act covers all. But, after this Bill is passed, will there be an Indemnity Act for those who, according to the provisions of the Test Act, have not taken the oaths of allegiance and supremacy within six months after the passing of the Act? If not, must not all civil and military officers, after this Bill has passed, take the oaths? This is what I want to know, and the answer to it will, in all probability, enable me to get rid of all objections. For if there is to be an Indemnity Act for all officers who shall not have taken the oaths, I am quite ready to admit that your Clause C. is an equivalent for it.

" There is very little feeling about the matter in this place. I have been very unwell for the last week and

confined to the house, and have seen nobody except
Van Mildert and Tournay. The latter is the representative of a very small body of individuals; the sentiments of the former are generally in unison with those
of the Church of England, and it is on this account
and from my personal regard for him, and my gratitude
for his uniform kindness to me, that I am anxious that
nothing may take place which may displease him or
oppose his principles. I am anxious to have him as a
warm and conscientious supporter, and if I can make
him so by a little explanation I shall think my time
well spent, for I am sure his opinions will influence those
of the whole Church.

" Always, my dear Peel,

" Most sincerely yours,

" C. O."

Bishop of OXFORD to Mr. PEEL.

" Christ Church, March 28, 1828.

" MY DEAR PEEL,

" I am much obliged to you for your letter, and
delighted by the Order of Council, which will settle all
difficulties and remove all objections. I have seen the
Warden of Wadham, who is quite satisfied, and whose
tongue is stopped; and I have no doubt that Van Mildert also will be content.

" I confess to you that it is no small delight to me
to feel that the measure may now pass not only with the
votes but with the goodwill of all whose opinions I respect. And I must trust to you to forgive me if I am

F

importunate on subjects on which opinions are afloat, and feelings are excited, which, if not watched, may ultimately be productive of much evil.

> "Always, my dear Peel,
> "Most sincerely yours,
> "C. O.

"Send a copy of the Bill to the Vice-Chancellor."

The proceedings in the two Houses of Parliament in reference to the repeal of the Test Laws are fully reported in the Parliamentary Debates. It will be seen that objections were taken to the power originally given to the Crown to name the offices on the appointment to which the Declaration substituted for the Sacramental test should be made. In the House of Commons those objections were obviated by providing that the specification of the offices should be an act of the King in Council. In the Lords the Bill was altered in this respect. All discretionary authority was taken away. As the general rule the Declaration was required to be made by all persons employed in the public service. There followed an exception from that rule, expressly inserted in the Act, in favour of naval and military officers below the rank of Rear-Admiral and Major-General, and of all persons whatever employed in the management or collection of the revenue.

Another more important alteration was made in the Bill in its passage through the Lords.

As the Bill was sent from the Commons the Declaration was not required to be made "on the true faith of a Christian." Those words, objected to at the time by Lord Holland, were inserted in the Lords at the suggestion of Lord Eldon and the Bishop of Llandaff.

The Bill as sent to the House of Lords from the Commons passed without any other important change.

Lord Eldon offered his most decided opposition to the Bill. He was greatly incensed by the conduct of the Bishops in giving it their support. In his published letters to his daughter he speaks of the Bill "as being, in his poor judgment, as bad, as mischievous, and as revolutionary as the most captious Dissenter could wish it to be." He says that "the administration have, to their shame be it said, got the Archbishops and most of the Bishops to support this revolutionary Bill."

In speaking in the House of Lords, Lord Eldon observed, "that he had voted against such a Bill before some of their Lordships now supporting it were born; and he might say the same of some of the Right Reverend Prelates who were so strangely showing their attachment to the Church. The last time the question was agitated in the House of Commons was in 1790, when there was a majority of 187 against it. Nothing had occurred since to make it less mischievous."

But I must remark, in vindication of the prelates and in my own vindication, that something had occurred since the period referred to by Lord Eldon, which it would not have been wise to exclude from the consideration, namely, that the majority of 187 which voted against the Bill in the year 1790 had been converted in 1828 into a majority of 44 in its favour.

It might be consistent with perfect fidelity and attachment to the Church to believe that with this decisive evidence of a change in public opinion, and considering the conscientious objections of many sincere friends of the Church to the Sacramental test as a qualification for office, it might be more for the real interests of the Church and of religion to consent to an alteration of the law than to commit a minority of the House of Commons, even with the aid of the Lords, to a conflict for its maintenance.

On the 8th of May, 1828, the Catholic Question was brought forward by Sir Francis Burdett.

He moved a Resolution to this effect—

"That it is the opinion of this Committee that it is expedient to consider the state of the laws affecting His Majesty's Roman Catholic subjects in Great Britain and Ireland, with a view to such a final and conciliatory adjustment as may be conducive to the peace and strength of the United Kingdom, to the stability of the Protestant Establishment, and to the general satisfaction and concord of all classes of His Majesty's subjects."

This Resolution was affirmed in a Committee of the whole House by a majority of 272 to 266, was adopted by the House, and communicated by its direction to the House of Lords at a conference.

There was thus for the first time in that Parliament (the Parliament of 1826) a majority of the House of Commons in favour of the Roman Catholic claims. At an earlier period of the Session the House of Commons, notwithstanding the opposition of the Government, had declared its opinion, by a still larger majority of 237 to

193, in favour of the repeal of the Test and Corporation Acts, and the Bill for their repeal had been assented to by the Lords, and had passed into a law previously to the vote on the Catholic Question in the House of Commons.

The mere fact that the House of Commons had, for the first time in that Parliament, voted for the removal of the Roman Catholic Disabilities, is not alone to be adverted to in considering the bearing of that vote upon the policy of continued resistance to concession. The character of the discussion, and the names and relative weight and authority of those who took part in it, must also be duly estimated.

It was remarked by Mr. Brougham, who closed the debate, that no single Member of those who had opposed the motion of Sir Francis Burdett had affirmed the proposition that things could remain as they were, and that it was impossible to conceal or deny the great progress which this question had made in Parliament and the much greater out of doors.

Among the speakers in favour of the motion were—

Sir FRANCIS BURDETT.
Mr. DOHERTY (the Solicitor-General for Ireland).
Lord FRANCIS EGERTON.
Sir JOHN NEWPORT.
Mr. WILMOT HORTON.
Sir JAMES MACKINTOSH.
Mr. BROWNLOW.
Mr. W. LAMB (the Chief Secretary for Ireland).
Mr. CHARLES GRANT (the President of the Board of Trade).
Mr. NORTH.
Mr. HUSKISSON (Secretary of State for the Colonies).
Mr. BROUGHAM.

The speakers against the motion were—

Sir CHARLES WETHERELL.
Sir N. TINDAL.
Sir ROBERT INGLIS.
Mr. WILLIAM DUNCOMBE.
Mr. GEORGE BANKES.
Mr. GEORGE MOORE.
Mr. LESLIE FOSTER.
Mr. PEEL.

Without depreciating the abilities or authority of those who concurred with me in resisting the motion, any one acquainted with the state of the House of Commons at that time would readily admit that the great preponderance of talent and of influence on the future decisions of the House of Commons was ranged on the other side.

Of several facts significant of the progress of public opinion, and of the ultimate issue of the contest, this was not the least remarkable—that many of the younger members of the House of Commons who had previously taken a part against the Roman Catholic claims, followed the example of Mr. Brownlow and admitted the change of opinion, and that it very rarely, if ever, happened that the list of speakers against concession was reinforced by a young Member even of ordinary ability.

Scarcely a week had elapsed after the vote in favour of Sir Francis Burdett's motion, when the discussion took place on the Bill for the disfranchisement of East Retford, which led to the retirement from office of Mr. Huskisson, Lord Dudley, Lord Palmerston, Mr. Grant, and Mr. William Lamb.

My own retirement at an early period would have

been determined by the vote on Sir Francis Burdett's motion. I should have taken this course in 1828, which I had wished and intended to take in 1825, and have declined to remain Minister for the Home Department and to lead the House of Commons, being in a minority on the most important of domestic questions.

The threatened danger to the Duke of Wellington's Government from the retirement of Mr. Huskisson and his friends, and the real difficulty of constructing, from any combination of parties, any other Government at that time, so recently after the breaking up of the administration over which Lord Ripon had presided, induced me not to insist upon retirement at the very moment when other members of the Government were withdrawing, upon totally distinct grounds, their cooperation from the Duke of Wellington.

The following letters passed between Mr. Lamb and me on the occasion of our political separation :—

Mr. LAMB to Mr. PEEL.

" Whitehall, May 26, 1828.

" DEAR PEEL,

" I send you an account of a most cruel and audacious outrage, which I received yesterday morning.

" I have further to inform you that I have just sent my resignation to the Duke of Wellington. Without giving any opinion upon the circumstances which have led to it, the fact of Huskisson's being withdrawn from the administration, with the other changes which must ensue, so entirely alters the aspect of affairs, and so

entirely subverts the principle upon which I understood
the Government to have been formed in January last,
that I feel it impossible that I should continue in office
with any regard to consistency. I cannot, however,
terminate our short official intercourse without expressing my high esteem for your character, and the perfect
reliance which I have always felt, and should always
feel, upon your honour and integrity.

" Yours faithfully,

" WM. LAMB."

Mr. PEEL to Mr. LAMB.

" Whitehall Gardens, Tuesday morning.

" MY DEAR LAMB,

"I deeply lament all that has recently occurred,
and certainly no part of it more than your secession
from office. There were few things that I looked forward
to in public life with more satisfaction than a cordial
union with you. I will not touch upon any other subject than my deep regret at our separation—excepting
indeed to say, that I should deprecate most sincerely
any change in the principle upon which the Government was formed in January last.

" With the truest esteem and regard, believe me, &c.,

" ROBERT PEEL."

Lord Anglesey remained in Ireland as Lord-Lieutenant, and Lord Francis Gower (now Lord Ellesmere)
accepted the office of Secretary in place of Mr. Lamb.

Amongst the offices vacated in consequence of the

recent schism in the Government, was that of President of the Board of Trade. It was offered to and accepted by Mr. Vesey Fitzgerald.

As the necessary consequence of Mr. Fitzgerald's appointment, the seat for the county of Clare became vacant, and events occurred in Ireland of deep importance, especially in their relation to the Catholic Question, and to other questions connected with the administration of affairs in Ireland, and with the legislation for that country, which, after the opinions of the House of Commons, so recently declared in favour of concession, could not be regarded separately from the Catholic Question.

For instance, I presume no one would have supposed it possible that the House of Commons, after the vote of the 12th of May, would consent to annihilate the forty-shilling franchise, and at the same time to leave in full force the civil disabilities of the Roman Catholics.

The election for the county of Clare took place in the latter end of June, 1828. It ended in the defeat of Mr. Fitzgerald and the return of Mr. O'Connell. It afforded a decisive proof, not only that the instrument on which the Protestant proprietor had hitherto mainly relied for the maintenance of his political influence had completely failed him, but that through the combined exertions of the agitator and the priest, or I should rather say through the contagious sympathies of a common cause among all classes of the Roman Catholic population, the instrument of defence and supremacy had been converted into a weapon fatal to the authority of the landlord.

However men might differ as to the consequences which ought to follow the event, no one denied its vast importance.

It was foreseen by the most intelligent that the Clare election would be the turning point in the Catholic question—the point—

" Partes ubi se via findit in ambas."

In a letter to his daughter soon after the event, Lord Eldon, after observing, " Nothing is talked of now which interests anybody the least in the world, except the election of Mr. O'Connell," makes these memorable remarks :—" As Mr. O'Connell will not, though elected, be allowed to take his seat in the House of Commons unless he will take the oaths, &c. (and that he won't do unless he can get absolution), his rejection from the Commons may excite rebellion in Ireland. At all events this business must bring the Roman Catholic question, which has been so often discussed, to a crisis and a conclusion. The nature of that conclusion I do not think likely to be favourable to Protestantism." It is clear therefore that Lord Eldon was fully alive to the real character and magnitude of the event.

He well knew that no Protestant candidate could hope to contest a Roman Catholic county in Ireland with greater advantages in his favour than Mr. Fitzgerald. He was personally popular ; had gained great credit by the manner in which he had discharged, at an earlier period of his political career, the duty of Chancellor of the Exchequer for Ireland ; had uniformly given his vote for the removal of Roman Catholic disabilities, and was supposed to have an influence in the county of Clare, from property, station, and past services to his constituents, which must ensure his triumphant return.

The following letters give an account of the signal defeat of Mr. Fitzgerald, of the excited state of the population, of the imminent danger to the public peace, and of the measures taken to preserve it :—

Mr. VESEY FITZGERALD to Mr. PEEL.

"Dublin, June 17, 1828.

"MY DEAR PEEL,

"I am sorry to tell you that my anticipations are but too likely to be anticipated,* and that I have every reason to fear a violent and exasperated contest.

"The Association has taken the field, and addresses are directed to be prepared to the Bishops, the clergy, and the population of Clare.

"On Sunday I am informed that exhortations were addressed to the congregations, and a circular letter is to be read at all the altars on next Sunday.

"I am told that, though there is a great schism among them, O'Connell and the violent ones have carried it all their own way. Mr. O'Connell says he cannot go down, but that I know is because he is afraid of personal risk and danger. I am now embarked in, and I must go through with it. I have been

* Plainly a slip of the pen for "fulfilled."—*Eds.*

greatly harassed by all this, and if I write incoherently
you must excuse it.   I only write because you desired
it, and because I know you will be anxious about me
and my prospects in this cursed affair.

" Ever yours affectionately,

" W. Vesey Fitzgerald."

Mr. Peel to Mr. Vesey Fitzgerald.

" Whitehall, June 21, 1828.

" My dear Fitzgerald,

" I shall be glad to hear from you when
you have had some little experience of the county of
Clare.

" Disregard entirely all personalities, whether proceeding from O'Connell or others of his stamp.

" It really is quite unnecessary for a gentleman and
a Minister of the Crown to notice the low slang of a
county election.

" It gives a vast advantage over the gentlemen of a
county if they are to place themselves on a level with
every blackguard who wantonly attempts to provoke
them.

" File an information against Mr. O'This or Mr.
Mac That, and every real gentleman will applaud the
true courage of doing so.   No one will misunder-
stand it.

" Ever, &c.

" Robert Peel."

Mr. VESEY FITZGERALD to Mr. PEEL.

(No date.)

" MY DEAR PEEL,

" Nothing can equal the violence here.

" The proceedings of yesterday were those of mad-men, but the country is mad, and they have been allowed to proceed in the career of revolution.

" It will not, cannot end well.

" As to myself and my election, I am now embarked, and must go through with it.

" I fear it will be a tremendous contest. You will judge of the spirit of this country, and of what I have to encounter, from the paper which I enclose to you.

" An ineffectual attempt was made to resist Mr. O'Connell, but all were borne down by the violence of the meeting.

" I leave this to-morrow.

" I only hope that some man whom I can notice without dishonour may repeat the calumnies and the language which Mr. O'C., in the impunity which he enjoys, has dared to address to me.

" Most affectionately yours,

" W. V. FITZGERALD."

Mr. GREGORY to Mr. PEEL.

(Confidential.)

" Dublin, June 27, 1828.

" MY DEAR PEEL,

" As I understand the Lord Lieutenant is in constant communication with you on the state of this country, I do not think it necessary to trouble you with letters from me.

" I apprehend very serious disturbances in Clare, and though any violation of the public peace is to be deprecated in such an ignited country as Ireland, yet the cause and the effects of the present contest are much more alarming. From the best information I can procure, Fitzgerald will not be returned. Every necessary precaution has been taken, by augmenting the military and police, to preserve the peace.

" I fear nothing will prevent the Orangemen of the North from walking in procession on the 12th of July. The persons of rank who formerly had influence over them have lost it, and they are in the hands of inferior men, who are as violent as the lowest of their order.

" Most truly yours,
" W. GREGORY."

Mr. GREGORY to Mr. PEEL.

(Private.)

" Phœnix Park, June 29, 1828.

" MY DEAR PEEL,

" I received by express last night a Resolution passed at a numerous meeting of magistrates and gentlemen of the county of Clare, requesting the Lord Lieutenant to afford such assistance to the High Sheriff as shall insure the freedom of election, and prevent all undue interference with the freeholders coming to the poll.

" The wishes of the magistrates had been anticipated

by the Lord Lieutenant two days previous to the receipt
of their application, and troops ordered to be advanced
to the county of Clare, with large reserves, to be called
upon if the High Sheriff and Magistrates shall think
necessary. Such a military force, aided by the police,
whose numbers Major Warburton may augment from
Galway according to his discretion, will be sufficient,
it may reasonably be expected, to suppress any disturbance. If O'Connell acted by those rules which would
guide other men, we might suppose it to be his interest
to prevent any tumult, and to attempt to prove that he
was not returned by violence and intimidation, but by
the quiet and peaceable choice of the people. However,
having excited the Roman Catholic population to madness, he will find it difficult to restrain them, even if he
is so inclined.

" I am informed that the gentlemen who support
Fitzgerald (and they all do) are determined to appear
at the hustings and give their votes, even though their
tenantry vote against them. I hope they may have
fortitude not to shrink from this resolution, as then will
be carried into effect the long-suspended threat of
numerical strength against property. Not that I anticipate any benefit to follow in the House of Commons,
but I do with the people of England.

" The accounts from Clare and Limerick, received
this day, are filled with great alarm at the preparations
making to receive O'Connell. He is to be met this
day at Nenagh after Mass, and escorted thence to the
borders of Clare by hundreds of horsemen and all the
trades of the city of Limerick, in which city his cause

is espoused by many respectable Roman Catholics
who never before interfered in the politics of the
Association.

" I have written to you a longer letter than I had
intended, and you will probably read all the details
much better given in the newspapers.

" I sincerely regret the disappointment and mortifi-
cation Fitzgerald must suffer.

" Most truly yours,

" W. GREGORY.

" Return to me the different papers sent to you by
the Lord Lieutenant yesterday."

Lord ANGLESEY to Mr. PEEL.

" Phœnix Park, July 1, 1828.

" MY DEAR MR. PEEL,

" I have had two letters from Ennis this morning—one from Mr. Fitzgerald : it is, I think, desponding, and appearing to think that he is not sufficiently
protected by a military force.

" I think he could not be aware of that by which he
is surrounded.

" Baron Tuyll sees things in a more favourable point
of view. He, however, calls for more military aid ; but
he too must have been in ignorance of the measures
that I have taken, and which moreover I desired to be
made known to the Inspector-General of the constabulary, to the Sheriff, and to the Magistrates.

There are at Ennis near . . 300 constabulary.
At Clare Castle (close at hand) 47 artillery, with 2 six-pounders.
                    120 cavalry.
                    415 infantry.
Within a few hours . . . . 183 cavalry.
                   1313 infantry.
Within 36 hours . . . . . . 28 cavalry.
                 1367 infantry.
                   2 six-pounders.

" These are placed at the disposal of the General Officer, as are also reserves, at a further distance, of one regiment of cavalry and above 800 infantry.

" If this cannot keep one county quiet, we are in a bad way; but I cannot persuade myself that there will be serious riot.

" I really believe the agitators are anxious to preserve order, and that they have the power as well as the inclination to accomplish it—it will be an additional triumph to them.

" I have not time to write to Lord Francis to-day.

              " Believe me, &c.,

                   " ANGLESEY."

Mr. VESEY FITZGERALD to Mr. PEEL.

           " Ennis, July 5, 1828 (at night).
" MY DEAR PEEL,

    " The election, thank God, is over, and I do feel happy in its being terminated, notwithstanding its result.

" I have polled all the gentry and all the fifty-pound freeholders—the gentry to a man.

" Of others I have polled a few tenants of ————*
only, my own, and not much besides what adhered to
me in that way.

" All the great interests broke down, and the desertion has been universal. Such a scene as we have
had! Such a tremendous prospect as it opens to us!

" My aim has been from the beginning to preserve
good temper, and to keep down the feelings of my
excited friends.

" The conduct of the priests has passed all that you
could picture to yourself.

" The Sheriff declared the numbers to-night. To go
on would have been idle. I have kept on for five days,
and it was a hopeless contest from the first. Everything
was against me. Indeed I do not understand how I
have not been beaten by a greater majority.

" The Sheriff has made a special Return, and you will
say a strange one; but it will force Parliament instantly
to take it up. It states that I was proposed, being a
Protestant, as a fit person to represent the county in
Parliament; that Mr. O'Connell, a Roman Catholic,
was also proposed; that he, O'Connell, had declared
before the Sheriff that he was a Roman Catholic, and
intended to continue a Roman Catholic.

" It states that a protest was made by the electors
against his return; as well as the certificate that he was
called to the Bar as a Roman Catholic.

" It states the numbers for each candidate—and thus
it leaves the Return.

———

* This word in the MS. is illegible, and was marked with a
" Query" by Sir Robert Peel.—*Eds.*

" I shall see you soon, I trust. I shall be able to get away from here, I hope, on Monday. I must have a day's rest, and one day to settle my accounts, and, as far as I can, arrange respecting them.

" I care not for anything since I have terminated the contest. For the degradation of the county I feel deeply, and the organization exhibited is so complete and so formidable that no man can contemplate without alarm what is to follow in this wretched country.

" Ever yours affectionately,

" W. V. FITZGERALD."

The last letter of Mr. Fitzgerald is especially worthy of remark. He says, "I have polled all the gentry, and all the fifty-pound freeholders—the gentry to a man." But he adds, " All the great interests (of the county) broke down, and the desertion has been universal. Such a scene as we have had! Such a tremendous prospect as it opens to us!"

A prospect tremendous indeed!

Can there be a doubt that the example of the county would not have been all-powerful in the case of every future election in Ireland for those counties in which a Roman Catholic constituency preponderated?

It is true that Mr. O'Connell was the most formidable competitor whom Mr. Fitzgerald could have encountered; it is possible that that which took place in Clare would not have taken place had any other man than Mr. O'Connell been the candidate; but he must be blind indeed to the natural progress of events, and to the influence of example in times of public excitement on the feelings and passions of men, who could cherish the delusive hope that the instrument of political power shivered to atoms in the county of Clare could still be wielded with effect in Cork or Galway.

The Clare election supplied the manifest proof of an abnormal and unhealthy condition of the public mind in Ireland—the manifest proof that the sense of a common grievance and the sympathies of a common interest were beginning to loosen the ties which connect different classes of men in friendly relations to each other—to weaken the force of local and personal attachments, and to unite the scattered elements of society into a homogeneous and disciplined mass, yielding willing obedience to the assumed authority of superior intelligence hostile to the law and to the Government which administered it.

There is a wide distinction (though it is not willingly recognised by a heated party) between the hasty concession to unprincipled agitation, and provident precautions against the explosion of public feeling gradually acquiring the strength which will make it irresistible.

" Concede nothing to agitation " is the ready cry of those who are not responsible—the vigour of whose decisions is often proportionate to their own personal immunity from danger, and to their imperfect knowledge of the true state of affairs.

A prudent Minister, before he determines against all concession—against any yielding or compromise of former opinions—must well consider what it is that he has to resist, and what are his powers of resistance.

His task would be an easy one if it were sufficient to resolve that he would yield nothing to violence or to the menace of physical force.

In this case of the Clare election, and of its natural consequences, what was the evil to be apprehended? Not force—not violence—not any act of which law could take cognizance. The real danger was in the peaceable and legitimate exercise of a franchise according to the will and conscience of the holder.

In such an exercise of that franchise, not merely permitted, but encouraged and approved by constitutional law, was involved a revolution in the electoral system of Ireland—the transfer of political power, so far as it was connected with representation, from one party to another.

The actual transfer was the least of the evil; the process by which it was to be effected—the repetition in each county of the scenes of the Clare election—" the fifty-pound freeholders, the gentry to a man," polling one way, their alienated tenantry another—" all the great interests of the county broken down "—the " universal desertion " (I am quoting the expressions of Mr. Fitzgerald)—the agitator and the priest laughing to scorn the baffled landlord—the local heavings and throes of society on every casual vacancy in a county—the universal convulsion at a General Election—this was the danger to be apprehended—these were the evils to be " resisted."

What was the power of resistance?

" Alter the law, remodel the franchise," was the ready, the improvident response.

If it had been desired to increase the strength of a

formidable confederacy, and, by rallying round it the sympathies of good men and of powerful parties in Great Britain, to ensure for it a signal triumph—to extinguish the hope of effecting an amicable adjustment of the Catholic question, and of applying a corrective to the real evils and abuses of the elective franchise—the best way to attain these pernicious ends would have been to propose to Parliament, on the part of the Government, the abrupt extinction of the forty-shilling franchise in Ireland, together with the continued maintenance of civil disability.

I well know that there are those upon whom such considerations as these to which I have been adverting will make but a faint impression. Their answer to all such appeals is the short, in their opinion the conclusive, declaration, " The Protestant Constitution in Church and State must be maintained at all hazards and by any means : the maintenance of it is a question of principle, and every concession or compromise is the sacrifice of principle to a low and vulgar expediency."

This is easily said—but how was Ireland to be governed ? How was the Protestant Constitution in Church and State to be maintained in that part of the empire ? Again I can anticipate the reply :—" By the overwhelming sense of the people of Great Britain—by the application, if necessary, of physical force for the maintenance of authority—by the employment of the organised strength of Government, the police, and the military, to enforce obedience to the law."

Is there in that reply any solution of the real difficulty ? The overwhelming sense of the people in

Great Britain was no aid to the executive Government in the daily practical administration of the law in Ireland.

If there were seditious libels to be punished, or illegal confederacies, dangerous to the public peace, to be suppressed, the offenders could only be corrected and checked through the intervention of an Irish jury, little disposed, if fairly selected, to defer, in the time of political excitement, to the authority of English opinion. But the real difficulty to be surmounted was not the violation of the law—the real difficulty was in the novel exercise of constitutional franchises—in the application of powers recognised and protected by the law—the power of speech—the power of meeting in public assemblies—the systematic and not unlawful application of all these powers to one definite purpose, namely, the organisation of a force which professed to be a moral force, but had for its objects to encroach step by step on the functions of regular government, to paralyse its authority, and to acquire a strength which might ultimately render irresistible the demand for civil equality.

No doubt all this was very offensive to public opinion in England and Scotland. But through what channel could that public opinion exercise any control over Irish agitation, or render any aid to the Government in resisting it? Was there any other except that of Parliament—except through such a manifestation of the strength of public opinion as should induce Parliament to alter the existing law, to control the liberty which was said to have been abused, and to extinguish the

franchise which the landlord could no longer command
or influence ?

I have attempted to show that no such alteration of
the law could have been expected from a House of
Commons which had decided that the experiment of
another remedy for the distracted state of Ireland,
namely, the establishment of civil equality, ought to be
tried without delay.

It may be said that the House of Commons did not
fairly represent the state of public opinion in Great
Britain. I will try to estimate, from other indications
than the votes of the House of Commons, the real
weight of this public opinion in Great Britain, and the
aid which it was likely to afford to the Government of
Ireland in maintaining (to use a common and intelligible phrase) Protestant principles in that part of the
United Kingdom.

As I observed in 1829, in proposing the Roman
Catholic Relief Bill—speaking of the Parliament
elected in 1826, of the representatives returned to Parliament by the following counties respectively—

YORKSHIRE,	DEVONSHIRE,
LANCASHIRE,	SURREY, and
MIDDLESEX,	KENT,

a majority voted against the maintenance of Protestant
principles—voted at least for the removal of civil disabilities.

The members for London, for Liverpool, for Nor-
wich, for Coventry, for Leicester, were equally divided
on the question.

The Members for Westminster, Southwark, New-castle-upon-Tyne, Preston, Chester, and Derby, voted unanimously for concession.

It may be said that Parliament might again have been dissolved. But what ground was there to expect that a House of Commons elected in 1828 or 1829, would come to a different conclusion on the Catholic question from the House of Commons of 1826?

The General Election of 1826 took place under circumstances especially calculated to call forth the manifestation of Protestant feeling throughout the country. It was in the year preceding that Election that the Commons, after long discussion and severe contest, had sent to the Lords, by a majority of 21, a Bill for the Repeal of Roman Catholic Disabilities.

Surely this was ample notice to the Protestant constituencies of Great Britain, that the hour for strenuous exertion on their part had arrived. It was with that notice that the Elections of 1826 had taken place.

If there was little hope in a renewed appeal to the constituencies of Great Britain, was the prospect of such an appeal in Ireland more satisfactory? Is there any sane man responsible for the public peace—any sane man sincerely anxious to support the Protestant interest in Ireland, who, after the events of the Clare election in June, 1828, would have advised a simultaneous appeal to all the Irish constituencies in the summer or autumn of that year?

If the Irish Government could neither turn for aid to the then existing Parliament, nor could cherish the hope of receiving it from one to be newly elected, could it

G

safely trust for the maintenance of its authority, for the punishment of acts which were illegal, or the counter-action of designs which, if not absolutely illegal, were manifestly dangerous to the public peace—to the extreme exercise of its ordinary powers, supported in case of necessity by the organized and disciplined force at its command, namely, the constabulary and military force?

This is a very delicate matter to discuss; but why have I deferred for twenty years this vindication of my conduct? Why have I consented to submit for that long period to every reproach which malice, or mistake, or blindness to the real state of affairs could direct against me, except in the hope that the time would come (I cared little whether I were in the grave or not when it should come) when delicate matters might safely be discussed, and when, without prejudice to the public interests, or offence to private feelings, the whole truth might be spoken?

I deliberately affirm, that a Minister of the Crown, responsible at the time of which I am speaking for the public peace and the public welfare, would have grossly and scandalously neglected his duty if he had failed to consider whether it might not be possible that the fever of political and religious excitement which was quickening the pulse and fluttering the bosom of the whole Catholic population—which had inspired the serf of Clare with the resolution and energy of a freeman—which had in the twinkling of an eye made all considerations of personal gratitude—ancient family connection —local preferences—the fear of worldly injury—the hope of worldly advantage, subordinate to the one absorbing sense of religious obligation and public duty ; whether, I say, it might not be possible that the contagion of that feverish excitement might spread beyond the barriers which, under ordinary circumstances, the habits of military obedience and the strictness of military discipline oppose to all such external influences.

This may appear to some the refined speculation—the needless misgiving of a civilian, to be repelled as derogatory to the military character, and utterly unworthy of serious regard by all who are practically conversant with the feelings and habits engendered by discipline—by the *esprit de corps*—by the sense of honour pervading all ranks of the British army.

But the Chief Governor of Ireland at that crisis of Irish history was not a civilian. He was a brave and distinguished soldier, well qualified to appreciate the feelings and habits of soldiers, and the confidence that might be placed in their fidelity. Of chivalrous honour himself, he was the last man to entertain a suspicion or hint a doubt injurious to the honour of that profession of which he was an ornament. But Lord Anglesey was also capable of estimating the force of other influences, operating at an extraordinary crisis, and in the following documents will be found the proof that he did not contemplate without anxiety their pernicious effects on the discipline, the harmony, the fidelity even—of some portions at least of the force in Ireland.

On the 11th of July Lord Anglesey addressed to me a confidential letter, from which the following is an extract :—

Lord ANGLESEY to Mr. PEEL.

"July 11, 1828.*

"Unless the King's Ministers (taking into consideration the alarming progress of organization, the unlimited power of the priests, and the complete control under which these are of the Association) should feel the necessity of no longer delaying their decision of the course to be pursued, I humbly conceive that the less notice is taken of the late occurrences in Clare the better, and I for one shall appear to treat it lightly, and as if it were an ordinary election contest.

"Its character, however, is far—very far otherwise, as Mr. Fitzgerald will fully detail to you. I need not enlarge upon this subject. I was almost tempted to send my aide-de-camp, Baron Tuyll, to make a report to you. I thought it possible that the high colouring Mr. Fitzgerald might be tempted to give to the transaction would be considered, partly at least, as the effect of disappointment, vexation, and injured feelings, and that a confirmation from the Baron, who was a calm and very observing witness, might take away all doubt of the facts which will be stated. I have, however, decided otherwise. His mission would be known and observed upon."

On the following day, however, Lord Anglesey announced his intention of sending Major Warburton to

* This, and the other letters of which extracts are here given, will be inserted *in extenso* at a subsequent part of this Memoir. —(R. P.)

London for the purpose of giving in person the information which he (Lord Anglesey) desired the Government to possess. On the 12th of July he writes,—

Lord ANGLESEY to Mr. PEEL.

"Phœnix Park, July 12, 1828.

" MY DEAR MR. PEEL,

"As I think I can manage to get Major Warburton to you without being missed on this side of the water, I am much inclined to send him off. He is capable of giving much useful information, which it is very important that the Government should receive. If he should present himself, I request you to see him with as little delay as possible, for I am desirous that his absence from hence should not be noticed.

"Believe me

" Very truly yours,

" ANGLESEY.

"No one but my private secretary knows of Major Warburton's departure."

Major Warburton, a very intelligent and trustworthy officer, and in whom (on account of the former relation in which I had stood to him when I was Chief Secretary for Ireland) I had entire confidence, held one of the chief appointments connected with the constabulary force in Ireland; and in July, 1828, had the command of that portion of the force which was stationed in the county of Clare during the Election. He had consequently the fullest opportunity of witnessing the progress of excitement, and of judging of the probability of its extension. He confirmed all the statements which we received from Mr. Fitzgerald as to the combined efforts of the lay and clerical agitators—the enthusiasm of all classes not under the control of authority, the indications (too clear to be mistaken) that even among classes under that control (I speak of the constabulary and the military force) the sympathies of a common cause political and religious could not be altogether repressed.

It was clearly the opinion of Mr. Fitzgerald and Major Warburton, founded on occurrences that had passed under their own eyes, that implicit reliance could not long be placed on the effect of discipline and the duty of obedience.

On the 20th of July, Lord Anglesey, after observing that he doubts whether the *chief* agitators were inclined to put their cause to the test of arms, and that he could not imagine how, without foreign aid, they could calculate upon success, proceeds thus: "I ought, however, to observe, that we hear occasionally of the Catholic soldiers being ill-disposed and entirely under the influence of the priests. One regiment of infantry is said to be divided into Orange and Catholic factions. It is certain that on the 12th of July the guard at the Castle had Orange lilies about them—the officer very properly took them away."

On the 26th of July Lord Anglesey wrote a letter from which the following is an extract:—

"The priests are using very inflammatory language, and are certainly working upon the Catholics of the army. I think it important that the depôts of Irish recruits should be gradually removed, under the appearance of being required to join their regiments, and that whatever regiments are sent here should be those of Scotland, or at all events of men not recruited in the south of Ireland. I desired Sir John Byng to convey this opinion to Lord Hill."

These and other letters from Lord Anglesey, which will hereafter appear, will show the deep impression made upon his mind by the passing events of which he had daily cognizance.

Before I refer to those letters, I must shortly advert to the proceedings in the House of Lords, which followed the communication to that House by the House of Commons of the Resolution of the 12th of May in favour of the Roman Catholic claims.

On the 9th of June Lord Lansdowne moved that the Lords should concur in the Resolution passed by the Commons.

In the interval between the discussion I had personal communication with the Duke of Wellington. I expressed great reluctance to withdraw from him such aid as I could lend him in the carrying on of the Government, particularly after the recent schism; but I reminded him that the reasons which had induced me to contemplate retirement from office in 1825, were still more powerful in 1828—from the lapse of time, from the increasing difficulties in administering the Government in Ireland, from the more prominent situation which I held in the House of Commons.

I told him, that being in a minority in the House of Commons on the question that of all others most deeply affected the condition and prospects of Ireland, I could not, with any satisfaction to my own feelings or advantage to the public interests, perform the double functions of leading the House of Commons and presiding over the Home department; that at an early period therefore my retirement must take place. I expressed at the same time an earnest hope that in the approaching discussion in the Lords, the Duke of Wellington might deem it to be consistent with his sense of duty to take a course in debate which should not preclude him, who was less deeply committed on the question than myself, from taking the whole state of Ireland into consideration during the recess, with the view of adjusting the Catholic question. The Duke of Wellington's sentiments did not differ from mine as to the embarrassment that must arise from the continuance of divided councils in the Cabinet, and as to the necessity of maturely considering the whole state of Ireland.

I shall advert, however, in more detail hereafter, to the communications which passed very shortly after this period between the Duke of Wellington and myself.

The Duke of Wellington and the Chancellor (Lord Lyndhurst) took part in the debates, and though they did not concur in the Resolution moved by Lord Lansdowne (which was rejected in the Lords by a majority of 44), the general tenor of the debate, of their speeches in particular, and the construction put upon them, may be inferred from the observations made by Lord Lansdowne in his speech at the close of the debate. He said, " My Lords, I shall forbear troubling your Lordships at any great length in reply. In what has fallen in the course of the debate, there have been many things that have encouraged me in my view of the subject. In the first place, I collect this encouragement from the tone of the whole debate. I have also collected encouragement not only from the supporters of the proposition, but from the suggestions furnished by the very enemies of the cause. I have even collected encouragement from the hints, cautions, and hesitations which fell from the Right Reverend Bench; and most of all, I have collected encouragement from that important admission from the noble Lord on the Woolsack, that he was aware of a great difficulty existing, and out of which he at present saw no outlet. This admission has been confirmed by the noble Duke, so that it will not now be denied that the Catholic Question has reduced this country to a state of great difficulty. This statement having been made by two noblemen so high in the confidence of the Sovereign, it almost necessarily follows that it is accompanied with their intention of looking at this question with a view to its final arrangement."

Lord Lansdowne also observed, " I therefore think that the noble Lord on the Woolsack, and the noble Duke, must have some such intentions as I have ascribed to them, because no one knows better than they do the danger of holding out expectations which cannot be realized."

The Session of 1828 was closed by the speech from the Throne on the 28th of July, and immediately afterwards the Duke of Wellington entered into communication with me on the subject of Ireland and the Catholic question.

Before I allude to the correspondence which passed between us, it will be necessary that I should call attention to such of my communications with Lord Anglesey of a date prior to that correspondence, as will fully explain the state of affairs in Ireland, and the impression made by the events that were occurring upon the mind of the Lord-Lieutenant.

Extracts from some of these letters have been previously given, but I feel it incumbent upon me (notwithstanding the repetition of certain passages) to insert continuously the whole of my correspondence with Lord Anglesey which has any bearing upon the political state of Ireland, as well out of justice to Lord Anglesey as from the desire to present without reserve every document in my possession which can throw light upon the motives and conduct of those who advised at that time the adjustment of the Catholic Question.

The letters and papers relating to the policy of continuing the Act of 1825 for the Suppression of Illegal Societies in Ireland, and some of the letters relating to the contest for the county of Clare, have been already given. The following correspondence extends from the 23rd of June to the 28th of the following month. There is an occasional reference to documents which (being sent in the original) were returned, but I believe they were not material, so far as the purpose for which the present correspondence is published is concerned. Every paper in my possession that appears to me of the slightest importance is here given.

Lord ANGLESEY to Mr. PEEL.

" Phœnix Park, June 23, 1828.

" MY DEAR MR. PEEL,

"I have read a short-hand report of the late proceedings of the Catholic Association. They are very violent and mischievous, but I do not think it would be wise to take up anything.

"O'Connell and his party are nearly driven to madness—he knows not which way to turn himself. He finds himself so much opposed by some of the most respectable of the Bishops, and by many of the lower clergy also, that he is quite wild. All the leaders are gone down to Ennis, and I have every reason to believe that he intends to stand himself. I know that he talked of it yesterday, and also know that to-day he expressed his determination to do so. The fact is, it has been strongly urged upon him that it is in vain to oppose Mr. Fitzgerald, and he thinks that the only chance is to stand himself. He says that he shall at all events sit until the first call of the House, and in the meantime he must trust to the chapter of accidents. The following extract of a letter from one of the most respectable Bishops to a person in my confidence will show that there is a good feeling among the higher clergy.

" 'Maynooth College, June 22, 1828.

" 'MY DEAR SIR,

" 'I found on my arrival here that the charge advanced against the Clare candidate, that he was an

enemy to this establishment, is considered extremely unjust, and that a strong feeling of gratitude towards him
exists in the house on account of his efficient exertions
on a former occasion to forward it. When an application was made some years ago for an increased grant
for the purpose of forming what is called the Dunboyne
Establishment, Mr. V. F. was the individual with whom
the secretary of the trustees corresponded in order to
bring about that object, and the application was completely successful. Dr. —— is now writing a statement
of this fact to Mr. O'C. The proposed measure regarding Clare is thought here to be most unwise, and
besides not likely to succeed. You can mention the
fact regarding the Dunboyne Establishment (not, however, on my authority) to any one who could render it
available at the meeting to-morrow. Perhaps Mr. O'C.
himself may acknowledge it.'

"I beg you to observe that the remark that 'the
proposed measure regarding Clare is thought here to be
most unwise, and besides not likely to succeed,' was
written without a knowledge of O'C.'s intention to stand
himself. This the Maynooth people will no doubt consider still more unwise ; nevertheless, I incline to think
he would be returned. I do believe he is losing ground,
and that he will lose still more ground, but he is still
very powerful, and the novelty of the attempt and the
very surprise at it may act in his favour.

"I fear you have not time to assist me in my various
projects. It would, however, be doing essential service
to make a beginning, and if the Coal Question could be

managed, it would give great popularity to your Government.

" Believe me, &c.,

" ANGLESEY."

Mr. PEEL to Lord ANGLESEY.

(Private.)

" Whitehall, June 28, 1828.

" MY DEAR LORD ANGLESEY,

"I have to apologise to you for not having written to you fully on the subject of your plans for promoting the employment of the poor in Ireland. I was obliged to leave town some days since to attend the funeral of a sister, and the arrear that accumulated in consequence of my absence, joined to the necessity of being in the House of Commons of late till three in the morning, almost every day, have compelled me to appear, I fear, very negligent.

" I have had more than one interview with the Duke of Wellington and the Chancellor of the Exchequer upon the subject. You shall hear very soon from me.

" I saw a very desponding letter to-day from V. Fitzgerald from Clare. The sentiments expressed in that from Maynooth College are very creditable, but every account we have in London seems to confirm the probability that Mr. O'Connell will effect his return for Clare.

" It seems not generally known that even a call of the House would not compel his attendance in Parliament. If he had been returned at a General Election, the call would have applied to him, but I understand that, according to the practice of the House of Commons, a Member returned during the existence of a Parliament, on such a vacancy as that which has occurred in Clare, would not be subject to a call of the House.

"Believe me, &c.,

" ROBERT PEEL."

Lord ANGLESEY to Mr. PEEL.

" Phœnix Park, June 28, 1828.

" MY DEAR MR. PEEL,

"I fear the Clare election will end ill. I enclose several communications from thence. There appear to be great violence and irritation, and the system of intimidation will have but too much effect upon the supporters of Mr. Fitzgerald.

"Dr. Doyle's letter to Mr. O'Connell is most mischievous: I however still hope that most of the other Bishops set their faces against his proceedings.

"I had long ago caused a considerable assembly of the Constabulary Force at Ennis under the pretence of inspection by Colonel Baron Tuyll, whom I have sent for that purpose, and I have increased the military force around the immediate scene of probable disturbance.

"I cannot discover that there is any settled plan of revolutionary movement.

"I believe, on the contrary, that the present sudden and very extraordinary effervescence is simply occasioned by the accidental circumstance of a new election in a Catholic county. I believe that even in Clare, if any one of less note and popularity had offered himself, Mr. Fitzgerald would have triumphantly carried his election, but the moment it was decided that O'Connell should present himself, I felt confident of his success, and every moment confirms me in this opinion.

"I write in much haste to save the morning post, as I think you will be anxious to receive the latest information. I request you to return the papers.

"Believe me, &c.,

"ANGLESEY.

"Some papers are not brought by Gregory. You shall have them by to-night's mail."

Mr. PEEL to Lord ANGLESEY.

"Whitehall Gardens, June 30, 1828.

"MY DEAR LORD ANGLESEY,

"I received this morning your letter, with its enclosures, respecting the Clare election.

"I have little more to say than that I think nothing can be more judicious than the precautionary measures which you have taken, and the instructions which you have given for the general conduct of the military.

"I am glad to see you reprimand my friend, Major Warburton, for illegible writing. It is really too bad that on matters of great importance such scrawls should be sent: serious mistakes might occur in consequence.

"The issue which now seems probable of the Clare election is not contrary to my expectations.

"Ever, &c.,

"ROBERT PEEL."

Lord ANGLESEY to Mr. PEEL.

"Phœnix Park, June 30, 1828.

"MY DEAR MR. PEEL,

"I have nothing particular to relate.

"There is, in the opinion of the General Officer in command at Limerick, who has now removed to Clare Castle, ample force to keep the peace and to ensure freedom of election.

"I believe O'Connell and his gang are very anxious to prevent riot, if it were only with the view to show the absolute control under which they have the priesthood, and by them the population. I am sorry to observe that the Bishops, many of whom are acting with much moderation, discretion, and goodwill, have much less influence than I had imagined.

"The post from Clare is this moment arrived: at its departure all was quiet.

"I remain, &c.,

"ANGLESEY.

"P.S.—Your letter of the 28th is this instant received.

"Believe me, I make ample allowance for your pressure of business, and for your distress of mind at

the loss of a sister.   You may be quite sure that Fitzgerald will be beat.   What will be said of a popular
representative who, being returned for a county, does
not present himself at the table of the House?   I do
not think O'Connell is doing himself any good.   I am
sure he is doing the Catholic cause much injury.   I fear
I shall have a good deal of trouble with the Orangemen
on the 12th.

" A."

Mr. PEEL to Lord ANGLESEY.

(Private.)

" Whitehall, July 3, 1828.

" MY DEAR LORD ANGLESEY,

"I return Baron Tuyll's letter, and am much
obliged to you for having sent it.   The views of a disinterested and unprejudiced stranger, in such cases as
those of the Clare election, are often the most satisfactory and often even the most correct.

"I must say that whatever happens, nothing has been
left undone by you to provide for the maintenance of
tranquillity, by effectual but temperate measures.

"I firmly believe that no persons are more interested
in preserving order during the contest for Clare, than
the agitators who are influencing the minds of the
people.   In case of a disturbance an agitator might feel
his own personal security more endangered than that of
any other person.

" We have an Irish question for discussion to-
night.

" Ever, &c.

" ROBERT PEEL."

Lord ANGLESEY to Mr. PEEL.

" Phœnix Park, July 11, 1828.

" MY DEAR MR. PEEL,

" Mr. Fitzgerald suggested that the presence of
the Irish Solicitor-General might be advisable in the
House of Commons. Of course he is ready to set off at
a moment's notice, and a letter from you by return of
post would enable him to be present upon Lord John
Russell's motion on the 17th.

" I have talked with Mr. Doherty about it, and I
have come to the conclusion that, unless the Government
is prepared to enter into the question, and to determine
upon some legislative measure regarding the Catholics,
his presence will be detrimental.

" Unless the King's Ministers (taking into consideration the alarming progress of organization, the unlimited
power of the priests, and the complete control under
which these are of the Association) should feel the
necessity of no longer delaying their decision of the
course to be pursued, I humbly conceive that the less
notice is taken of the late occurrences in Clare, the
better ; and I for one shall appear to treat it lightly,
and as if it were an ordinary election contest. Its character, however, is far, very far, otherwise, as Mr. Fitz-

gerald will fully detail to you. I need not enlarge upon the subject.

"I was almost tempted to send my aide-de-camp, Baron Tuyll, to make a report to you. I thought it possible that the high colouring Mr. Fitzgerald might be tempted to give to the transaction might be considered, partly, at least, as the effect of disappointment, vexation, and injured feelings : and that a confirmation from the Baron, who was a calm and very observing witness, might take away all doubt of the facts that will be stated. I have, however, decided otherwise. His mission would be known and observed upon ; and as I doubt of the possibility of the Cabinet coming to any conclusion upon Irish politics, or (if it did) of the House of Commons being willing to remain assembled long enough to complete any measure, I think it more prudent to show no anxiety upon the subject. During the recess there will be ample time to consider the actual state of this country, and it is well worth considering. I do not calculate upon immediate danger. I continue to feel confident that tranquillity will not be materially disturbed at present, and that you will have time to deliberate ; but I repeat that we must not long attempt to remain as we are. I have closely watched the proceedings of the agitators since I have been in this country. It is very daring and very insulting. I have often appealed to the law authorities as to the practicability and the policy of prosecutions for acts committed or words spoken, but I have always been assured that nothing that had occurred could be laid hold of. I took the opportunity of the presence of Mr. Fitzgerald to have the opinion of the Attorney-General upon this point, and he then repeated what he had said before.

" Mr. Gregory has this moment brought me the letter and opinion I enclose respecting the eligibility of Mr. O'Connell to sit in Parliament. You are of course well aware of all that is stated, but Mr. G. wished that it should be sent to you.

" When I speak with confidence of continued tranquillity, I must be understood to mean that there is no immediate intention on the part of the leaders of the Catholics to break the peace. But I will not answer for it if any extraordinary occurrence should produce collision.

" To-morrow, for instance, being the 12th of July, may, and I am afraid will produce many violent scenes. Every precaution has been taken to engage the Orangemen to be quiet, but I believe they are in a very high state of excitement.

" It is not thought that O'Connell will present himself at the House during the Session. If he does, and he is rejected, or if the House takes any step in consequence of the petition of the freeholders of Clare to exclude him, then it is possible that great violence may ensue. But, barring these occurrences, I think we shall have a tranquil summer.

" I remain, &c.,

" ANGLESEY."

Mr. PEEL to Lord ANGLESEY.

(Most private.)

" Whitehall, July 13, 1828.

" MY DEAR LORD ANGLESEY,

" I hasten to reply to your letter of the 11th, which I have just received.

" A considerable difference of opinion prevails among many who under ordinary circumstances would support Lord John Russell's motion* as to the policy of bringing it forward at this period of the Session. Some probably think that any legislative declaration of opinion in favour of the Roman Catholics following so closely the recent events in Clare would be ill-timed. I know that earnest representations have been made to Lord John against the agitation of the question at present. What effect these representations may have I know not. But independently of any other considerations, while there is a doubt as to the question being brought forward, I should feel very reluctant to call Mr. Doherty away from Ireland.

" I yesterday received from the Duke of Wellington the letter which you wrote to Lord Francis Gower some days since, extracts from which Lord Francis had previously communicated to the Duke and to me.

" As that letter concludes with a wish that it should be communicated to me, and through me to the members of the Government, I of course considered it as partaking

* The intention of bringing forward this motion was not persevered in.—(R. P.)

of the character of a formal official communication, so far
at least as concerns the obligation of making it known to
my colleagues.

" I received the letter yesterday morning, and in the
course of the day it was read at the Cabinet. We were
all of opinion that the King ought to be apprized of it;
and the Duke of Wellington, who was to see his Majesty
on other business to-day, will take your letter with him
to Windsor.

" The course which it may be ultimately fitting for the
King's advisers to pursue involves so many considerations,
each of so much importance, that I am confident you will
not expect from me at the present moment any declaration of opinion.

" You will see that I have with the utmost promptitude
submitted your views with respect to the present state of
Ireland, and the only effectual remedies for it, to those
to whom they ought to be made known.

" The opinion of my colleagues was, I think, unanimous
that Lord John Russell's motion would be very unwise
and ill-timed, and is much more to be deprecated from
the probable bearing of it upon public interests than
from any prejudice it could do to the Government.

" The warmest advocate for concession might deprecate
with you any sudden declaration which, made at the end
of the Session, unexpectedly, without due notice, in the
absence of most of the Irish Members, must appear to be
the result of the recent occurrences in Clare, and to be
extorted from the Legislature by the apprehension of an
immediate danger.

" Our impression is, that the best course will be—if

the motion is persisted in—to put it aside, on the general
ground of the unfitness of the period and of the circumstances for its discussion, and to avoid, as far as we can
avoid, lengthened debate.

" We had some conversation—I mean in the Cabinet—
on the questions arising out of Mr. O'Connell's Return.

" The Return is not objectionable in point of form, and
it has been notified in the ' Gazette.'

" I apprehend it to be quite clear that Mr. O'Connell
cannot possibly take his seat as a Member of Parliament.
He will have no opportunity of making any harangue.
If he appears, the Speaker will desire him to take the
oaths required by law, and if he declines to take them,
will treat him as a stranger and intruder, and listen to
nothing that he has to say.

" He probably is quite aware of this, and will remain
in Ireland.   Is it prudent to step out of the usual course,
and to compel his attendance by an order of the House
for the express purpose of bringing the question to an
issue ?

" On the one hand it is alleged that it is indecorous
and impolitic for the House of Commons to acquiesce
for the period of six months in a notorious evasion of the
intention of the law, and to permit a man who appears
from the return of the Sheriff to have publicly declared
that he will not, and cannot qualify as a Member of
Parliament, to assume the character, and exercise some
of the privileges of a Member.

" On the other hand, it must be borne in mind that if
the House of Commons once commits itself in a contest

with Mr. O'Connell, it must persevere to the last. It cannot separate without coming to a final decision.

" Some time might elapse before Mr. O'Connell's appearance could be compelled. He might make plausible excuses for not obeying the summons. He would, in the event of disobedience, be brought in custody. On being so brought, he would decline to take the oaths, and a new writ would issue; but I apprehend the refusal to take the oaths would not disqualify him from again presenting himself to the electors of Clare, nor would it invalidate a second Return by the Sheriff.

" The effectual remedy against such a Return would be to pass a law enabling the same oaths that are to be taken at the table of the House to be tendered to a candidate previously to the election, and thus to disqualify the man who cannot be a Member of Parliament from being a candidate.

" There is nothing unreasonable in this; but our impression, after the discussion in Cabinet of yesterday, was, that more public inconvenience would arise from keeping Parliament sitting until the case of Mr. O'Connell could be finally and effectually disposed of, than from adhering, for the present at least, to the ordinary course pursued in respect to the return of a Member to Parliament.

" I am writing this without having seen Fitzgerald. I have more than once sent to his house, but he is not yet arrived.

" He may have information to give which may alter

our impressions, and induce us at least to reconsider this matter.

> "Believe me, &c.,
>
> "ROBERT PEEL.

"P.S.—I hope that the 12th of July was as un-favourable a day for public processions in Ireland as it was with us. It rained here almost the whole morning.

"I am obliged to send this letter without keeping a copy of it. Will you be good enough either to send me a copy of it or to return it to me for a day, that I may have a copy taken."

The following is the letter from Lord Francis Egerton, with the extracts from Lord Anglesey's letter to him, which is referred to in mine to Lord Anglesey of the 13th of July. My reply to Lord Francis is also given.

Lord F. L. GOWER to Mr. PEEL.

(Private.)

"Sudbrook, July 6, 1828.

"MY DEAR MR. PEEL,

"Lord Anglesey has desired me to communicate to the Duke of Wellington and yourself the strong expression of his opinion on the present state of Ireland, which you will find in the enclosed extracts from his letter. I thought I could not do better than to convey his sentiments in his own language, and accordingly sub-

H

mitted to the Duke yesterday the extracts which I now forward to you.

" I must confess that I should feel some reluctance to trouble you with a mere argument on that unfortunate question, which has so often called forth the deliberate expression of your opinion on its merits. I wish therefore to state the feeling with which I now execute Lord Anglesey's desire, and which would in my own case dictate the tone of my own correspondence with yourself as far as regards that question. I should think it idle to trouble you with the repetition of any argument not drawn from the particular circumstances and events of the time and of the country; but I shall always, with your permission, communicate without reserve my own impressions as to the existing situation of Ireland, whether they may appear to me to strengthen my views of the case in that obnoxious question or not.

" I am sure you will acknowledge in such communications, as in that which I now forward, the distinction between arguments which may be culled from debate and those which are suggested by the observation of things as they are or as they seem at least to be.

" Believe me, my dear Mr. Peel, &c.,

" F. LEVESON GOWER."

EXTRACTS from Lord ANGLESEY's LETTER to Lord FRANCIS LEVESON GOWER, 2nd July, 1828.

" I will give you my opinion upon the state of things and upon the great question.

" I begin by premising that I hold in abhorrence the Association, the agitators, the priests, and their religion ; and I believe that not many, *but that some* of the Bishops, are mild, moderate, and anxious to come to a fair and liberal compromise for the adjustment of the points at issue.   I think that these latter have very little, if any, influence with the lower clergy and the population.

" Such is the extraordinary power of the Association, or rather of the agitators, of whom there are many of high ability, of ardent mind, of great daring (and, if there was no Association, these men are now too well known not to maintain their power under the existing order of exclusion), that I am quite certain they could lead on the people to open rebellion at a moment's notice ; and their organization is such, that, in the hands of desperate and intelligent leaders, they would be extremely formidable. The hope, and indeed the probability of present tranquillity, rests upon the forbearance and the not very determined courage of O'Connell, and on his belief, as well as that of the principal men amongst them, that they will carry their cause by unceasing agitation, and by intimidation, without coming to blows.   I believe their success inevitable—that no power under heaven can arrest its progress.   There may be rebellion, you may put to death thousands, you may suppress it, but it will only be to put off the day of compromise ; and in the mean time the country is still more impoverished, and the minds of the people are, if possible, still more alienated, and ruinous expense is entailed upon the empire.

" But supposing that the whole evil was concentred in the Association, and that if that was suppressed all

would go smoothly; where is the man who can tell me
how to suppress it? Many, many cry out that the
nuisance must be abated; that the Government is
supine; that the insolence of the demagogues is intolerable; but I have not yet found one person capable
of pointing out a remedy. All are mute when you ask
them to define their proposition. All that even the
most determined opposers to emancipation say is that
it is better to leave things as they are than to risk any
change. But will things remain as they are? Certainly not. They are bad; they must get worse; and
I see no possible means of improving them but by
depriving the demagogues of the power of directing the
people; and by taking Messrs. O'Connell, Sheil, and the
rest of them from the Association, and placing them in
the House of Commons, this desirable object would be
at once accomplished.

"*July 3rd.* The present order of things must not,
cannot last. There are three modes of proceeding:—

" 1st. That of trying to go on as we have done.

" 2nd. To adjust the question by concession, and such
guards as may be deemed indispensable.

" 3rd. To put down the Association, and to crush the
power of the priests.

" The first I hold to be impossible.

" The second is practicable and advisable.

" The third is only possible by supposing that you
can reconstruct the House of Commons; and to suppose
that is to suppose that you can totally alter the feelings
of those who send them there.

" I believe nothing short of the suspension of the

Habeas Corpus Act, and Martial Law, will effect the third proposition. This would effect it during their operation, and perhaps for a short time after they had ceased, and then every evil would return with accumulated weight.

" But no House of Commons would consent to these measures until there is open rebellion, and therefore until that occurs it is useless to think of them. The second mode of proceeding is then, I conceive, the only practicable one, but the present is not a propitious time to effect even this.

" I abhor the idea of truckling to the overbearing Catholic demagogues. To make any movement towards conciliation under the present excitement and system of terror would revolt me ; but I do most conscientiously, and after the most earnest consideration of the subject, give it as my conviction that the first moment of composure and tranquillity should be seized to signify the intention of adjusting the question, lest another period of calm should not present itself."

Mr. PEEL to Lord F. L. GOWER.

(Private.)

" Whitehall, July 7, 1828.

" MY DEAR LORD FRANCIS,

" You will not only be performing your duty, but will be giving me a proof of your confidence, by communicating to me at all times, without the slightest reserve, your impressions as to Irish affairs, and as to

the bearing of present or future circumstances upon the
Roman Catholic question.

" I have thought it right to send in circulation to all
my colleagues those papers that relate to the Clare
election. I mean the letters which you have sent me
from Major Warburton, Baron Tuyll, &c. &c. It is
fit they should know the real state of things in the
county of Clare.

" Believe me, &c.

" ROBERT PEEL."

Mr. PEEL to Lord ANGLESEY.

(Secret.)

" Whitehall, July 14, 1828.

" MY DEAR LORD ANGLESEY,

" Although the letter which I received from you
yesterday intimates an expectation on your part that the
tranquillity of Ireland may in all probability be maintained, I am unwilling to permit Parliament to separate
without a more particular consideration of the expediency
of arming the executive Government of Ireland with
powers beyond those which they at present possess.

" We have determined not to renew the Act which
was intended for the suppression of the Roman Catholic
Association, and which expires at the close of the present Session.

" Experience has proved that it is no difficult matter
to evade it; and I think there can be little doubt that
its existence on the Statute-Book would give the Govern-

ment little, if any, power which they would not possess either under the common law or the Convention Act.

" In case of any danger so imminent as to require the decided interference of the Government of Ireland, we have a firm reliance that all the powers of the Government would be exerted, under your superintendence, with that combined prudence, energy, and firmness most likely to make the exercise of them effectual for its purpose; and you may depend upon receiving every support from His Majesty and his advisers.

" If you should be of opinion that powers might be given to you by law enabling you to take precautions against future danger—powers differing in character or degree from those which without any express authority from the Legislature every Government must exercise in cases of extreme emergency—I will without delay bring the subject under the consideration of my colleagues. The inconvenience of keeping Parliament together would no doubt be very great. The nature of the evil to be guarded against, and the probable efficacy of the remedy to be applied, ought to be very maturely considered; but still, if you should be of opinion that material advantage would result from giving to the Government of Ireland, by a law to be passed without delay, powers which it does not at present possess, at the hazard of any inconvenience this important matter should be taken into serious deliberation before Parliament is allowed to separate.

" I shall be glad to hear from you, as soon as you can write to me on this point. Under ordinary circumstances Parliament would probably be prorogued about

the 26th of July.   The House of Commons might ad-
journ on Tuesday of next week, I apprehend.

                           " Believe me, &c.,

                                " ROBERT PEEL."

            Lord ANGLESEY to Mr. PEEL.

                           " Phœnix Park, July 16, 1828.
" MY DEAR MR. PEEL,

       " I write a hasty line to acknowledge the receipt
of your letters of the 13th and 14th, and to inform you
that I have no desire, that, on the contrary, I should
object to being armed with any power beyond that
which the Government already possesses.

       " I will write more fully by this night's post.

                           " Believe me, &c.,

                                " ANGLESEY."

            Lord ANGLESEY to Mr. PEEL.

                           " Phœnix Park, July 16, 1828.
" MY DEAR MR. PEEL,

       " I wrote in much haste this morning, merely to
state that I was averse to being armed with any power
beyond that which the Government possesses already.

       " I have now to reply more fully to your letters of the
13th and 14th.

       " I fear I have not adopted the most convenient or
correct course in making my communications.

       " I have not made a distinction between private and
official information.   I have often doubted whether I

should address myself to you or to the Chief Secretary
for Ireland. My notion has been that you would receive from him, at times the most convenient to you,
such communications as I might make, and that you
would be the best judge of what in those letters, as well
as in those addressed to you, it might be necessary to
lay before the Cabinet. I was, however, desirous that
the whole of my letter to Lord F. L. Gower of the 11th
should be seen by your colleagues, because it expressed
my sentiments upon the state of Ireland, as far as it
is affected by the Catholic Question, the mischiefs with
which it is threatened, and the only means that have
occurred to me of averting them. I was desirous of this
because when the King and the members of His Majesty's Government became thus fully acquainted with
my opinion, they would judge of my fitness to carry into
effect the measures they might decide upon adopting.
I was therefore pleased to learn that you had produced
the letter, although I now feel that it ought to have
been drawn in a more official form, and that it might
perhaps with more propriety have been addressed to you.
You must excuse my failure upon these points, and at-
tribute them to my unofficial habits, and I feel bound to
apologise for the unconnected and desultory nature of
the correspondence.

"The sum, I believe, of what I have written from
time to time amounts to this—that I do not apprehend
the tranquillity of the country will be immediately endangered; that there is no necessity for the enactment
of new laws to strengthen the arm of Government; that
no coercive legislative measures, unaccompanied by con-

cession, will get rid of existing evils; that such an attempt would produce infinite irritation, and might create a crisis, the actual existence of which would alone justify their adoption; that if rebellion were to break out, there is a sufficient force to meet its first attempts and probably to quell it; that then, and not till then, coercive laws might be called for, and, if called for, nothing short of the suspension of the Habeas Corpus Act would put down the Association and curb the priests; that such a measure would only produce temporary tranquillity; that at this moment there is no ground to justify an application for a coercive law, and that, if it existed, I could not use it; that the King's Government may depend upon my being watchful and ready to make full, vigorous, yet prudent use of the power as it now is, if unfortunately there should occur any tangible infringement of the law.

" After fully reflecting upon the sentiments I have from time to time expressed upon the Catholic Question in the course of my correspondence, I feel apprehensive that I may possibly be considered as having become a partisan in the cause.

" I can solemnly assure you that this is not the case. I have endeavoured to weigh the question with an impartial hand, and I can conscientiously assert, that if even I had taken an opposite view of it, I should have felt it to be my duty to pursue the same line of conduct, and to have made the same statements. Perhaps, indeed, I have been more jealously watchful of myself from feeling that my judgment might be warped by the opinion I entertain, and I have therefore omitted no opportunity of resorting to the legal advisers of the Crown for their opinions upon the practicability and the expediency of commencing prosecutions, and also of suggesting laws for the more effectual preservation of public tranquillity.

"The result is, that it has not been found practicable to commence any prosecution, or expedient to ask for any further power.

"Believe me, &c.,

"ANGLESEY."

Mr. PEEL to Lord ANGLESEY.

"Whitehall, July 16, 1828.

"MY DEAR LORD ANGLESEY,

"I have no doubt that your attention will have been called to a report of speeches professing to have been delivered at the New Catholic Association on Saturday the 12th of July.

"A Dublin newspaper, called the 'Morning Register,' of the 14th of July, contains a report of those speeches.

"I have sent this newspaper to the Law Officers of the Crown here, and desired to have their opinion as to the liability to prosecution of the parties concerned in the delivery or the publication of these speeches, in order that time might be saved, should the Law Officers of the Crown in Ireland (as has sometimes been the case) wish for a reference to the Crown Officers of this country.

"I enclose a copy of the confidential letter* which I

---

* This letter is thus endorsed :—" I have not a copy of the enclosure in this letter."—(R. P.)

nave addressed to the latter, and I will of course apprise you without delay of the answer which I receive to it.

" Believe me, &c.,

" ROBERT PEEL."

Mr. PEEL to Lord ANGLESEY.

(Private.)

" Whitehall, July 19, 1828.

" MY DEAR LORD ANGLESEY,

"I have this morning received your letter of the 16th. I assure you most sincerely that I have not only not the slightest objection to the form of communication which you adopted in writing to Lord Francis Gower, and requesting him to communicate your letter to me, but that I very much doubt whether there is not more advantage in the free and unreserved intercourse that can be carried on through the medium of private letters than in a formal, official correspondence.

" I have already proved to you that I do not consider your letters, whether addressed to Lord Francis or to me, as *private* in that sense which would prevent the disclosure of them to those who ought to be apprised of their contents; and if you concur with me as to the benefit of a free and informal correspondence, I will continue to address you as I have hitherto done.

" Believe me, &c.,

" ROBERT PEEL."

Lord ANGLESEY to Mr. PEEL.

"Near Kingstown, July 20, 1828.

" MY DEAR MR. PEEL,

"Upon the receipt of your letter of the 16th, I placed it, together with that you had addressed to the Attorney and the Solicitor-General of England, in the hands of the Attorney and Solicitor-General of Ireland, desiring their opinion upon the case stated. I have this moment received it, and it is enclosed herewith. My attention had already been called to the speeches delivered at the Catholic Association on the 12th; and in a letter I wrote to Lord F. L. Gower on the 14th I desired that he would read Mr. Sheil's speech. It struck me as being clever, ingenious, and remarkably mischievous, but that he had artfully guarded himself against prosecution. This opinion is confirmed by that given by the Attorney and Solicitor-General, and there, I conceive, ends the question.

"Mr. Sheil is the least likely man of all the agitators to be caught. He is in the habit of writing and well weighing what he means to speak. Mr. O'Connell, O'Gorman Mahon, Lawless, and several others, are carried away by their feelings and thirst for popularity, and are very unguarded. ——, you probably know, is a determined republican, without a guinea and of some nerve. ——, if a rebellion should break out, will be a very prominent character in the field.

"Coupling the communication you have received from Paris with the circumstance of Major Warburton's having met, upon his journey to London, many foreigners proceeding with great expedition to Ireland, and amongst whom he believed he saw the Duke of ——— (I forget the title, but the name is Macdonald), it appears not improbable that there may be an attempt to introduce arms, and finally insurrection. I am quite sure the disaffected are amply organised for the undertaking. They are partially, but ill armed. Pikes, however, to any amount, and at very short notice, would easily be manufactured, if they are not already made and secreted. Still I cannot bring myself to believe that the ruling characters are at all inclined to put their cause to the test of arms; and if they do, I cannot imagine how, without foreign aid, of which there appears no fear, they can calculate upon success.

" I ought, however, to observe that we hear occasionally of the Catholic soldiers being ill-disposed and entirely under the influence of the priests. One regiment of infantry is said to be divided into Orange and Catholic factions. It is certain that on the 12th of July the guard at the Castle had Orange lilies about them; the officers very properly took them away.

" Party feeling is thought to be at its height. There is a sullen, gloomy discontent amongst the Catholics that surpasses everything that has been hitherto known. I collect this from various parts. Lord Forbes is just returned from the assizes at Longford. He has been in the habit of holding much intercourse with the priests and their flocks. They formerly were communicative, and gave him much useful intelligence. They are now *all* silent and reserved   No money will tempt any one of them to make a single disclosure. There is a general impression amongst them that some great event is at hand.

" You have not yet had time to answer the propositions I submitted to you for the improvement of Ireland. I am much pressed to give an opinion upon the probability of their being favourably received, but I have not felt authorised to give one.

" I wish I had been enabled to make a beginning in the formation of roads through some of the most disturbed parts of the country. It would have given employment to its lawless people, and would have at the same time proved to them that they will be closely looked after.

" Believe me, &c.,

" ANGLESEY."

(Enclosure.)

OPINION of Mr. JOY and Mr. DOHERTY, July 19, 1828.

" We have read in the ' Morning Register ' a report of the speeches made at a meeting of the Roman Catholic Association held on the 12th instant, and are of opinion that there is nothing in those speeches which would justify us in recommending a prosecution. It is perfectly clear that no criminal proceeding ought to be attempted against any member of the Association without at least a reasonable prospect of success. The speech of Mr. Sheil, which appears to be the most worthy of attention, professes to give a description of what the speaker alleges to be the present state of things in Ireland, and to give that description, not for the purpose of creating danger, but of warding it off. This is the professed object of the speaker, and it would be competent to him, upon the trial, to insist that such was his real object. It is manifest therefore that a line of defence would be open to him which, if a jury were favourably inclined, would afford an obvious ground on which to found a verdict of acquittal. Under these circumstances we are of opinion that a prosecution in this instance would not be successful, and therefore that it would be inexpedient to attempt it.

" H. JOY.
" JOHN DOHERTY."

Mr. PEEL to Lord ANGLESEY.

(Private.)

" Whitehall, July 23, 1828.

" MY DEAR LORD ANGLESEY,

" The enclosed letter * to you ought, as you will see by the date, to have been sent on Saturday, but the delay is immaterial.

" I think it very probable that the opinion of the Law Officers here will be in conformity with that which you have sent me, as to the inexpediency of founding a prosecution on the speeches reported to have been delivered at the Roman Catholic Association on the 12th of July. Still I am glad the reference was made, as those speeches excited much attention and provoked

---

* There is no paper enclosed in the copy of this letter.—(*Eds.*)

great indignation; and it is useful to be enabled to show that the propriety of interference in respect to them on the part of the Government had been duly considered.

" I presume that the precautions which were taken in Lord Wellesley's time as to evidence against the Association, in case prosecution should be necessary, are continued. The reports of speeches in the newspapers would not, I apprehend, be available as evidence against the speakers. A short-hand writer used to be in attendance at the Association, employed by the Government, who would have been prepared, in case of necessity, to prove the words spoken. Without such assistance there might be great difficulty in adducing proof in a Court of Law against the speaker of any speech, however seditious.

" The foreigner whom Major Warburton passed was, according to his belief, the Duke de Montebello (Lasnes, not Macdonald). The Duke was in Ireland some time since. He is known to so many persons that it will be easy to discover whether he is actually in Ireland or not. I should rather be inclined to doubt it.

" I agree with you that the object of those who have laboured so hard and so successfully to excite the people in Ireland, must probably be to avoid, for the present at least, actual commotion. Still they may not be able to control the passions they have inflamed. In case of any sudden burst their situation will be a very hazardous one. They must choose between the danger of heading those whom they have goaded on—

committing themselves to all extremities—and the
odium of abandoning the cause at its crisis from considerations of personal safety.

" Whatever are our hopes that there will be no
actual collision, it is true policy and true mercy to be
well prepared.   All parties will agree that any attempt
at insurrection must be promptly and effectually put
down—the more promptly and the more decisively, the
less would be the ultimate evil.

" Believe me, &c.

" ROBERT PEEL."

Mr. PEEL to Lord ANGLESEY.

(Private and confidential.)

" Whitehall, July 24, 1828.

" MY DEAR LORD ANGLESEY,

" In conversation the other day with Lord
Beresford, he mentioned that there was only a very
small proportion of the Militia and yeomanry arms in
charge of the Ordnance in Ireland. The remainder
is, I suppose, in store in the several counties. Great
caution might be necessary in removing them, but
unless they are in safe custody it would be desirable to
provide for it.

" I have little doubt that all these things have
occurred to you; still, even if my caution is superfluous,
it will do no harm.

" Ever, &c.

" ROBERT PEEL."

Lord ANGLESEY to Mr. PEEL.

" Rich View, July 26, 1828.

" MY DEAR MR. PEEL,

" I have received your letters and enclosures of
the 24th. The subjects shall be attended to. Everything
that regards the arms had been anticipated. I have
already desired inquiry to be made as to the embarkation of Irish labourers for the English harvest, and I will
give you the information I may receive.

" I am put into rather an awkward predicament by an
application on the part of Mr. O'Connell for an audience.
He first requested to see Lord Forbes, and to him he
expressed a desire to wait upon me. The ostensible
object is to engage me to send down a commission of
inquiry for the purpose of investigating a case of murder
committed by the collision of parties of Orangemen with
Catholics on the 12th of the month. I shall get rid of
this by saying that the ordinary course of law is the best
method of dealing with the case.

" I have no doubt, however, that Mr. O'Connell has
other objects. It has been considered whether I should
receive him, and universally agreed that I ought not to
object.

" It will be my business to be very patient, very
guarded, but not severely reserved, and whilst he is
endeavouring to penetrate me, to try if I can make
anything out of him.

" I give you this information in advance, as I am
aware that this occurrence may and probably will be
invidiously commented upon. To guard as well as I can

against his misrepresentations, I shall take care to have a witness present.

" A person much connected with the leading agitators inquired of one who is known to be high in my confidence if it would be satisfactory to the Government that the Association should cease to meet for the next four months.

" A general reply was made that it must of course be satisfactory to all those who loved their country to observe any tendency towards the suppression of violence and the allayment of irritation.

" Although I never receive a post without many reports of the alarming state of the public mind, and urgent applications for the augmentation of the military force, yet I cannot persuade myself that immediate danger is to be apprehended; at the same time I cannot say that it would surprise me if insurrection were to break forth at once. The priests are using very inflammatory language, and are certainly working upon the Catholics of the army. I think it important that the depôts of Irish recruits should be gradually removed, under the appearance of being required to join their regiments, and that whatever regiments are sent here should be those of Scotland, or, at all events, of men not recruited in the south of Ireland. I desired Sir John Byng to convey this opinion to Lord Hill.

" You will, I am sure, appreciate the motive that engages me to revert again to the great question. Few, very few, even of the reputed Orangemen, now dispute the fact that it must at no distant period be adjusted. Every hour increases the difficulty of adjustment. What would have been considered as a perfect boon but a few years—I may say but a few months ago—would not, I apprehend, be now very gratefully received ; and that which might by possibility be effected now, whilst we have external peace and internal plenty, would in all probability be rejected with disdain at some future time, and under opposite circumstances.

" If I should fortunately be enabled, by the advice and the warnings I give, to keep this country in a quiet state for a little time longer—if the Association should cease to agitate, and there were to be anything like an appearance of moderation, I most seriously conjure you to signify an intention of taking the state of Ireland into consideration in the first days of the next Session of Parliament.

" I hold it to be my duty thus freely to express my opinion, but I beg you to be assured that I never commit myself or the King's Government by holding out to any one that the question will be entertained.   It is perfectly well known that I have no authority to discuss it, still less to negotiate upon it.   Negotiation indeed would be beneath the dignity of the State.   We must legislate, not negotiate.

" Believe me, &c.,
" ANGLESEY."

The accompanying letters of the 26th of July from me to Lord Anglesey were in reply to one written by him on the 16th of May preceding, enclosing two letters, one from the Attorney-General of Ireland, the other from Mr. Gregory, and suggesting plans for the improve ment of Ireland. I have no record of this communication from Lord Anglesey, which I am sure was dictated by the sincerest desire on his part to combine with the repression of disorder and the punishment of crime measures for the melioration of the condition of Ireland and the development of her natural resources.

The general nature of the measures suggested will be collected from the reference to them in the accompanying letter :—

Mr. PEEL to Lord ANGLESEY.

" Whitehall, July 26, 1828.

" MY DEAR LORD ANGLESEY,

"I at length send you an answer to your letters containing suggestions for the improvement of Ireland.

"I am afraid I am giving you as much reason now to accuse me of prolixity as I did before of delay.

"Ever most faithfully yours,

"ROBERT PEEL."

Mr. PEEL to Lord ANGLESEY.

"Whitehall, July 26, 1828.

" MY DEAR LORD ANGLESEY,

"I cannot approach the subject on which you have repeatedly addressed me—your suggestions for the improvement of Ireland—without repeating to you my regret that I have been compelled by the severe pressure of the Parliamentary business of the Session to postpone

for so long a period any answer of at all a definitive
nature. The delay has arisen from no insensibility on
my part to the importance of the subject, but from a
desire maturely to consider proposals that involve in
them very important principles.

" Your letters and the various documents which you
sent me relate principally to three points which I will
refer to in the order in which I now state them.

" First. The expediency of encouraging manufactures
in Ireland by a direct interference on the part of Government, and principally by a guarantee to be given by
Government to the proprietors of such manufacturing
establishments as may be set on foot against loss from
arson or from other malicious injuries to property.

" Secondly. The claim of Ireland, in point of justice,
as well as in point of policy, to the repeal of the existing
duties upon the import of coal.

" Thirdly. The policy of opening new lines of communication through inaccessible districts by the aid of
public money; thus finding temporary occupation for a
lawless and unemployed people, and facilitating the
future improvement of the country, together with the
maintenance of public tranquillity.

" To the adoption of the first suggestion—that of
guaranteeing private individuals against loss from malicious injuries to property of a certain description—we
see very serious objection.

" There are at present two species of security against
such loss open equally to all the subjects of His
Majesty;—the insurance of property at the insurance
offices, and the remedy against the district.

" In the first case every motive of pecuniary interest is in operation to guard against fraud, either in the valuation of the property insured, or in regard to the circumstances under which claims of indemnity are preferred on the insurers.

" In the second—the remedy against the district—the inhabitants have a common interest in the preservation of property against wilful damage, on account of the liability to which they are subject to make good the loss that may be sustained.

" We cannot think that it would be advisable for the Government, with a view to the encouragement of manufactures, to undertake that the public should either relieve individuals from the cost of insurance, or the district from the responsibility to which it is now subject.

" It might be very difficult to reconcile such a guarantee, given with respect to certain specified manufactories, with strict justice to other parties engaged in the same branches of manufacture.

" The guarantee would be neither more nor less than a pecuniary premium; and the principle of such a premium would excite great jealousy, and not unjustly, on the part of those who did not benefit by it.

" The precedent would also be a very embarrassing one to the Government.

" In the manufacturing districts of this country losses are occasionally sustained from the acts of unlawful combinations, against which no precaution of the proprietors of manufacturing establishments can guard.

" The Luddites, some years since in Nottinghamshire,

the hand-loom weavers more recently in parts of Lancashire and Yorkshire, did great mischief to the property of innocent persons, and mischief for which no sufficient compensation was probably ever made.   Now we should, without hesitation, refuse, and we did actually refuse, either to compensate such sufferers for the past, or to indemnify them for the future.   A similar decision would in future cases be acquiesced in most reluctantly, if it were known that we had given a guarantee of indemnity from loss to persons engaged in similar undertakings in another part of the empire.   Again, if the Government were to undertake to repay the loss that might accrue from fire, or other malicious injury, could it have the effectual security which it ought to have against the possibility of a fraudulent demand?   Suppose a manufactory to which its guarantee had been given to be burnt under circumstances at all suspicious, the situation of the Government would be most embarrassing, between its desire on the one hand to adhere to its engagements, and on the other to resist an attempt at imposition.

" The Attorney-General of Ireland, in his letter to your Excellency of the 11th of May, proposes that the manufacturer should have the security of Government for the safety of his factory, by Government agreeing to reimburse him his loss, and to stand in his place as to his remedy against the county under the Presentment Law.

" Now if the Government should recover from the county the exact amount of the sum which they had paid to the sufferer in case of loss, there appears little advantage in the arrangement.

I

" If in the much more probable case the Government should recover little or nothing from the county, the effect would be to benefit, at the expense of the public, the district previously responsible for the loss sustained, and at the same time to diminish that stimulus to active exertion in the prevention of violence and outrage, which it was the general policy of the law to hold out by imposing local responsibility.

" On the whole, there is such embarrassment on so many grounds in the Government interfering in the encouragement of individual mercantile speculations—its means of effectual superintendence are so limited—its guards against fraud so ineffectual—the remote consequences of such interference upon other establishments which rely exclusively on private exertion are so difficult to be foreseen, that we cannot advise a departure from the general principle upon which the trade and manufactures of this country have been so long conducted.

" I proceed to the duty upon coals.

" The encouragement which would be given to the manufactures of Ireland by a reduction in the duty upon coals imported into Ireland from England is a perfectly legitimate encouragement, open to none of the objections in principle which I have urged in regard to the encouragement of industry through the special interference of the Government in individual cases.

" It is necessary, however, that I should state distinctly, that the claim for the reduction of this duty, which is founded on an appeal to the provisions of the Act of Union, appears to us to be untenable.

" The Attorney-General of Ireland expresses an opinion that the maintenance of the duty on coals contravenes the sixth article of the Act of Union. But I cannot help thinking that there are circumstances connected with the imposition of this duty subsequently to the Union, of which the Attorney-General may not have been fully aware when he addressed your Excellency upon this subject.

" I believe the following is a correct statement of these circumstances.

" Before the Union coals imported into Ireland paid on exportation from Great Britain 10*d*.; on importation into Ireland, 10*d*.; making 1*s*. 8*d*. in the whole. By the Union it was stipulated that articles should be exported from one country to the other without duty on such export; in consequence the duty of 10*d*. on exportation of coals to Ireland necessarily fell to the ground.

" The Act of Union, however, provided that coals on importation into Ireland from Great Britain should be subject to *burthens* not exceeding those to which they were then subject.

" Those *burthens* were, as before stated, 10*d*. on export and 10*d*. on import, or 1*s*. 8*d*. in the whole.

" The export duty was to cease under the former article of Union, and therefore in 1801 an additional import duty was imposed to make up the *burthen* on coals imported into Ireland equal to what it had previously been, viz., 1*s*. 8*d*. in the whole.

" The following extract from a speech delivered by Mr. Corry, then Chancellor of the Exchequer, in 1801, is material, as showing the intention with which the additional import duty of 10*d.* was imposed in that year.

" ' Having stated the Ways and Means, Mr. Corry next called the attention of the Committee particularly to the article of coals. He said he was extremely anxious not to be misunderstood upon this subject, because any misconception might create considerable alarm. There was heretofore a duty in this country upon that article exported into Ireland of 10*d.* per ton, which produced a revenue of about 17,000*l.* a-year. This duty could now, in consequence of the Union, no longer be collected in England ; and it was proposed to collect it in Ireland, thereby giving the benefit of the produce to that country ; whereas it had heretofore been levied upon the consumer in Ireland, for the benefit of the British Exchequer. There was therefore no increase in the duty upon coals ; it was merely collecting the same duty in Ireland, which before the Union had been collected in England ; and if the coal trader in Ireland should attempt to make this a pretext for raising the price of the article, it would be impossible for him to avoid detection, and that disgrace which would belong to such imposition.'

" That the word *burthens* applied to coals was intended to include more than import duties is evident from its being applied to coals only, while to all other articles the word duty is applied. Coal was the one upon which an export duty was paid in addition to an import. The two are fairly construed, as they were by Mr. Corry in 1801, as making up the *burthen* on coals : it was, before the Union, 1*s.* 8*d.* ; it is now the same.

" With respect to the 'Wide Street Duty,' to which the Attorney-General refers, it must be recollected that money was borrowed on that duty to the amount of above 200,000*l.* That sum of 200,000*l.* was laid out in the improvement of Dublin; and in some way or other Dublin ought to provide adequate security for the payment of the interest of the debt incurred, according to the engagement originally made with the lenders.

" I have thought it absolutely necessary to enter into these details respecting the duty on coals, because, from communications received respecting it, there appears to be a strong impression in Ireland that the continuance of the duty is contrary to the spirit at least, if not the letter of the Act of Union.

" We are, however, perfectly ready to admit that the policy of continuing the coal duty in Ireland is a consideration quite apart from that to which I have been last adverting. The subject is one which will undergo deliberate investigation during the Recess; and that investigation will be entered upon with a strong disposition to consult the interests of Ireland by the encouragement of her manufacturing industry.

" The last subject to which I have to advert is your Excellency's proposal that a certain sum of public money should be applied to the construction of barracks for the accommodation of the constabulary force in disturbed and lawless parts of the country, and to the making of roads through mountainous and at present inaccessible districts.

" Before I particularly advert to these suggestions, I will make a few observations on the statement which has been transmitted to your Excellency by the Society for the Improvement of Ireland, and which accompanied your letter to me of the 18th of May.

" From the proposals of the Society that the aid of public money should be granted for promoting the opening of communications into remote districts, for coast improvements, and the extension of fisheries, and also from the reference which they make to the case of Scotland, and to the encouragement which that country has received from the Legislature, I am inclined to think that the Society is not fully aware of the extent to which Parliamentary aid has been granted, and particularly of late years, with the view to foster and extend the spirit of local improvement in Ireland.

" The two great canals of Ireland, the Royal Canal and the Grand Canal, have received very large grants of public money from the Legislature.

" When I filled the office of Chief Secretary to the Lord-Lieutenant of Ireland, in one year the sum of 300,000*l.* of public money was voted by Parliament, one moiety of which was employed in the completion of the Royal Canal, and the other was appropriated to the relief of the Grand Canal Company from a state of the greatest pecuniary embarrassment.

" In the five years ending the 1st of January, 1828, a sum of not less than 2,149,000*l.* has been advanced from the public funds for roads and other public works in Ireland, on the security of presentments of tolls, &c. &c.

In the year ending 1st January, 1824 . £304,544
,,   ,,   1825 . . 327,411
,,   ,,   1826 . . 533,258
,,   ,,   1827 . . 546,922
,,   ,,   1828 . . 437,753

Total £2,149,888

" During the same period there have been absolute grants of Parliament for public works in Ireland that are not to be repaid, to the amount of 251,842*l*.

" The total of advances and of grants in the last five years amounts therefore to the sum of 2,400,000*l*.

" While I admit the melancholy fact that there is a great want of employment for the poor in Ireland, and admit also that an increase in the demand for labour would be of the utmost advantage to society in that country, I must at the same time express a doubt whether ultimate advantage would arise from the creation of such a demand by the continual application of large sums of public money.

" In voting the public money in aid of local improvements, it must be borne in mind, that with the best intentions on the part of Government, it is not easy to prevent occasional abuse in the expenditure ; and that if there be such abuse, there is a moral evil attending it, independent of the mere waste of money.

" It must also be borne in mind, that too great a facility on the part of Government in applying the public money in aid of local improvements has a tendency to discourage local exertions, and to afford an excuse for the indifference and neglect of those who ought to apply some part of their influence and their wealth in promot-

ing the improvement of their country. There is danger
also that the demand created for labour in consequence
of the interference of Government may be merely temporary ; and by anticipating in some degree the natural
demand, which would gradually arise without that interference, may cause increased languor and depression at
some future period.

" Even independent therefore of the consideration of
economy, the grant of public money for the purposes
above mentioned, unless most judiciously applied and
vigilantly superintended, is not free from objections.

" The above observations apply rather to the statement presented to your Excellency by the Society for
the Improvement of Ireland than to the specific proposal
which you have made respecting the construction of
public barracks, and the opening of roads through mountainous districts.

" You observe in your letter to me of the 16th of
May, that two or three police barracks will cost from
about four to six hundred pounds ; and in that of the
2nd of June, enclosing one from Mr. Griffiths respecting roads in Tipperary, is the following paragraph :

" ' You will observe that for the roads, a most material object, not more than 10,000*l.* will be wanted,
and the advantage to be expected from them is very
great indeed.'

" After the communications which I have had with
the Duke of Wellington and Mr. Goulburn, I feel
myself warranted in giving to your Excellency an authority to apply the sums above mentioned to the objects
to which you propose to apply them.

" Mr. Griffiths states that thirty miles of road through lawless parts of the county of Tipperary can be made at the expense, including bridges, &c., of 20,000*l*.   He very properly suggests that under the provisions of 1 George IV., chap. 81, one moiety of the expense should be defrayed by the Government, and that the county should contribute the other.

" We think it of great importance that any grant made by your Excellency should be in conformity with this suggestion, namely, in aid of local advances of at least equal amount.

" As we give you the authority to expend the sum of 10,000*l*. without having had the previous sanction of Parliament, we are most anxious that that sum should not on any account be exceeded ; and we suggest to your Excellency, that in making any engagement with the Grand Jury, or other parties, respecting these roads, the best plan would be to undertake to advance, on the part of Government, a definite sum of money on condition that they should advance the remainder ; and not to undertake to defray a moiety or any other portion of an estimated and uncertain expenditure.

" We shall be very glad if the whole sum to be applied shall be placed under the exclusive control and superintendence of your Excellency, as in that case we have every confidence that it will be judiciously and economically applied.

" I have, &c.,
" ROBERT PEEL."

I interrupt the series of the Irish correspondence

for the purpose of adverting to that which passed shortly after the date of the last letter from Lord Anglesey between the Duke of Wellington and me.

At the close of the Session of 1828 it became incumbent upon me to decide without delay on the course which I ought to pursue. All the material facts and documents which could influence that decision have been brought under review.

It was open to me to retain office, or to relinquish it—persisting in either case in offering continued resistance to concession. There could be little doubt (considering that the King was opposed to concession, and that a clear majority of the House of Lords was opposed to it) that notwithstanding the recent vote of the House of Commons in its favour, resistance to concession would for a time prevail.

It would so far prevail as to obstruct the final settlement of the Catholic Question, but the same sad state of things must continue; a divided Cabinet, a divided Parliament, the strength of political parties so nicely balanced as to preclude any decisive course, either of concession on the one hand, or the vigorous assertion of authority on the other.

I maturely and anxiously considered every point which required consideration, and I formed a decision as to the obligation of public duty—of which I may say with truth, that it was wholly at variance with that which the regard for my own personal interests or private feelings would have dictated.

My intention was to relinquish office; but I resolved not to relinquish it without previously placing on record

my opinion that the public interests required that
the principle on which the then existing and preceding
Governments had been formed should no longer be
adhered to ; that the Catholic Question should cease to
be an open question; that the whole condition of Ireland, political and social, should be taken into consideration by the Cabinet, precisely in the same manner
in which every other question of grave importance was
considered, and with the same power to offer advice
upon it to the Sovereign.

I resolved also to place on record a decided opinion
that there was less of evil and less of danger in considering the Catholic Question with a view to its final
adjustment than in offering continued resistance to that
adjustment, and to give every assurance that after retirement from office I would in a private capacity act upon
the opinion thus given.   The impressions under which I
came to the resolution, and the motives for the advice
which I gave, will be better judged of by the confidential and unreserved communications which took place
with the Duke of Wellington at the time, than by any
thing which I can now say in their justification.

I left London for Brighton very soon after the close
of the Session of 1828, having made a previous arrangement with the Duke of Wellington that he should send
to me a Memorandum explanatory of his views on the
state of Ireland and on the Catholic Question, and that
I should write to him fully in reply.

On the 9th of August the Duke wrote to me the
following letter :—

Duke of WELLINGTON to Mr. PEEL.

                                "London, August 9, 1828.
" MY DEAR PEEL,

" I now send you the Memorandum which I sent
to the King upon the state of Ireland ; the letter which
I wrote to him at the same time ; his answer ; a Memorandum upon the Roman Catholic Question which I
have since drawn ; and a letter which I wrote yesterday
to the Lord Chancellor. I am to see him again this
afternoon, and will write you a line before the post goes
out ; and I hope to hear from you on Monday.

" I will either then, or this evening with the Lord
Chancellor, fix a time at which we shall meet to talk
over this subject, previous to my having any further
communication with the King.

            " Believe me,
                " Ever yours most sincerely,
                            " WELLINGTON.

" I have seen the Lord Chancellor, who thinks the
arrangement would answer if there is not a religious
objection on the part of the Roman Catholics to the
licences.

" He thinks, however, that we ought to limit the
number of offices as well as the number of seats in
Parliament, and to pass the law for seven years, meaning then to revise it. We might except the Lord Chancellor of England, the Lord Lieutenant of Ireland, the
First Lord of the Treasury, as possessing Church patronage, but nothing else.

" The Chancellor and I are going to Windsor on

Tuesday. We will afterwards fix a time to meet you. In the mean time let me hear from you."

The papers which accompanied the above letter I returned to the Duke of Wellington without having taken copies of them.

On the 11th of August I wrote to the Duke the letter which follows :—

Mr. PEEL to the Duke of WELLINGTON.

" Brighton, August 11, 1828.

" MY DEAR DUKE OF WELLINGTON,

" I have read with the greatest attention the papers which I received from you yesterday, consisting, independently of the private letters, first, of a proposal to the King that the state of Ireland shall be considered by his Government with a view to the settlement of the Catholic question ; and secondly, of the outline of a plan for the settlement of that question which you have communicated to the Lord Chancellor.

" I shall give you without the slightest reserve my opinions upon the whole subject. They are necessarily (as I am writing by return of post) committed to paper very hastily ; but I have no wish, in communicating with you, to weigh expressions, or to conceal anything which occurs to me.

" I have uniformly opposed what is called Catholic Emancipation, and have rested my opposition upon broad and uncompromising grounds.

" I wish I could say that my views upon the question

were materially changed, and that I now believed that
full concessions to the Roman Catholics could be made,
either exempt from the dangers which I have apprehended from them, or productive of the full advantages
which their advocates anticipate from the grant of
them.

" But, whatever may be my opinion upon these points,
I cannot deny that the state of Ireland under existing
circumstances is most unsatisfactory; that it becomes
necessary to make your choice between different kinds
and different degrees of evil—to compare the actual
danger resulting from the union and organization of
the Roman Catholic body, and the incessant agitation
in Ireland, with prospective and apprehended dangers
to the constitution or religion of the country; and
maturely to consider whether it may not be better to
encounter every ·eventual risk of concession than to
submit to the certain continuance, or rather perhaps the
certain aggravation, of existing evils.

" Take what view we may of the Catholic question,
we must admit that we labour under this extreme and
overwhelming embarrassment with reference to the present condition of Ireland : that the Protestant mind is
divided and very nearly balanced upon the most important question relating to Ireland.

" We cannot escape from the discussion of that question, and we cannot meet it without being in a minority
in one branch of the Legislature.

" In the House of Commons in 1827 there was a
majority of four against concession ; in 1828 there was
a majority of six in its favour.

" The change certainly was not effected by any other cause than the progress of uninfluenced opinion. The actual number therefore in the House of Commons in favour of the measure is on the increase. The House of Commons of the last Parliament, and the House of Commons of this Parliament, have each decided in favour of the principle of concession. The majority of the House of Lords against the principle, looking at the constitution of that majority, is far from satisfactory; but if it were much greater, the evil of permanent disunion on such a question between the two branches of the Legislature would be extreme, and the parties that would gain dangerous strength from its continuance would be those in whose favour the House of Commons have decided.

" Whatever be the ultimate result of concession, there would be an advantage in the sincere and honest attempt to settle the question on just principles, which it is difficult to rate too highly in the present state of affairs.

" The Protestant mind would be united, not at first, for the party opposed to concession would probably under any circumstances be a powerful one. If, however, concession should tranquillize Ireland and produce the effects predicted by its advocates, that party would gradually and rapidly acquiesce in it. If concession on just principles were rejected by the Roman Catholics— or if it were abused—if they were put clearly and undeniably in the wrong—then the Protestants of all shades of opinion would be united into one firm and compact body, and would ultimately overbear all opposition.

" The present state of affairs in Ireland is such, the
danger is so menacing, that it is an object of great
importance to lay the foundation of cordial union and
co-operation among the Protestants of the empire—supposing you should fail in establishing the more general
and more desirable union among all classes of the
King's subjects.

" I have thus written to you without reserve upon the
first and great question of all—the policy of seriously
considering this long-agitated question with a view to
its adjustment. I have proved to you, I trust, that no
false delicacy in respect to past declarations of opinion
—no fear of the imputation of inconsistency—will prevent me from taking that part which present dangers
and a new position of affairs may require. I am ready,
at the hazard of any sacrifice, to maintain the opinion
which I now deliberately give—that there is upon the
whole less of evil in making a decided effort to settle
the Catholic question, than in leaving it, as it has been
left, an open question—the Government being unde-
cided with respect to it, and paralyzed in consequence
of that indecision upon many occasions peculiarly requiring promptitude and energy of action.

" I must at the same time express a very strong
opinion that it would not conduce to the satisfactory
adjustment of the question, that the charge of it in the
House of Commons should be committed to my hands.

" I put all personal feelings out of the question.
They are, or ought to be, very subordinate considerations in matters of such moment, and I give the best
proof that I disregard them by avowing that I am quite

ready to commit myself to the support of the principle
of a measure of ample concession and relief, and to use
every effort to promote the final arrangement of it.

" But my support will be more useful if I give it
(with the cordiality with which it shall be given) out of
office.

" Any authority which I may possess as tending to
reconcile the Protestants to the measure would be increased by my retirement.

" I have been too deeply committed on the question
—have expressed too strong opinions in respect to it—
too much jealousy and distrust of the Roman Catholics
—too much apprehension as to the immediate and remote consequences of yielding to their claims—to make
it advantageous for the King's service that I should be
the individual to originate the measure.

" It may be right to decline negotiation or consultation with the Roman Catholics, but the more you can
conciliate them by the *mode* of proposing the measure
the better ; the more of good will and of satisfaction that
you can extract from it, the greater is the prospect that
the adjustment will be a permanent one.

" The very same measures, whether of concession to
the Roman Catholics or of security for the Protestants—
proposed by one who has taken so decided a part in
opposition to the question as I have—would be regarded in a very different light by the Roman Catholics
from that in which such measures would appear to
them if proposed by a person less adverse to concession
than I have been.

" It may be said, on the other hand, that the proposal of those measures by me would tend to reconcile the Protestant mind to concession. But that advantage would perhaps be even more fully secured by the explicit declaration of my opinion out of office as a Member of Parliament, and by my zealous co-operation in the attempt to effect a settlement.

" You must also bear in mind the state of parties in Parliament. The Government ought to take every precaution that any measure of relief which may be proposed shall not only be carried by majorities, but shall have as far as possible the decided and unequivocal sense of Parliament expressed in its favour.

" You must look therefore at the character and constitution of the majority by which you are to carry it.

" You will have a reluctant assent on the part of many of the best friends of the Government—a decided opposition perhaps from some.

" The great mass of support must be looked for from the ranks of those who are, if not habitually opposed to the Government, at least under no tie of support to it, and perhaps not favourably disposed towards it. Can you depend upon them for zealous co-operation in the carrying of the measure ?

" In the principle of it they will no doubt concur. They will go with you in establishing the equality of civil privileges ; but there will be many details little less important than the principle : there are, for instance, the securities which (be they what they may) it will be of the utmost importance to carry with a general assent, and by a commanding majority.

" If carried otherwise, the seeds for future discontent and agitation are sown.

" Consider these things well.   If the question is to be taken up, there is clearly no safe alternative but the settlement of it.

" Every consideration of private feelings and individual interests must be disregarded.   From a very strong sense of what is best for the success of the measure, I relieve you from all difficulties with respect to myself.

" I do not merely volunteer my retirement at whatever may be the most convenient time ; I do not merely give you the promise that out of office (be the sacrifices that I foresee, private and public, what they may) I will cordially co-operate with you in the settlement of this question, and cordially support your government ; but I add to this my decided and deliberate opinion, that it will tend to the satisfactory adjustment of the question if the originating of it in the House of Commons, and the general superintendence of its progress, be committed to other hands than mine.

" I am, my dear Duke of Wellington,

" Ever most faithfully yours,

" ROBERT PEEL.'

Twenty years have elapsed since the above letter was written. I read it now with the full testimony of my own heart and conscience to the perfect sincerity of the advice which I then gave, and the declarations which I then made—with the same testimony also to the fact that that letter was written with a clear foresight of the penalties to which the course I resolved to take would expose me—the rage of party—the rejection by the University of Oxford—the alienation of private friends— the interruption of family affections.

Other penalties, such as the loss of office and of Royal favour, I would not condescend to notice if they were not the heaviest in the estimation of vulgar and low-minded men, incapable of appreciating higher motives of public conduct.

My judgment may be erroneous. From the deep interest I have in the result (though now only so far as future fame is concerned), it cannot be impartial ; yet surely I do not err in believing that when the various circumstances on which my decision was taken are calmly and dispassionately considered—the state of political parties — the recent discussions in Parliament — the result of the Clare election, and the prospects which it opened—the earnest representations and emphatic warnings of the chief Governor of Ireland—the evil, rapidly increasing, of divided councils in the Cabinet, and of conflicting decisions in the two Houses of Parliament— the necessity for some systematic and vigorous course of policy in respect to Ireland—the impossibility, even if it were wise, that that policy should be one of coercion— surely I do not err in believing that I shall not hereafter be condemned for having needlessly and precipitately, still less for having dishonestly and treacherously counselled the attempt to adjust the long litigated question that had for so many years precluded the cordial co-operation of public men, and had left Ireland the arena

for fierce political conflicts, annually renewed without
the means of authoritative interposition on the part of
the Crown.

The following Memorandum, which accompanied my
letter of the 11th of August, is a commentary upon
that which had been sent by the Duke and returned
by me.

The latter has no doubt been preserved by the Duke.
The general tenor of the suggestions which it contained
may be inferred from my remarks upon them.

Mr. PEEL'S MEMORANDUM, August 11, 1828.

(Most private and confidential.)

" Whenever it is once determined that an attempt
should be made by the Government to settle the Catholic
question, there can be, I think, but one opinion—that
the settlement should be, if possible, a complete one.

" Partial concessions would be of no use : they
would give power to the Roman Catholics without giving
satisfaction. If you once make up your mind to relax
the present system of exclusion, you ought at the same
time to look at the whole question in all its details, and
be prepared for the discussion and arrangement of every
branch of it.

" But each branch of the question requires the most
mature consideration, and I should earnestly deprecate
a positive decision upon any branch without minute inquiry and full deliberation.

" If it be once known that the King's Government

mean to attempt the adjustment of the question upon
enlarged and just principles, there will be no necessity
for an immediate and irrevocable decision upon any of
the details.

" The three great points which present themselves
most prominently in the consideration are these :—

" *First*. The footing on which the Roman Catholics
shall be placed in respect to the enjoyment of civil privileges.

" *Secondly*. What arrangement shall be made with
respect to the elective franchise in Ireland ?

" *Thirdly*. What shall be the future relation of the
Roman Catholic religion to the State ?

" Of these three most important subjects, the last
involves by far the greatest difficulties.

" I will consider each in the order in which I have
above presented them.

" My answer to the first query—What shall be the
condition of the Roman Catholics in respect to civil
rights—is a very short one.   I should answer at once,—
equality, equal capacity with other classes for the enjoyment of the offices and distinctions of the State.

" I do not mean to say that there must be no exception as to particular offices ; but I think the ruling principle must be equality of civil privilege.

" By any material departure from that principle, you
would gain nothing in point of security ; you would
resign the grace and the advantage of concession, and
you would deprive your arrangement of the character of
permanency.   The Roman Catholic in Ireland is at
present eligible for almost every office, excepting the

judicial office, and the higher offices which constitute the Government.

"If you are to open any of these to him, where are you to draw the line, unless you open all? You would make your arrangement upon no intelligible principle; and the absence of such a principle would be a fatal defect in it.

"After you have abandoned the present system of exclusion by law, the great security against the possession of undue power and influence by the Roman Catholics (so far as civil office confers power and influence) must be in the discretion of the Crown and its advisers.

"The Roman Catholics will be eligible, not entitled, to office; and whether they be eligible to this office or that, is a matter of no great importance. If the Crown and the Government be inclined unduly to favour them, the exclusion by law from five or six offices would be of little avail when fifty or sixty would be open, with privileges attached to them capable of great perversion and abuse.

"No arrangement would be complete in the present state of affairs by which the Roman Catholic continued excluded from Parliament.

"It would be manifestly unwise to admit him to Parliament, and exclude him from the favour of the Crown.

"There is a question, however, connected with this branch of the subject, which will deserve great consideration.

"Shall there be any limitation upon the number of Roman Catholics entitled to sit in Parliament at the same time? or shall there be—as has been proposed lately—any restriction upon the rights of individual Roman Catholic members of Parliament with respect to voting upon particular questions relating to the Established Church?

" I do not conceive that a limitation of the number of Roman Catholics sitting at the same time in Parliament would infringe the great principle of equality of civil privilege.

" You limit the number of Members sitting for Ireland and for Scotland, and you have a right to limit the number representing a particular class if you see sufficient reason for the limitation.

" I think, of the two proposals above mentioned, the limitation of numbers is much less open to objection than the other, by which the discretion of a Member of Parliament is to be fettered, or rather taken away on certain and not very definite questions.

" With respect to the House of Lords, no limitation would probably in any event be necessary. You know the present number of Roman Catholic Peers.

" Conversions to the Roman Catholic faith are not much to be apprehended, and the Crown can prevent an increase to the number by the refusal to create a Roman Catholic Peer.

" In the House of Commons, however, you might have, and in my opinion you very soon would have, a very considerable number of Roman Catholic Members. If the spirit of party should continue in Ireland after the concessions to the Roman Catholics had been made—if there still should remain, as I think it probable there will, separate interests and separate views—

make what regulation you will as to the elective franchise, you must calculate on the ultimate return of many Roman Catholic members.

" You may strike off the lower class of voters in counties, but in a great part of Ireland the majority of the voters under any constitution of the right of voting will remain Roman Catholics.

" If you strike off the indigent voters, you increase the influence of the class above them; a class perhaps a little more independent of the priest, but also more independent of the landlord.

" It must be recollected also, and it is generally forgotten in calculating the probable numbers of Roman Catholic Members, that there are other places besides Irish counties and Irish boroughs that may return Roman Catholics to Parliament.

" Why may not the Duke of Norfolk acquire as large a borough influence as Lord Darlington or Lord Hertford?

" I very much doubt whether a Roman Catholic Peer or Commoner of great wealth would not have stronger motives for increasing such an influence than the Protestant.

" The party struggling for advancement—for equality, not only of privilege but of power—is more active than the party in possession; and the existing state of the elective franchise in England would admit of a larger return of Roman Catholics for the boroughs of England than would be proportionate to their relative wealth, or influence, or numbers.

" It may be urged on the other hand, that you take

K

no precaution against the return of an undue number of
Presbyterians, or Dissenters of any description ; that any
combination of Roman Catholic Members to advance
Roman Catholic interests would be met by a much more
powerful counter combination ; and that the Crown
might exercise the same influence over Roman Catholics
to withdraw them from any dangerous confederacy
which it exercises over other individuals and parties.

" Still the actual limitation of Members might be very
useful as a security satisfactory to the Protestant feeling ; and any security, compatible with the great object
of permanently settling the question, that would abate
the uneasiness and apprehension of the Protestants, ought
to be favourably considered.

" On this ground, no security that has been proposed
by the advocates of the Roman Catholic claims ought
to be lightly rejected.

" The Duke of Wellington's Memorandum suggests
the annual suspension, so far as Parliament is concerned,
of the laws which exclude Roman Catholics from Parliament.

" Would there not be great difficulty in a constitutional point of view in giving to a Member of Parliament by express enactment a tenure of his seat other
than the usual tenure — the duration of a Parliament ?

" Great care should be taken not to embarrass the
question with any constitutional difficulties not necessarily incidental to it.

" The revision of the oaths is an important point, but
one of subordinate importance. The present oaths con-

tain disclaimers that might probably be dispensed with, and imply suspicions against which, even if they were well founded, they supply very imperfect precautions.

" There would be little advantage in requiring persons whom you were willing to admit to an equality of civil rights, to deny that the Pope could excommunicate and depose a King, or relieve them from the obligation of a solemn oath.

" Some more appropriate, yet shorter declaration, might possibly be substituted for those at present required.

" *Secondly.* As to the elective franchise.

" The Duke of Wellington's Memorandum proposes that no elector shall vote who does not contribute to local charges of some kind or other five pounds annually.

" The principle is a very good one, but it could not be applied practically without much previous consideration and inquiry as to the effect which it would produce in different counties of Ireland.

" I have no doubt but that it will be absolutely necessary to take some such criterion of property. It would not suffice to deprive the owner of a forty shilling free hold, held on a life interest, of his right of voting, and leave the right of voting with the possessor of a freehold interest in fee simple of the same amount.

" You would soon have a body of forty shilling fee simple freeholders, as open to objection as the present voters.

" But there is this difficulty in taking a given sum of contribution to local charges as the qualification for voting, that it would be a very uncertain and imperfect test of actual property in Ireland.

" The valuation of lands, by which the county charges are regulated, is of old date; and the consequence is a presumptive and very unequal distribution of the burden. In one county, or in one part of a county, a man of very inferior wealth might contribute five pounds to the county rate; while in another county, or in another part of the same county, a person of much larger property might be excluded from the right of voting from not being assessed according to its true value.

" There would also be this difficulty. The county, the expenditure of which was well managed, would have fewer voters in proportion than the county which was careless and profuse in the application of its rates, and the effect of economy and reduction of the county expenditure would be to disfranchise some of its voters.

" I believe that five pounds would be much too large a sum to take as the qualification of the right of voting; but it would be very difficult to determine on any particular sum, without very full inquiry as to the practical effect which the assumption of it would have in different counties.

" *Thirdly.* The regulations to be established with respect to the exercise of the Roman Catholic religion and its relation to the State.

" I have before observed, and I repeat, that here is the great difficulty of the question; and it ought to be well considered as a point preliminary to all others in reference to this branch of the subject.

" Whether it would be better to leave the Roman

Catholic religion on the footing that it stands at present, tolerated, connived at, but not encouraged by the State, or to give it a partial establishment and that degree of sanction and authority which must be inevitably given by the payment of its ministers by the State.

" So far as the Roman Catholics are concerned, you are, I conceive, at perfect liberty to leave the Roman Catholic religion as you find it. It may be policy to act otherwise, but there is no ground for complaint if you do not.

" Those subjects of the King who are not of the established religion may have a very urgent claim for the equality of civil privileges, but they can have no claim of right that the ministers of their religion should be paid by the State.

" The admission of any such claim on the part of the Roman Catholics would produce similar claims on the part of Dissenters in this country, who contribute in like manner to the support of their own religion, and that of the established religion also ; and even suppose you distinctly deny the claim of right, the consequences of the precedent must be well considered.

" If you pay 300,000*l.* a-year for the support of the Roman Catholic priesthood in Ireland, will not the Protestant Dissenter of England remonstrate against being made to contribute his share towards the support of two Churches, unless you take the case of his Church also into consideration ?

" Will there not be among the religious classes of the community a very great repugnance, founded on higher motives than the unwillingness to be taxed, against contributing in any manner to the propagation or maintenance of the doctrines of the Church of Rome? The very designation of our own faith is derived from protestation against those doctrines, and very great caution must be used to prevent the excitement of a religious feeling—more difficult to combat than political apprehensions or anticipations.

" But every part of this subject is full of difficulties— I will not say insurmountable difficulties—but I refer to them to show the absolute necessity of very extended and minute consideration.

" If the State undertakes to pay the Roman Catholic priest, will you allow him, or not, to receive dues, Easter offerings, &c. &c., from his parishioners?

" Can you effectually prevent him, considering the influence he possesses, from receiving such payments?

" If he receives them in addition to his stipend, will not his condition be better than that of the minister of the Established Church in many of the parishes of Ireland?

" But suppose you effectually prevent him from receiving any such payments, you will then provide by law that there shall be a gratuitous administration in Ireland of the ceremonies of the Roman Catholic Church —of baptism, marriage, &c. &c.

" The possible effect of this on the lower classes of Protestants and in all cases of intermarriage between Protestant and Roman Catholic must not be overlooked. The nonpayment of any fee may be a very powerful stimulus to the conversion of a labouring man.

" Supposing, however, that it were conceded that the

political advantages of providing for the Roman Catholic priesthood are such that every difficulty above referred to must be surmounted, I think some much more extensive arrangement than the mere grant of licences to officiate by the Crown would be requisite.

" I am referring to the suggestion in the Memorandum of the Duke of Wellington.

" I doubt whether the mere grant of a licence would not soon degenerate into a form—a nominal power, never to be exercised, giving no real control to the Crown, but investing the person licensed with a sanction and authority derived from the Crown.

" Could the licence ever be refused, except in some most notorious case of unfitness?

" If the Parliament were to vote such a sum as 300,000l. annually for the support of the Roman Catholic priesthood, and the Government were to apply that vote to the payment of the ministers of the Church of Rome in Ireland, granting a licence for the performance of their spiritual functions, would not such an arrangement, without any express enactment, be a virtual and complete supercession, if not repeal, of the laws which prohibit intercourse with Rome?

" Part of the sum voted must probably be allotted to the payment of Roman Catholic prelates: if it is not, will the arrangement be of any avail?

" If it is so allotted, can the State affect to be ignorant that the Bishop whom it pays derived his right to be a bishop from the See of Rome?

" The mode of appointment, and every particular connected with it, are detailed in the evidence given by the Roman Catholic prelates before Parliamentary Committees.

" If, being possessed of that information, you pay those prelates without asking any further question or suggesting any further regulation, could you subsequently, with any fairness, in almost any conceivable case, call into action the dormant penalties of the Statute of Præmunire? It does appear to me that the grant of licences by the Crown to Roman Catholic prelates and Roman Catholic priests to exercise their spiritual functions, accompanied by a provision for their payment out of the public funds, would be a virtual recognition of so much of the authority of the See of Rome as is essential to the exercise of those functions.

" What we grant we grant with notice on the records of Parliament, that there is a constant intercourse between the Church of Ireland and the See of Rome.

" I will not inquire whether any important advantage would result from the inspection and regulation of that intercourse; all that I say at present is, that I doubt whether the inspection and regulation of it would imply any stronger recognition of the authority of the See of Rome than the grant of licences and the payment of the priesthood by the Crown.

" I conclude this Memorandum by observing that I have written it very hastily, and that I mean it rather to suggest topics for very full inquiry and consideration than to express decided opinions on the points to which I have adverted.

" ROBERT PEEL.

" Brighton, August 11, 1828."

The Duke of Wellington acknowledged the receipt of my communication to him in the following letter :—

Duke of WELLINGTON to Mr. PEEL.

" London, August 13, 1828.

" MY DEAR PEEL,

" I did not answer your letter upon the Roman Catholic question yesterday, as I was obliged to go to Windsor at an early hour, and I wished to communicate what you had written to the Lord Chancellor, whom I was to meet at the Royal Lodge.

" I will not now pretend to discuss the different topics in your letter and paper, but will do so at a future moment when I shall be more at leisure.

" In the mean time I tell you that I have communicated your papers to the Chancellor alone ; Goulburn is not in town, and I had not shown him my papers, nor done more than merely mention the subject to him.

" Moreover I told the King that it should go no farther than to you and the Lord Chancellor in this stage.

" I have not told the King what you think, or even anything beyond the first paper.

" The Lord Chancellor will sit in Chancery until the 19th or 20th, and it would not be convenient to him to enter upon the discussion of this question for some days after that time.

" I have been advised to go for a short time to Cheltenham ; and if it should not be inconvenient to you, I

K 3

would fix some day in the first week of September for
you and the Lord Chancellor and I to meet.

"Ever, my dear Peel, &c.,

" WELLINGTON."

I left it to the Duke of Wellington to determine the
mode and the period in which communications could
best be made to the King and members of the Government on the subject of our recent correspondence.

I did this not only from the consideration due to the
Duke's position as head of the Government, but from
my unbounded confidence in his integrity and discretion.

Precarious as I deemed my tenure of office to be,
I felt it to be my duty while I retained it to conduct the
correspondence with Ireland and to discharge the other
functions of the Home Department without the slightest
reference to any such consideration.

I now revert to the letters received from the Lord-
Lieutenant and his Chief Secretary, and will insert consecutively all those which are of political importance,
together with the letters in reply. They embrace a
period extending from the 14th of August to the end of
the year 1828.

Whatever tendency this correspondence may have
had to confirm the decision communicated by me to
the Duke of Wellington on the 10th of August, being
of a subsequent date it could not of course have influenced that decision.

It will probably be recollected, or may be ascertained
by a reference to Lord Anglesey's letter to me of the

26th of July, previously inserted, that at the conclusion
of that letter Lord Anglesey had repeated very empha-
tically the expression of his opinion that the Catholic
question ought to be taken into consideration by the
Government without delay, observing that "few, very
few, even of the reputed Orangemen, now dispute the
fact that it must at no distant period be adjusted;" and
that "every hour increases the difficulty of adjustment."

In the letter which is at the commencement of the
following series I advert to the above passage in the
letter of Lord Anglesey.

Notwithstanding the confidential communications I
had then had with the Duke of Wellington, I did not
feel myself justified in giving any more specific assurances
in respect to the course of the Government than those
which my letter conveys.

With the exception of the Lord Chancellor, no member
of the Government was then aware of what had passed
between the Duke of Wellington and me; nor had the
King's consent been obtained for any departure from the
principle on which the then existing, like preceding administrations, had been formed in relation to the Catholic
question.

EXTRACT from my LETTER to Lord ANGLESEY of the
14th August, 1828.

"Upon the concluding part of your letter of the
26th of July I beg to observe that I have no doubt that
the advisers of the King will continue to direct their
most serious consideration to the whole state of Ireland;

will weigh most maturely all the circumstances connected with its present condition, and determine some
time before the commencement of the next Session of
Parliament what advice it may be proper to offer to
his Majesty as to the course fitting to be pursued,
and the declarations to be made when Parliament shall
assemble.

" ROBERT PEEL."

Lord ANGLESEY to Mr. PEEL.

" Rich View, August 31, 1828.

" MY DEAR MR. PEEL,

"Being much occupied, I desired Lord F. Leveson to inform you that I had not found it necessary to
release Mr. M'Donnell on the morrow, as I had expected. He is certainly very ill, but I could not ascertain that his life is in immediate danger, and an imper-
tinent Memorandum sent by him to Lord F. L., in
which he *demands* a copy of the report of the physicians,
in order that he may lay his case before the King, whilst
about the same time some of the agitators at the Munster
meeting were again bringing his case before the public,
has not tended to expedite his release. As, however, his
symptoms may rapidly change, and as, moreover, you
may in your answer to my first letter encourage his
liberation, I leave an order of discharge in the hands of
Lord Francis Leveson, to be used at his discretion,
during my absence at Carlingford, whither I am going
for a few days.

"I have nothing very particular to inform you of.

The reports of individuals continue to be very formidable in respect to the proceedings of the Catholics in the South, and of the Brunswick associations everywhere. Yet with all these unpleasant appearances I have little doubt of present tranquillity, but again I say that things must not, indeed they will not, remain as they are. You must legislate with decision and with promptitude. If you are prepared to meet the great question of Catholic emancipation, I have very little doubt that such terms might be given to the people of that Church as would fully satisfy them without outraging the feeling of the Protestants. At this instant I have every reason to believe that a satisfactory arrangement might be made.

"I think there would be no real difficulty with the Bishops; that an arrangement might be made for the payment of the clergy; and that even the most formidable of all the difficulties, the suppression or rather the gradual extinction of the forty-shilling freeholders, might be adjusted. But of this I am quite certain—that every hour of delay will increase the difficulty of adjustment.

"I am aware that I am addressing one whose sentiments upon this frightful question are very different from those I entertain, yet I feel it my duty to revert to them from time to time, because I cannot see the smallest chance of ever turning this country to any good for the empire at large but by settling it.

"I have almost pledged myself for the tranquillity of the country until the meeting of Parliament, but, I protest, I dare not encourage the hope of its continuance beyond that period, unless there is a determination on the part of the Government to settle the question of Emancipation.

" Believe me, &c.,

" ANGLESEY."

Lord ANGLESEY to Mr. PEEL.

" Rich View, September 17, 1828.

" MY DEAR MR. PEEL,

" Lord Erne being dead, I have sent a circular recommending Lord Dunally for the Representative Peerage.

" I am sorry to say that Lord Kingston is dangerously ill—I believe he has dropsy.

" I wish to understand at once what Peer would be preferred in case of another vacancy.

" The following are candidates, and I place them as I would recommend them :—

Marquis of WESTMEATH.
Earl of LLANDAFF.
Earl of DUNRAVEN.
Earl of GLENGALL.
Viscount CASTLEMAINE.

" I name them as I think their consequence entitles them to be placed, but I have no predilection.

" Frightful reports from the South! It is now imagined that the priests have no longer power to control the people. I have all along thought that there is more of a revolutionary than of a religious spirit afloat, but I cannot persuade myself that the *leading* agitators have any view beyond the carrying of their great cause, and if that is so, I do not comprehend how there can be any simultaneous or very formidable rising.   It is right, however, to observe that many persons of great local knowledge and sound judgment (Lord Donoughmore, for instance) are of a different opinion.   He and a great many others think there is very serious reason for alarm.

"Happen what may, I know of no other mode of proceeding than that I am adopting—that of keeping a good look out—of avoiding the evil moment as long as possible, but of being ready to act, and of acting vigorously if necessary.

"They are very feverish in the North.   The two parties there, being more fairly balanced, are ripe for strife.   This may be turned to account in the event of general insurrection.

"These combatants might keep each other employed or in check whilst the great body of troops were concentrated in the South.   But I must not anticipate evil. I hope, and I really do believe, that nothing serious will occur at present.

"Believe me, &c.,

"ANGLESEY."

Lord ANGLESEY to Mr. PEEL.

(Private.)

"Rich View, —— September, 1828.
" MY DEAR MR. PEEL,

"I have no particular information to send.   You get the reports from the provinces, and I have nothing to add to them.

"It seems to be agreed on all sides that the public

feeling has never been at so high a pitch of excitement as at present.

"The language of the respective parties is violent in the extreme, and both appear to be ripe for action.

"The organization of the Catholics is very complete. They carry banners; they form and they march by word of command, and in good order, but they commit no outrage, and I discourage interference or display both of the military and of the constabulary. The carrying of party flags is illegal; but is it expedient to put the law in force? What is to be gained?

"Some of the ringleaders might be taken. The assemblies would then be instructed by the agitators through the priests to obey the law, and to discontinue to display their flags. They would be obeyed, and the flags would disappear, but the meetings, the great grievance, would continue, and in suppressing the minor one you would increase irritation and bad feeling towards the laws.

"The speeches continue to be very inflammatory. Expressions might possibly be noted that would admit of prosecution; but in general the language, although violent, is nicely measured, and so equivocal as to admit of an explanation that might be strained into an excess of loyalty and a nervous warning to the State of the dangers to which it is exposed. I have yet heard of nothing that might lead to a favourable verdict.

"On the other hand, the Orangemen, or I suppose I am now to call them the Brunswickers, are rivalling the Association both in violence and in rent. Two Associations and two Rents are rather formidable.

" The latter establishment is certainly not very flattering either to the King, or to his Ministers (I put myself quite out of the question), or to his army, since they deem it necessary to take the whole under their special protection.

" This is a most distressing state of things, and I defy any one to pronounce the result. But this I know, that it must not remain so long. I cannot see far before me—I can only guess at what is likely to happen for a very few months.

" I calculate upon a quiet winter (in acts, but not in language).

" I ground my opinion upon this—that the Catholics are persuaded the Brunswickers will bring on collision if they can, with the view of committing the Government against them. This is what the leaders will endeavour to avoid, and with the power they possess over the minds of the multitude, I think they will succeed. There will be probably even less crime and nightly outrage than has been usual.

" Even if there be any project of insurrection, which I do not believe, the winter would not be the chosen season. I can imagine nothing less inviting than a rebel bivouac during a long dreary winter's night. Therefore it appears probable that you will have time to legislate before we begin to fight.

" Believe me, &c.,

" ANGLESEY."

Mr. PEEL to Lord ANGLESEY.

" Drayton Manor, September 22, 1828.
" MY DEAR LORD ANGLESEY,

" In your letter of —— September, 1828, from
Rich View, you advert to a subject which appears to me
to require immediate and most serious consideration—
namely, the continued and systematic assemblage of
large bodies of Roman Catholics, which traverse the
country under apparently very frivolous pretexts—forming and marching by word of command, and assuming,
so far as they can assume it, by the carrying of flags
and the wearing something like a rude uniform, the
appearance of military bodies.

" You suggest that, although the carrying of the
flags is contrary to law, there would be little advantage
in interference on the part of the Government ; because,
while the flags would be withdrawn in obedience to the
injunctions of the Government, the meetings, which are
the great grievance, would continue in existence, with
increased irritation and bad feelings, on account of the
enforcement of the law in respect to the exhibition of
party insignia.

" Now it appears to me that the following very important questions arise for our consideration :—

" First, Are these meetings, in point of fact, as you
assume them to be, tolerated by the law ?

" Secondly, If they are contrary to law, is there not
that danger in continued forbearance that it becomes
the imperative duty of the Government to interfere ?

" Thirdly, Supposing the law not to give the power

of suppressing the meetings themselves, is there not more of evil in conniving at a flagrant infraction of the law by large bodies of disciplined men (taking it for granted that the carrying of flags is such an infraction) than in the temperate, but decided, exercise of the lawful authority of the Government?

" The first point to be ascertained is the precise state of the law; and I earnestly recommend that the immediate attention of the Law Officers of the Crown in Ireland should be called to this subject; that they should be put in possession of the most accurate information which can be laid before them with respect to all the circumstances accompanying the assemblages of which we have lately heard—the numbers ascertained or calculated to have been present on different occasions—the pretexts for which they were assembled—the mode in which they conducted themselves, and all the particulars in regard to dress, banners, and the forming and marching by word of command.

" The Law Officers should be required to give their opinion whether such assemblages are punishable either by the Common Law or by Statute; and whether the executive Government, having reason to apprehend their continuance, would not be warranted in cautioning by proclamation all persons against joining or being concerned in them; and in expressing its determination, in the event of a disobedience of the proclamation, to enforce the injunctions of it.

" The Law Officers will of course refer to the proceedings which took place with reference to the Manchester riots in 1819, and to the opinions that were pronounced in Parliament by eminent legal authorities as to the general power of the Government to prevent the assemblage of large bodies of men, calculated to cause extreme alarm to the peaceable and well-disposed subjects of the King, if not to incur the imminent risk of immediate and serious disturbance of the public peace.

" I propose to consult without delay the Law Officers in this country on the same point, according to the practice in cases of equal importance.

" Having ascertained as clearly as we can what is the nature and extent of the authority possessed by the Government, it will then be for us to determine whether that authority shall be exercised, and in what manner; and, with the view of preventing unnecessary delay, let us assume for the present that the meetings will be pronounced by our legal advisers contrary to law, and that the Government will, in their opinion, be justified, in a legal point of view, in interfering for their suppression.

" On this assumption I must say that my present impression is, that it is the duty of the Government to interfere—to interfere in the first instance by warning— by the issue of a proclamation pointing out the danger of such assemblages, declaring their illegality, and announcing the fixed intention of the Government to suppress them.

" I am fully aware of all the possible consequences of the issue of such a proclamation. I bear in mind that the disobedience of the proclamation may leave no alternative but the employment of actual force, and its employment in the most decisive manner; but if these meetings are to continue, I do not see what we gain by forbearance. Such forbearance carried beyond a certain length would be imputed to fear by those who are disposed to favour violent measures, and the impression would only serve to make them more presumptuous and more daring in their exhibitions and menaces of organized force. The Protestants and well-affected of all classes would gradually lose their confidence in the ability or the desire of the Government to protect them, but they would not tamely submit to the menaces or the numbers of the opposite party. They will confederate, in fact, they are now confederating, in their own defence, and under the combined influence of hatred and alarm will become perfectly uncontrollable.

" Is there not reason to hope that the manifestation of a decided intention on the part of the Government to vindicate the authority of the law will avert some of these evils?

" Are the demagogues prepared to commit themselves at present to the support of such assemblages as those of which we are speaking, after they shall have been publicly denounced as illegal by the Government? and if they are not, will not the mischievous influence of the demagogues be lessened by their apparent abandonment, at its crisis, of the cause in which they have embarked?

"In some of the papers which Lord Francis has sent me it is stated that the old priests are adverse to the meetings, and have done what they could to discourage them. It would appear, also, that intimidation is used in order to swell the numbers attending the meetings, and to collect money for defraying the expenses of them ; and I should think that most persons having property, however violent the language of some of them may be, must see with alarm the organization of physical strength, and must be well aware how difficult it is to limit the application of that strength to the ostensible object which in the first instance it may exclusively profess to attain.

" It is not improbable, therefore, that many who are prepared to go certain lengths in the attainment of a common object, would view with secret favour, if they did not openly approve, the intention of the Government to interfere for the purpose of maintaining the public peace and protecting the well-disposed.

" The leading agitators would be placed in the very awkward predicament of having to choose whether they would abandon to their fate the wretched creatures whom they had been inflaming to frenzy, or whether they would incur the risk of personal danger by placing themselves at their head. The confidence of the peaceable and well-affected would be restored, and they might be induced either to trust exclusively to the Government for protection, or to place themselves, if their co-opera-tion should be requisite, under its immediate control. It would of course be most desirable that any measure adopted by the Government should be, as far as possible, incapable of misconstruction or misrepresentation ; that it should appear to be not a declaration in favour of one party against another, but the exercise of the lawful authority of the Government against combinations formidable to the public peace, and endangering the property and personal security of all respectable classes of society.

"Supposing a proclamation to be issued and obeyed, not only would the immediate object of it be attained, but the moral influence and strength of the Government would be greatly increased by the successful manifestation of a disposition to enforce the law.

"If the proclamation should not be obeyed, and if the meetings should be continued in open defiance of it, there will be no alternative, I apprehend, consistent with the maintenance of the authority of the Government and of the law, but the dispersion of such meetings at any hazard by actual force.

"That alternative is so painful a one, and the consequences of it may be so important, that we are bound not to take any step that may impose the necessity of having recourse to it without a firm conviction that such a step is justifiable in point of law, and demanded by an urgent case of danger.

"The policy of interfering, however clear the legal right may be, will in a material degree depend upon the prospect there is of the continuance of the meetings in question; and upon this, and upon all other matters connected with it, I shall of course be most anxious to hear your opinion in detail.

"I think there cannot be a doubt that, suppose we determine on interference, the first step should be the issue of a proclamation. It should be couched, in my opinion, in temperate, but, at the same time, very decisive language; should have all the authority that it is possible to give to it from the number and weight of the names of the Privy Councillors attached to it, and should leave no doubt whatever as to the fixed resolve of the Government to act with the utmost decision in the event of disobedience.

"The moment that it is determined to issue such a proclamation, every preparation would of course be immediately made to meet the contingency of resistance.

" I adverted in the beginning of this letter to another and a separate consideration, namely, the policy of interfering to prevent the exhibition and carrying of banners, supposing it to be clearly established that the meetings at which such banners are borne are not in themselves illegal.

" This certainly is a matter subordinate in importance to that which I have been previously discussing. If, however, it is perfectly clear that these banners are borne in open violation of the law, I doubt whether there would not be great advantage in enforcing it, at least whether there is not considerable evil in overlooking a notorious and perhaps intentional infraction of the law, by large bodies of men assembled avowedly for the purpose of demonstrating and consolidating their force.

" If the meetings cannot be suppressed, the mere prohibition of the banners would scarcely be a fit subject of itself for so formal an act as a proclamation by the Lord Lieutenant in Council, and there might be great objection to the issue of a proclamation which, interdicting as illegal one out of many acts threatening the public peace, might appear by its silence to admit the legality of the rest.

" But any triumph of the law would be, in my opinion, valuable under existing circumstances, and, supposing the law against the carrying of flags to be effectually enforced in the ordinary manner, I doubt whether the advantage resulting from it would not be an ample set off against any irritation or annoyance which it might give to the parties who had transgressed the law and were compelled to obey it.

" I have thus given you, without reserve, the result of my consideration of the intelligence which has lately reached me from Ireland.

" I am writing under the impression that there is yet time maturely to deliberate on the course which it may be fitting to pursue with respect to the assemblages to which I have referred.

" But I cannot read the reports which I have received without foreseeing that paramount considerations of the public safety may compel you to act on the instant, and that cases of necessity may occur in which a Government must take upon itself the responsibility of providing for that safety by the extreme exercise of all its authority.

" It would be idle to discuss what these cases are. They must be judged of when they actually occur, and by those who are on the spot. In the event of their occurrence, I am confident that His Majesty and his Government will bear in mind all the difficulties of your situation; will cheerfully bear their full share of any responsibility that may be incurred; and will cordially sup-

L

port you in every measure that it may be necessary to
adopt for the repression of violence and the vindication
of the authority of the law.

" Believe me, &c.,

" ROBERT PEEL."

Lord ANGLESEY to Mr. PEEL.

" Dublin Castle, September 20, 1828.

" MY DEAR MR. PEEL,

" I know that Lord Francis Leveson has been in
full communication with you lately upon the state of
this country, and I have from time to time sent you
such information as I deemed it important to put you in
possession of.

" It is most distressing to me to feel that I may now
be compelled to bring on a crisis which it has been my
most anxious wish to avoid.

" Until within a very few days I had much hope that
it might be averted, or at all events deferred, but the
complexion of the public mind has undergone a very
rapid and a very alarming change, and I can no longer
encourage the hope that the country will remain quiet
unless measures of precaution are immediately taken.

" You have been apprised that about two months ago
the people in three of the southern counties, Tipperary,
Limerick, and Clare, commenced holding meetings in
various districts, under the pretext of reconciling ancient
feuds which had existed amongst themselves. These
assemblies, both from their numbers, their military organization, and the banners which they displayed, were

calculated to excite alarm; but it was thought more prudent not to interfere with them, or to attempt to disperse them by force, a confident expectation having been entertained that, after one or two such meetings, the people would of themselves discontinue them.

"I regret, however, to state that I have been disappointed in this expectation. These meetings have now become more frequent, more numerously attended, and have assumed altogether a more formidable appearance; and I fear I can no longer permit them to take place without imminent danger to the peace of the country.

"In one district in the county of Tipperary no less than three such meetings took place on Sunday last. The accounts which I have received of them from various quarters represent (and I believe without exaggeration) that at Templemore there were between two and three thousand persons dressed, with colours, flags, and music, &c., and attended by nine or ten thousand others, bearing green boughs, and marching in military array. At Killenaule, about fifteen hundred dressed, attended by six or seven thousand others. At Cahir, seven hundred cavalry, three hundred infantry, and about twelve thousand attendants. I have been informed too, that in their ranks are to be found some of the most abandoned characters in the country, men who have notoriously been concerned in the perpetration of murder, and for the apprehension of whom a large reward has in vain been offered by the Government. The terror which these assemblies have produced among the peaceable, the well-disposed of the Catholics as well as of the Protestants, is, as may be supposed, very great; for although, hitherto, these assemblies have contented themselves with meeting, with marching in military array, and have abstained from any one act of violence, yet it is hard to pronounce that such a body, composed of such materials, actuated by such various passions, and confident in their own strength and numbers, may not in a moment be directed to acts of outrage, vengeance, or crime, at the instigation or suggestion of any individual.

" I am informed that a very considerable meeting of a similar description is expected to take place either at Clogheen or Clonmel to-morrow, and it is important to observe that those priests who have hitherto maintained their influence by having supported the agitators, interfered and remonstrated in vain. They were unable to prevail on those whom they addressed to refrain from attending the meetings on Sunday last. This gives a much more formidable character to the assemblies, as there is every reason to fear that both the priests and the leading agitators have lost all control over these infuriated people.

" Under the circumstances I have described, I am anxious to call the attention of the Cabinet to the course I think it will be prudent to adopt. It will, no doubt, agree with me, that these assemblies can no longer be permitted to take place without danger to the peace of the country. It then becomes a question in what manner they can be most prudently and at the same time most effectually checked or suppressed.

" It would occur to me that before any attempt to disperse them by force, the people should have full notice of the illegality of such assemblies, and warning of the risk they expose themselves to by attending them. This could, I presume, be best effected by a proclamation; but it is obvious that such a proclamation should not be put forward by the Government without a fixed determination to enforce it, and to disperse the meetings if they should take place after the notice given.

"Were the people, in defiance of the proclamation, and relying upon their own strength and the smallness of the military force stationed in that part of the country, to persevere in meeting, additional troops would be required, and in the present state of Ireland I do not feel that I could safely remove a sufficient number from other parts; the more especially as I could not calculate upon their speedy withdrawal from the South: for if once moved there in order to prevent such meetings, they could not, I should think, be withdrawn without danger that the people would immediately revert to their meetings again.

"In the event of the people evincing a determination to disregard the proclamation, and to persevere in their meetings, troops would be required in a district of country extending from Carrick to Limerick, a distance of not less than sixty miles. Under the circumstances I have described, when the population can assemble so large a force in any appointed place at short notice, the army cannot be stationed in small detachments. I have indeed already caused many of these to be called in, and I should think that not less than three battalions, and one regiment of cavalry, or four battalions, would be requisite to give a sufficient force upon the points that it will be necessary to occupy.

" As long as there is a chance of tranquillity, I would prefer that the troops destined as a reinforcement should remain on the opposite shore; but as they may be wanted at a moment's notice, I beg to suggest that it may be advisable to give me authority to put them in motion without waiting for an order from the Horse Guards.

" Believe me, &c.,
" ANGLESEY."

Lord ANGLESEY to Mr. PEEL.

" Rich View, September 23, 1828.

" MY DEAR MR. PEEL,

" Lord Francis Leveson has sent you a copy of an important letter from Clonmel. I now forward three more,* that are worth your notice, and I request you to return them. I beg you to consider as most confidential that from Lord Donoughmore to Lieutenant-Colonel Gosset. Lord Donoughmore has rather altered his tone. I do not disguise from you that it was in consequence of some former communications from him, I was at length and very reluctantly induced to suggest the probable expediency of issuing a proclamation. Now he is very decidedly against it; but after giving due consideration to his valuable opinions, and weighing them fairly against the reports that are almost hourly reaching me, I fear it may be necessary to have recourse to some act of vigour. You may trust to my delaying

---

* *Note on the MS. letter:* " Original enclosures returned October 7."

the crisis as long as I possibly can, because I feel it may possibly lead to very destructive consequences; but there is a point beyond which forbearance cannot go, and I now incline to believe that we are approaching it rapidly. Another Sunday or two (if so much time is given us) will probably determine this.

"I have apprised the Duke of Wellington that Lord Castlemaine is canvassing against the Government candidate. He probably does not know that I have adopted the recommendation of the King's Ministers, and fancies that he is merely opposing my wishes.

"It gives me great pleasure to tell you (and I am bound to do so, after having expressed my doubt of the prudence of the appointment) that I find in Lord Francis Leveson a very able and zealous assistant, and I have no doubt that everything will go on most satisfactorily between us.

"Believe me, &c.,
"ANGLESEY."

Mr. PEEL to Lord ANGLESEY.

"Whitehall, September 26, 1828.
"MY DEAR LORD ANGLESEY,

"The very important subjects discussed in the letters which I have recently received from you and from Lord Francis Gower have undergone the serious consideration of His Majesty's confidential advisers.

"If you have reason to expect the continuance of meetings of the same character with those which have been of late assembled in the counties of Tipperary and

Limerick, his Majesty's Government entirely concurs in
the opinion which you express in your letter of the 20th
instant, that the time is come when the Government
must actively interfere for the prevention or suppression
of such meetings.

"I informed you some days since that I should consult the Law Officers of this country on the state of the
law as it affects meetings of this description. This
morning I had a personal conference with the Attorney
and Solicitor-General, who left with me the report of
their opinion, of which I enclose a copy. In the opinion
therein given, the Lord Chancellor, who was present at
the Cabinet assembled this day, entirely concurs.

"I communicated to the Lord Chancellor and the
Law Officers the draft of a proclamation which Lord
Francis Gower sent to me, and fully discussed with them
the purport and the form of it.

"I return another draft of a proclamation, in which
you will observe some omissions and variations which
were considered by my colleagues, and were deemed to
be improvements on the original draft.

"You will of course consider, in concert with the Law
authorities in Ireland, the terms suggested in this draft,
and will give their due weight to any observations which
it may occur to them to offer in respect to those terms.
The form of the proclamation as applicable to Ireland
may require alterations in some particulars. This will
be readily determined by a reference to precedent.

"Directions will be forthwith given to the commanders
of the troops stationed on the West coast of this country
to obey any orders which they may receive from you for

embarkation of troops for Ireland ; and all the necessary information in respect to the present stations of such troops and other military details will be sent to you from the Horse Guards.

" If you should determine upon the issue of a proclamation, it is needless for me to suggest the importance of every previous precautionary measure, not merely calculated to enforce obedience to the injunctions of such a proclamation, but to discourage all resistance to them.

" Having the discretionary authority to call for military aid from this country, you will maturely weigh the comparative advantages of having that aid or any part of it in Ireland previously to the issue of the proclamation, or keeping it in reserve in this country, ready to be called over in case of actual necessity.

" As the general view taken of the important subject of these meetings in my letter of the 22nd of this month meets with the concurrence of my colleagues, it is not necessary for me on this occasion to write to you more in detail, or to do more than to assure you of the cordial support and co-operation of His Majesty's Government throughout any difficulties in which you may be placed by the absolute necessity of a decisive exercise of the powers of Government.

" I am, &c.,

" ROBERT PEEL."

OPINION of the ATTORNEY and SOLICITOR-GENERAL of

ENGLAND.

" We have given to the several accompanying documents with which we have been furnished, and to the

L 3

very important and delicate questions arising from them,
every attention which they necessarily require, and the
result of our best reflection upon the whole subject is,
that meetings of the description contained in the letter
of Major Carter of the 17th of September, and in the
memorial of the Sovereign and Magistrates of Fethard
of the 15th of September, are by the common law unlawful assemblies.   For we conceive that meetings having
no definite object sanctioned by law, consisting of such
large numbers, formed with such apparent concert and
organization, and attended with such other circumstances as to strike a well-grounded fear and alarm
into the peaceable and well-disposed inhabitants of the
neighbourhood where they meet, are by the common
law of the land held to be unlawful, although no act of
violence takes place.

"Such was the opinion of Lord Chief Justice Holt
in the case of the Queen *v.* Soley, 11 Modern Reports,
116; and such also was the opinion of the Court of
King's Bench in the late case of the King *v.* Hunt and
others, where the point left for the consideration of the
jury had been whether the meeting was of such a description as to inspire well-grounded fear in the inhabitants of
Manchester; and this principle is likewise recognised by
Hawkins and other text-writers upon the criminal law.

"Applying this principle, which we assume to be
clear, to the meetings above referred to, we conceive
that they have all the character of unlawful assemblies.
For as to the three meetings of peasantry held simul-
taneously on the 14th of September, at Templemore, at
Killenaule, and at Cahir, they have numbers sufficient

to inspire dread and terror; they have a certain degree
of military array and discipline; and they have no
apparent object sanctioned by law to call them together.
It tends still further to confirm the illegal character of
these meetings, that a considerable portion of the persons constituting them are mounted; a circumstance not
called for by any apparent object of the meeting itself,
and which, if occasioned by the distance from whence
the parties came, is the stronger evidence of concert and
organization. And it forms a very important proof of
preconcert, that those meetings, at three places so remote from each other, took place at the same time. The
same observations apply in nearly a similar degree to
the assembly mentioned in the memorial of the Sovereign
and Magistrates of Fethard, with the additional circumstance that it appears they were assembled on that occasion from different districts, and the individuals com-
posing them were designated with a certain uniformity
of dress or other symbol.

" With regard to the next question submitted to our
consideration, namely, whether the Government would
be justified in issuing a proclamation declaring such
meetings to be illegal, warning all persons against
encouraging or joining in them, and announcing the
fixed intention of Government to put a stop to them;
we are of opinion that the Government would be justified in issuing such proclamation: for although by itself
it would not operate to render meetings illegal, if in
any particular instance they could be excused or justified,
yet undoubtedly it would have the effect of giving notice
and warning to well-affected and unwary persons, who

might otherwise be seduced to join such meetings. It
may be a question, to which we shall afterwards refer,
whether in point of discretion such a step shall, under
all the circumstances of the case, be advisable.

" We come now to the last, and by far the most
important and delicate, point submitted to us, viz., whether, in the event of disobedience to such a proclamation, the Government would be justified in dispersing
such meetings by force.

" In contemplating this question, we must beg leave
distinctly to call the attention of the Government to the
consequences of the proposed dispersion of such meetings
by force. It should seem not improbable that such
resistance would ensue as would end in bloodshed, or in
personal injury to some of the parties assembled. In
that case the individuals suffering injury, or in case of
death their friends, will have the right, of which they
cannot be divested, of trying with the Government, in
some Court of Law, the question whether the meeting,
in the particular case, was or was not an unlawful
assembly, within the principle we have above explained.
From what we have before stated, it is our opinion the
Government would be justified in dispersing such meetings by force (supposing force becomes necessary), whatever consequences may ensue ; but as the question may
be submitted to the juries of Ireland, in the same manner
as has already occurred in England in the Manchester
case and others of a similar nature, we think it right to
call the attention of the Government to that circumstance, and to the possible course which a trial arising
out of such an occasion might take in Ireland.

" With regard to the practical mode of applying force for the dispersion of any such meeting, it is proper here to state distinctly, that any measure of violence ought not to be resorted to until the ordinary means of putting down the assembly by the interference of magistrates and other civil authorities have been found ineffectual; and that in no case would it be advisable to resort to force, until, as a matter of further precaution, the requisites of the Act against riotous and tumultuous assemblies (27 George III., chapter 15, Irish) have been duly observed. And we beg further to add, if necessity requires force to be used, such case should be selected in the first instance as presents the most clear and unanswerable evidence of the several circumstances which denote and designate the illegal character of the meeting.

" In conclusion, we have only to advert again to the question as to the expediency of issuing a proclamation by the Government, upon which point we have to observe, that in our judgment it would not be expedient for the Government to issue it, unless, after full consideration of the circumstances above suggested, they come to the final determination of carrying the proclamation into full effect, whatever may be the consequences.

" CHARLES WETHERELL.

" N. C. TINDAL.

" Lincoln's Inn, September 26, 1828."

Mr. PEEL to Lord ANGLESEY.

(Secret.)

"Whitehall, September 27, 1828.

"MY DEAR LORD ANGLESEY,

"I enclose the copy of a confidential communication which I have just received from the Horse Guards.

"You will learn from it that six regiments of infantry and two of cavalry have received orders to hold themselves in readiness for embarkation for Ireland, and that directions have been given to the commanding officers at the places where these regiments are stationed to attend to any requisition which they may receive from you.

"Believe me, &c.

"ROBERT PEEL."

Mr. PEEL to Lord ANGLESEY.

"Drayton Manor, September 29, 1828.

"MY DEAR LORD ANGLESEY,

"I have just received your letter dated 26th September, Dublin Castle.

"I did not suggest the expediency of a numerous attendance of Privy Councillors at the Council, at which a Proclamation should be issued, with a view of dividing the responsibility with the Executive Government of the issue of such a Proclamation, but in order that a Proclamation pronouncing decided opinions on very important legal points might have all the weight which the signature of high legal authorities would unquestionably give to it.

" If a Proclamation be issued, I doubt much whether it would not be advisable, even at the expense of some little delay, to issue it in the usual form, and not as the single act of the Lord-Lieutenant.

" I make this observation with reference to your remark, that under certain circumstances ' you will not hesitate one moment in issuing a Proclamation entirely on your own responsibility, provided you are pressed and have not time to assemble a respectable Privy Council.'

" If there be any portion of the Press in Ireland at the same time receiving public money and misrepresenting and villifying you, why should not the countenance of Government be withdrawn from it ?

" You say that some portion of it is ' *paid by Government*.' Would it not be expedient to inquire what are the newspapers which receive any aid either from the Vote for Proclamations or from any other source, and apply at once the remedy, which is in the hands of the Irish Government, without assigning any reason ?

" I am confident that no Irish newspaper has any connection with the Government here.

" Lord Francis Gower's letter with an account of the proceedings of the Roman Catholic Association on the 25th September has reached me.

" The Resolutions respecting the meetings in the South of Ireland owe their origin no doubt to no better motives than the fear of personal danger, and the impression that meetings so composed are an unfavourable mode of demonstrating that physical strength, to which the constant appeal has been made by the very movers of these Resolutions.

" If by the voluntary discontinuance of the meetings, or by their assuming such a character that they can be dealt with effectually by the ordinary course of law, the formal and extraordinary interference of the Government is not called for, it is no doubt prudent to abstain from an unnecessary demonstration of vigour, and not to deaden the moral influence of acts of authority by the useless resort to them.

" At the same time I have a strong impression that the Government ought to persevere in its course— whatever that course may be—uninfluenced as far as possible by any Resolutions or acts of such a body as the Roman Catholic Association.

" If it had been determined, previously to the appearance of the Resolutions entered into by that body on the 25th of September, to issue a Proclamation for the suppression of the meetings, those Resolutions would in my opinion rather supply an additional motive for adhering to the course on which the Government had resolved, than for abandoning or deviating from that course.

" Believe me, &c.,

" ROBERT PEEL."

"P.S. The letter of Mr. Carter from Cashel, dated the 23rd September, is one of the strongest which I have seen in proof of the necessity of interference. It describes the meeting of the 21st September to be composed of two divisions of cavalry of 600 men, and three divisions of infantry of 9000 in the whole, appearing, to use his expression, under admirable command. He adds that this meeting was addressed in very inflammatory language by a brewer of the name of Egan, who requested these people 'to meet him on the Sunday following in the King's County to prove that they were not afraid to assemble anywhere they pleased.'

"I wrote to Lord Francis on Saturday as to my direction for the next few days.

Lord ANGLESEY to Mr. PEEL.

"Rich View, October 2, 1828.

"MY DEAR MR. PEEL,

"I have received your letters of the 29th of September from Drayton Manor, and of the 30th from Whitehall.*

"I have no doubt of Lord Dunally's success, now that it is known he is supported by the King's Government.

"In respect to the proclamation, I have to observe that it was decided to issue one in the name of the Lord Lieutenant alone, because the very few Privy Councillors who could have been brought together, independently of those who are immediately connected with the Government, would have given it little weight.

"The Chancellor had not arrived, and was not expected, and the Law Officers conceived there was strong objection to making the two Chief Justices parties to it,

* No copy of this last letter appears among these MSS.—(*Eds.*)

when they might be called upon to try persons who
should disobey it.

" I own I thought the measure might have been
delayed, or even perhaps avoided altogether; but as the
opinions of others entitled to the highest consideration
were of a contrary persuasion, and thought that a day
ought not to be lost, I acquiesced.

" The proclamation was immediately issued, and I
acknowledge that there is every reason to believe it will
be attended with the best effect.

" As for the manifesto of the Catholic Association, I
have not the least doubt that it was dictated by personal
fear and from a conviction that the Government has
firmly resolved to tolerate the meetings no longer.

" I wish the Protestant clubs had taken the same
course. It is impossible to persuade them that the
Government is watchful to protect their interests, their
persons, and their property, whilst it declines to become
a partisan of their principles.

" It is only in that part of the country where, from
their numbers, they are in no danger from the machina-
tions of the Catholics, that the Protestants unite for
mutual protection. My greatest, and, indeed, my only
alarm is lest a conflict should be provoked by the strong
power of the Protestants in the North, which would
produce a dreadful retaliation in the South upon their
weaker brethren. It shall be my incessant care to avert
so horrible a crisis by every possible precaution.

" I really think there is no danger of formidable
disturbance in the South. Two additional battalions,
and a regiment of cavalry, with a couple of guns (if

they could be conveniently spared), to place along the line of Tipperary, Limerick, and Clare, would even prevent much of the partial outrages that may be expected in the winter ; and if the leaders of the Brunswickers could be prevailed upon to set their faces against the organization and the assembly of the Protestants, if they would trust to the power of the Government, to the wisdom of the King's Ministers, and to the judgment of Parliament, instead of attempting to dictate to all, then this unhappy country might hope for comparative rest.

· " The proclamation, it is true, is equally applicable to both parties, but I would fain avoid all interference.

" The advice of a few prudent and moderate men (if there are any such in Ireland) would tranquillize the whole country,—at least until the time when the great question is to be determined upon by the Legislature.

" Believe me, &c.,

" ANGLESEY."

Lord F. L. GOWER to Mr. PEEL.

(Private.)

" Dublin, October 2, 1828.

" MY DEAR MR. PEEL,

" I have to apologise for not having sent yesterday a copy of the proclamation as it went to the press. In the hurry of transmission of other letters it escaped my recollection. The only novelty of any importance which, with the advice of the Law Officers, the Lord-Lieutenant has ventured to introduce into the draft as sent by you, and on which, therefore, we had no opportunity of taking your opinion, is the paragraph which describes the meeting in the North. We considered that the opinion of the Law Officers in England had been taken, and your form of the document mainly founded, on the case of the Tipperary meetings, and that this addition was in the present state of things indispensable. I certainly in my own person must plead guilty to the having suffered my attention to be occupied somewhat too exclusively with the South. I can account for this by the circumstance that communications reached me every moment from persons of all classes in that quarter; while in the North the magistrates have in very few instances condescended to communicate with us at all, and when they have, as in the cases of General Archdall and Mr. Shirley (who, by the bye, is not a magistrate), their accounts have been, in the opinion at least of the Law Officers, vague and unsatisfactory. I am neither surprised nor piqued at the apparent want of confidence on the part of the magistracy which I suspect exists in the North; but it is detrimental to the public service, and you may depend upon it that everything in the power of the Lord-Lieutenant and myself will be done to alter and amend this state of feeling. I feel convinced that we shall have much more difficulty through the winter in the northern counties, where the two parties are more intermixed, than we shall have with the bedizened chivalry of Tipperary,—albeit 'they march in perfect order to the Dorian mood, &c.'

" Already complaints have reached me from Ballibay that the yeomanry, without a magistrate to control them, are making grievous abuse of their victory over Mr. Lawless, nor is it possible to imagine that men of their stamp and feeling should forego any part of their triumph, insulted, attacked, and threatened as they have been on their own soil. I doubt whether any Government will be able to regulate their passions, or secure a firm administration of justice in that quarter for some time to come. I trust that our measures will have a tendency at least to tranquillize the Protestant mind.

" With regard to the Catholics of the South, it is right to calculate upon the worst supposition, viz., that some large body or bodies may resist the proclamation, and measures have been taken with a view to that contingency, but I do not expect in the least that this will be the case. I think the neck of the system was broken at Shinrone last Sunday. Still Lord Oxmantown's calculation of what would probably have been the numbers attending there, viz., 50,000, bears me out in the opinion which I stated some time since, that if the North and South were to be allowed to go on mutually acting and reacting on one another, a blow struck in one quarter might call out 100,000 men in another, certainly ill-armed, but capable of executing much mischief before they could be effectually checked. It is surely better to err in cases like these on the safe side, if at all, and to act as you have done, in granting such liberal military aid, than to run the thing too fine, and to rely upon a force which may be amply sufficient to punish and suppress if put to the test, but may be possibly too small to prevent.

" A few days and I confidently hope that the crisis may be considered as over ; if not, at least it will be met promptly and decidedly. In any case, I fear we must look to a gloomy winter, for I do not expect that the Magpies and Black Hens will roost very lovingly together through the long nights, and I doubt not the police will have plenty of employment.

. . . .

" Believe me, &c.,

" F. LEVESON GOWER."

Mr. PEEL to Lord F. L. GOWER.

" Manchester, 1 o'clock, P.M.,
" October 2, 1828.

" MY DEAR LORD FRANCIS,

" I have just received the box and letter brought by your messenger.

" I have a strong impression that, under present circumstances, the resolution to issue a proclamation is a wise one ; that it will not increase the hazard of party conflicts or of insurrections ; and that it will relieve the Government from the difficulties in which I think it would be involved by inaction, either in the event of the complete success of the recent proceedings of the Roman Catholic Association, or in the event of the failure of those proceedings to effect their professed objects, namely, to prevent the continuance of the meetings in the South, and the necessity of interference on the part of Government.

"I well know the trying difficulties of the Lord-Lieutenant and of your own situation, and believe me that, throughout those difficulties, every assistance and support which I can render shall be most cordially rendered. But I am sure you will consider it perfectly consistent with that determination to give my opinion unreservedly to the Lord-Lieutenant and to you upon any matter that may occur.

"I doubt the policy of the issue of the proclamation as the act of the Lord-Lieutenant alone. I write under the impression that all proclamations of a similar nature have been issued in Ireland by the Lord-Lieutenant with the advice and concurrence of the Privy Council; and if that be so, I think there would ultimately be found greater advantage in adhering to the established usages and forms than in departing from them.

"I am bound to express this opinion to you, but you will probably not receive it until after a course different from that which I would recommend shall have been actually adopted. It shall never affect in the slightest degree my cordial support of the measure taken.

" Ever, &c.,

" ROBERT PEEL."

Lord F. L. GOWER to Mr. PEEL.

" Dublin, October 6, 1828.

" MY DEAR MR. PEEL,

"I cannot consider myself in condition by this day's post to give you positive assurance of the discon-

tinuance of all illegal meetings, but every account which
has had time to reach me induces me to believe that the
Protestants of the North will now be disposed to place
a proper degree of reliance on the disposition and ability
of the Government to give them protection. They have
been left in a state of excitement which cannot be expected to subside instantaneously, and which will require
careful watching on the part of Government.

" Strong complaints have reached us of the conduct
of the yeomanry at Ballibay since the departure of Mr.
Lawless. The Lord-Lieutenant has sent Major D'Arcy
down, with directions to furnish an accurate report of
the state of that place, and upon his statement we shall
be able to judge whether interference is really called for
and in what shape. The numbers of the assemblages of
both parties have been, as may well be supposed, much
exaggerated. It has been stated that 40,000 Protestants assembled at Armagh. I have reason to think
that their real numbers were between 6000 and 7000 of
all ages, and very imperfectly armed.

" At Ballibay about 1700, with about 600 stand of
fire-arms of all descriptions. I am sorry to find that
the alarm excited in England is so great, but I do not
see what we could have done to avoid exciting it.

" Mr. Lawless is in Dublin, and is, I have no doubt,
revising his correspondence with me for the press.

" The Lord-Lieutenant desires me to repeat on his
part what I had previously conveyed on my own, that
he is most grateful for the free expression of your opinion
on the subject of the form of the proclamation. I had

intended to have written further on that topic, but some previous communication is necessary with the Attorney-General, who has been unwell for the last two days.

" Believe me, &c.,

" F. LEVESON GOWER."

Mr. PEEL to Lord F. L. GOWER.

(Private.)

" Drayton Manor, October 17, 1828.

" MY DEAR LORD FRANCIS,

" *You* sent me the letter which contained an account of the High Constable of a certain Barony sitting on the box of Mr. Lawless's carriage, not as the custos of that worthy gentleman, but as a friend and supporter. You will find the original, the copy of which you sent me, in the correspondence from the neighbour-hood of Carrickmacross, about ten days or a fortnight since. I think the letter which gave the account was written either by Major D'Arcy or the chief constable of police.

" I had a letter from the Duke of Wellington yesterday, dated the 13th of October, and written therefore before he received Lord Anglesey's letter respecting Lawless, urging strongly the prosecution of Lawless and the person who led the mob in the King's County, and Mr. Steele.

" I presume the Duke refers in the two latter instances to the Shinrone affair, and to Mr. Steele's conduct at Limerick.

M

" The Duke adds, that the King had mentioned these
three cases to him; had expressed great indignation at
the conduct of the parties, and some impatience for the
enforcement of the law against them.

" Mr. Lawless we have disposed of.

" I certainly am not prepared to recommend the prosecution of Mr. Egan (for I conclude he is the person to
whom the Duke refers), or Mr. Steele, upon the recollection which I have of their proceedings, but be good
enough to refer to the evidence which you have bearing
upon their share in the transactions in which they were
respectively engaged in the King's County and Limerick,
and consider with the Lord-Lieutenant and the Law
authorities whether it would be advisable to prosecute.

" The experience of the last fortnight confirms most
strongly my previous impressions, that the surest way to
prevent collision and bloodshed, and to add strength
and influence to the Government of Ireland, is to enforce
the law against seditious acts, seditious speeches, and
sedition in every shape. The enforcement of the law
compromises no opinion on political questions, and it
enables the Government to speak with a tone of authority, not only to the party against whose acts the law
may be immediately directed, but to other parties, who
may be carried beyond due bounds in their preparations
for resistance or self-defence. It deprives them of the
pretext that the law does not afford protection or
redress.

" At the same time I quite feel that prosecutions
must not be hastily and indiscriminately instituted.
The evidence must be well weighed, and the chance of

failure duly considered; but I think of late years rather too much importance has been attached to the consequences of failure in a justifiable prosecution. I doubt whether it would not be better in every case of flagrant sedition to appeal to the law (when it is believed that an honest jury ought to convict), and to incur the risk of failure, rather than to leave it totally unchecked and unnoticed.

" Ever, &c.,

" ROBERT PEEL."

Mr. PEEL to Lord ANGLESEY.

" Whitehall, October 23, 1828.

" MY DEAR LORD ANGLESEY,

" The renewal of the meetings of the Roman Catholic Association, the language which they hold as a body, and the speeches delivered by individuals, make it important that we should be enabled fully to consider whether we have the power by law to interrupt the meetings of that body, and whether it is advisable to exercise that power.

" The first point to be ascertained is the authority of the Government in point of law to interdict the continuance of the meetings of the Association.

" It appears to me that it would be desirable to call the immediate attention of the Law Officers of the Crown in Ireland to this subject, in order that we may exactly understand, having a detailed report of their opinion, what is the bearing of the law upon the Association.

M 2

" The Act that was intended to provide for the suppression of the Association has expired.

" The question therefore is, whether the Association offends against the Common Law, or against any of the Statutes in force in Ireland directed against dangerous assemblies, and more particularly the Convention Act.

" I apprehend that an Association may transgress the provisions of the Convention Act in one or other of two ways.

" It may be illegal in its origin by the mode of its appointment, by owing its constitution to some sort of delegation—or, not offending in respect to its constitution, being in the first instance an association of individuals belonging to it merely in their individual capacities, it may perform acts or assume an authority which give to it a representative character, and bring it within the express enactments of the law.

" The several acts of the Roman Catholic Association ought therefore to be considered with this view.

" There have been recently published by the Association two addresses or proclamations, one discountenancing organized meetings in the South of Ireland, the other professing to give advice to the Roman Catholics of Ulster. The terms and general tenor of these addresses should be carefully examined. Can they be considered in any other light than as the addresses of a body assuming and avowing a representative character ?

" The immediate object of the addresses in question may be to counsel forbearance and present submission to the law ; but the nature of the advice given in such addresses ought not to withdraw our observation from

the assumption of authority which the giving of it involves, from the principle which it establishes, from the
facility with which the habitual submission to plausible,
or even really good advice, can be in an instant converted to the worst purposes.

" Apart from these considerations, but bearing on the
continued existence of the Association, is the recent
arrest of Mr. Lawless. He was their agent. Did he
exceed his authority? Do they disavow the measures
taken or the language holden by him at Ballibay?
They, or at least one of themselves, Mr. Sheil, declares
that they *recalled* Mr. Lawless, thus directly admitting
that he was an agent; but Mr. Sheil does not say
that he was recalled because he exceeded his instructions.

" If there had been, or should be, a distinct avowal by
some public declaration of the Association that Mr.
Lawless was their instrument, that they were the di-
rectors of his measures, or parties to them, could we
avoid making them take their full share of the legal
responsibility incurred by these measures?

" The resolutions moved at the last meeting of the
Association by Mr. Sheil, and I presume adopted by the
meeting, though referring immediately to Mr. Lawless's
mission and the events of Ballibay, bear also materially
upon the question whether the Association has not done
acts and assumed a character which bring it within the
Convention Act.

" The first resolution declares that Mr. Lawless had
been *recalled* by the Association.

" The third offers a reward of 500*l.* for the apprehension of an 'Orange Assassin,' no reward having been offered by the Government.

" The speech of the individual by whom these resolutions are moved, the declaration that 'The Association had entered into a league with the Government,' and other declarations of a similar nature, would, I presume, be admissible as evidence to show the character of the assembly adopting such resolutions.

" Whatever course may hereafter be determined on, we are bound, I think, to ascertain from the best authority what is the exact relation in which the law of the land and the Roman Catholic Association stand towards each other.

" Believe me, &c.,

" ROBERT PEEL."

Lord ANGLESEY to Mr. PEEL.

" Phœnix Park, November 6, 1828.

" MY DEAR MR. PEEL,

" I have delayed acknowledging the receipt of your letter of the 23rd of October, because I have expected each day to be enabled to send the opinion of the Law Officers upon the several points to which that letter refers. I have not yet received it.

" After much consultation with the Chancellor, the Chief Secretary, and the Attorney and Solicitor-General, I have come to the conclusion that a sufficiently strong case cannot be made out against Mr. O'Gorman Mahon to justify me in causing him to be removed from the magistracy.

"I have no event of consequence to report. The country is quiet.

"Believe me, &c.,

"ANGLESEY."

OPINION of the ATTORNEY and SOLICITOR-GENERAL of IRELAND.*

"In obedience to your Excellency's command, we have proceeded to consider the subject on which our opinion has been required by Mr. Peel in his despatch of the 23rd Ultimo. The different points to which our attention ought to be directed have been put forward in that despatch with great distinctness and perspicuity. The subject is one which has long engaged our most anxious attention. If even we had been disposed to view the proceedings of the Catholic Association with unconcern, the public feeling on that subject, which vents itself in daily upbraiding of the Attorney-General for suffering that body to continue in existence, must have called our attention to it. But, though individual members have by their speeches, in our opinion, afforded just ground for prosecution, yet, as everything relating to the subject has ceased to be of merely local, and become of imperial concern, we have thought it our duty to submit to the imputation of inefficiency rather than by adopting any proceeding on our own judgment to risk embarrassing the Government, or the contravening

* The following is the legal opinion referred to in Lord Anglesey's letter of Nov. 6, but not yet at that time received.

any general system of policy which it may deem it expedient to adopt.

" Having made these preliminary observations, which we have deemed necessary for our own justification, we shall proceed to give your Excellency our opinion on the important questions proposed to us. That opinion should have been sooner had, if Mr. Peel had not called for a ' detailed report,' and recommended our attentive consideration of the several acts of the Association.

" We have therefore thought it necessary to read over the reports of the proceedings of the Association for the last six months, within which period the character (at least the ostensible character) of that body has undergone an alteration, or at all events its views have been more clearly developed, and its assumption of power has been more open and undisguised. An additional cause of delay has arisen from our not having been able to procure from the short-hand writers, until this day, the authentic reports of all the recent proceedings of the Catholic Association.

" We are not aware of any Statute which can bear on this case, except the Convention Act (33 George III., chapter 29, Irish). That Act was intended (as far as the preamble is evidence of such intention) to meet only the case of associations constituted by election or delegation ; but the enacting words go beyond the preamble, and embrace not merely societies which have been elected and constituted to represent, but those also which have assumed or exercised a right or authority to represent, the people, or any class or description of them. It is manifest that these two descriptions of the character of the Society were not intended to apply to the same thing, and that if the right of the first to represent is founded on an authority given to the Society in its original inception and by its original constitution, that of the latter is one which has not been conferred on it in its original creation, but one which it has assumed subsequently of itself, and by its own proper motion. It is clear that the Roman Catholic Association is not of the first description, as the Catholic Convention of 1811 clearly was. It remains to be considered if it be of the latter description; and with respect to that we would observe that there are but two ways in which an assembly can evince that it has assumed and that it exercises such right and authority, viz., by its acts, or by the speeches of its members. From both of these sources we think there may be drawn evidence on which a jury would be well warranted in finding that the Catholic Association had assumed and exercised a right or authority to represent the Roman Catholics of Ireland. We shall select some out of many instances of both, in order that our view of this case may be corrected if it be erroneous.

" First—Resolutions of the Association, purporting to direct the conduct or express the feelings and sentiments of the Roman Catholic people—addresses in the nature of proclamations to the Roman Catholics, enjoining them to a particular line of conduct, and in one of which (that recently addressed to the Catholics of Tipperary) they style themselves the virtual representatives of the Catholics of Ireland.

" Secondly—Speeches delivered by members in the

M 3

Catholic Association. We have thought it more satisfactory to transmit herewith some of the volumes containing the authentic reports of the short-hand writers,
and we have noted in the first page references to some
of the passages in the speeches which appear to us to be
the most important.

" But though we are of opinion that the evidence
which we have alluded to would warrant a jury in finding that the Catholic Association had assumed or exercised a right or authority to represent the Roman
Catholics of Ireland, yet we think it right to observe
that that necessarily supposes that the question on the
evidence must be submitted to a jury, whose verdict may
be influenced by many considerations, and whose feelings
may be acted on in a variety of ways, which may be
readily conceived, but which it is here unnecessary to
detail. We may also add, that this particular branch
of the Convention Act has never undergone any judicial
determination. These considerations necessarily preclude
the possibility of pronouncing with certainty what may
be the result of any proceeding founded on the Convention Act. In addition to which we cannot omit
observing, that the length of time during which the
Association has been suffered to exist, and the enactment
of a Statute (6 George IV., chapter 4, now expired)
deemed necessary, it must be presumed, for the purpose
of its suppression, present topics of defence which might
be urged with considerable effect before a Court and a
jury, upon a first attempt to treat that assembly as a
violation of the Convention Act, however strongly we
may be impressed with the opinion that the recent acts

of and speeches at the Association show it of late to
have more undisguisedly assumed a representative character.

" With respect to the question whether the Association offends against the Common Law, we are of opinion
it is not, in that view, an unlawful assembly. This
opinion that the Catholic Association is not an unlawful
assembly by the Common Law, is perfectly consistent
with the notion that certain members of it may have
exposed themselves to a prosecution at Common Law ;
and, notwithstanding the novelty of the case, the pecu-
liarity of many of the circumstances attending it, and
the consequent absence of precedent, it appears to us
that the principles of the offence of conspiracy are sufficiently comprehensive to comprise those members.

" In this view of the case we think that an information or indictment might be maintained against the
leading members of the Catholic Association for a
conspiracy: the objects of which might be charged to
be, the compelling of the Legislature, by intimidation
and the show of force, to alter the existing law ; the
exciting disaffection and discontent amongst certain
classes of His Majesty's subjects ; and the creating
dissatisfaction in the minds of the people by misrepresenting the mode in which justice is administered : the
acts and proceedings of Mr. Lawless (sanctioned and
adopted as they have been by a vote of approbation)
would thus, like other parts of the conduct of the Association, be valuable and persuasive evidence of the
nature of the conspiracy charged.

" In adopting this view we do not depart from what

has hitherto taken place preparatory to the prosecution of Mr. Lawless; on the contrary, the proceedings taken against him have been purposely so framed (by containing in the informations which have been sworn against him a charge for a conspiracy with divers other persons who are not named) as to leave us at liberty to include in the indictment any other members of the Roman Catholic Association whom it may be deemed expedient to prosecute.

" F. Joy.

" J. Doherty.

" Dublin, November 17, 1828."

Lord F. L. Gower to Mr. Peel.

(Private.)

" Dublin, December 2, 1828.

" My dear Mr. Peel,

" I am anxious to communicate to you the general impression as to the state of this country which I have derived from the various sources of information which are open to me here. I entertain a serious apprehension that the appetite for disturbance which notoriously exists among the peasantry in certain parts of Ireland, most especially in Tipperary, must be gratified sooner or later, and that it will not subside till the unfortunate and deluded people shall have found by bitter experience that Government is the stronger party.

" This opinion I believe I hold in common with Sir J. Byng, Mr. Gregory, and others whose minds are not

influenced and whose apprehensions are not exaggerated
by considerations of a personal nature. Major Miller
and Mr. Carter, with whom I have had personal
communication, agree in describing the peasantry of
Tipperary as perfectly organized, and impressed to a
man with the notion that some great object is shortly to
be effected by force in their favour. They are of opinion,
however, that both in point of arms and leaders the
people have at no previous period been so ill-provided.
Mr. Griffiths, the engineer, states that the men in his
employment universally consider the time to be at hand
when they are to be independent of any such means of
subsistence as that employment affords.

"From another part of the country, the county of
Mayo, I have a letter from Sir F. Blosse, Lord Plunket's
son-in-law, of which I shall forward a copy. It gives
some curious information as to the formation of some
religious societies in that quarter, which I am told are
very similar to some which were prevalent previously to
the rebellion of 1798.

"I have little doubt that the peasantry of the South at
present look forward to the period of O'Connell's ex-
pulsion from the House of Commons as the time for
rising, but any occurrence in the interval which should
appear to be adverse to the interests of the Roman
Catholic body might precipitate this result. I do not
believe that there is a man in Ireland more alarmed at
this aspect of affairs than O'Connell. Sheil has for some
time sedulously kept away from the Association.

"I have not made the above statement of my opinion
with any view of suggesting the adoption of measures.

I do not conceive it possible, by any precaution, absolutely to prevent an explosion, if the course of events should lead to it ; and I am not aware of any measure of precaution or of preparation to meet the consequences which has been neglected.

" I mentioned some time since that a violent spirit of resistance to the law had shown itself at Doneraile. I was glad to hear from Major Miller that, by a system of nightly patrol in that neighbourhood, he had succeeded in effectually checking that system.

" Believe me, &c.,

" F. LEVESON GOWER."

Mr. PEEL to Lord ANGLESEY.

(Secret.)

" Whitehall, December 14, 1828.

" MY DEAR LORD ANGLESEY,

" I lose no time in sending you the opinion of the Law Officers in this country on the points referred to in my letter to you of the 23rd of October. You will no doubt communicate this opinion to the Law Officers in Ireland. I send it immediately after its receipt, and before I have had an opportunity of conferring with my colleagues upon it.

" Believe me, &c.

" ROBERT PEEL."

OPINION of Sir C. WETHERELL and Sir N. TINDAL.

" Lincoln's Inn, December 10, 1828.

" SIR,

" We have been honoured with your commands to peruse your letter to the Marquis of Anglesey respecting the Roman Catholic Association, and to report our opinion to you on the matters therein contained.

" In obedience to your commands, we have the honour to report that we have considered the general substance of your letter, and also the particular points to which our attention was thereby directed, for the purpose of coming, as well as we are enabled, to a practical conclusion as to what measures could be legally taken, and, admitting the legality of the measures, what it would be prudent and expedient to take on the part of the Government for its suppression.

" In the first place, as to any direct step of interference for the purpose of preventing the continuance of its meetings, we had formerly the honour of reporting to you our opinion that, although it might be justified in law, we conceive it would be too hazardous for the Executive Government to take such a step upon the grounds which we then stated, and we continue to be of the same opinion.

" With respect to any course of legal proceeding, the subject falls under two considerations: first, whether the Catholic Association is an illegal assembly within the meaning of the Convention Act (33 Geo. III. chap. 29, Irish) ; secondly, whether it be an illegal meeting by the Common Law.

"Upon the first of these questions it is truly remarked by the Law Officers of Ireland that there has been no judicial determination upon the Convention Act to settle or define its precise bearing and construction with respect to a body of persons meeting and conducting themselves as the Catholic Association have done. The preamble and enactment of that Statute are expressed in the following terms:—'Whereas the election or appointment of assemblies purporting to represent the people, or any description or number of the people of this realm, under pretence of presenting or preparing petitions, complaints, remonstrances, and declarations, and other addresses to the King or to both or either Houses of Parliament, for alteration of matters established by law, or redress of alleged grievances in Church and State, may be made use of to serve the ends of factious and seditious persons, to the violation of the public peace, and the great and manifest encouragement of riot, tumult, and disorder; be it declared and enacted by the King's Most Excellent Majesty, by and with the advice and consent of the Lords Spiritual and Temporal and Commons in Parliament assembled, and by the authority of the same, that all assemblies, committees, or other bodies of persons elected, or in any other manner constituted or appointed to represent, *or assuming or exercising a right or authority to represent* the people of this realm, or any number or description of the people of the same, are unlawful assemblies.'

"Now it must be admitted that the Catholic Association is not a meeting 'elected, constituted, or appointed to represent the people of the realm, or any number or description of them, &c.,' but that it is an aggregate meeting of persons, attending merely in their individual character. It has not, therefore, the character of representation as derived from the direct mode by which it is formed or constituted, and therefore cannot be said to fall within the preamble of the Act or the first branch of the enactment. The question, however, still is, whether it does not come within the meaning of the second branch of the enactment, by 'assuming or exercising a right or authority to represent,' &c., in which case, although not comprehended within the mischiefs described in the preamble, it would still be clearly an offence against the Act. Now here we would observe that the expressions 'or assuming,' &c., are capable of bearing a double construction : either they may mean that the species of meeting declared to be unlawful is one which assumes to be '*elected, constituted, or appointed*' to represent, though in truth it were not so formed, or they may mean simply that the self constituted meeting assumes to represent the opinions and interests of the people, or any description of the people. Now if the former should be held to be the legal construction of these terms, we think the evidence would not be sufficient to bring the Catholic Association within the second branch of the enactment so construed ; for it should seem that they do not, properly speaking, assume or assert themselves to have the right or authority of persons 'delegated, elected, or appointed to represent,' &c. as if they stood in the direct or personal relation which exists between electors and elected, or of representatives and constituents. But if the true construction of the Act is, that the assuming a

general representation of opinions and interests and
acting thereon will bring the meeting within the meaning
of the Act, the point then to be discussed is whether
there is a sufficient body of evidence to bring the case
before a jury of the country for their consideration and
decision. This difference between assuming the right
and authority of the representative character in the
proper sense of delegation from constituents, and assuming an undefined representation of the opinions and
interests of the Catholic body, though it may be indiffe-
rent with reference to the mischievous nature of the
Society, is, as we have already stated, a point of considerable moment with regard to its falling within the
legal purview of the Convention Act, and is, as we conceive, the very point upon which the success or failure of
any proceedings under the Act would hinge.

" The continuance of the meetings of the Association
without molestation under the Convention Act, and the
subsequent passing of the Act of the 6th George IV.
(lately expired), would furnish plausible topics for con-
tending that such an assembly was not within the scope
of the Convention Act. On the other hand, it would be
matter of strong observation that it is only very recently
that the Association has, by its addresses, speeches, and
other measures, furnished any overt acts of assuming this
character of representation in the personal sense, and this
line of argument is correctly brought forward in the
opinion of the Law Officers of Ireland.

" Upon the whole, on the question whether the
Catholic Association can be brought within the legal
enactments of the Convention Act, we strongly in-

cline to the opinion that speaking in the abstract, and looking merely to the strict and dry construction of the Statute, a Court and jury might hold it to be an unlawful assembly.

"But at the same time, taking into consideration the grounds of argument which we have above adverted to, and the great danger that the minds and temper of the jury may not be of that even, unbiassed, and firm character which would be indispensably requisite for the just determination of a question which has caused so much excitement throughout Ireland, we cannot think an attempt to bring the case within the penalties of the Convention Act would be attended with success.

"With respect to the question whether the Association can be treated as an illegal assembly at Common Law, we conceive that looking at the Association collectively as a Society from time to time meeting, it would not be an unlawful assembly by the principles of the Common Law; but even if in legal theory it could be so considered, the observations we have above made as to its continuance, as to the passing of the Convention Act itself, and as to the lately expired Act of 6 George IV., would induce us decidedly to say that the attempt of recurring to the Common Law at this time of day in order to establish against it the character of an illegal assembly ought not to be made.

"The last point of view in which we have considered this subject (the same in which it has been treated by the Law Officers of Ireland) is, whether certain individual members of the Association might not be legally proceeded against for a conspiracy of a seditious nature to

intimidate the Government, and excite discontent and
disaffection in the manner they have suggested.

"Now, we concur in the opinion of the Law Officers
of Ireland, that in point of law an indictment or information against particular persons for such a purpose might
be supported, and it appears to us that such proceedings
of the Catholic Association as have had a direct tendency to further and promote such a design would be
evidence against A, B, or C, the particular members prosecuted, in support of a charge against them individually for a conspiracy of the above nature, the bearing of
the evidence against them being that they contrived or
availed themselves of the acts and proceedings of the
Catholic Association collectively in furtherance of their
own conspiracy, and as it were made use of them as a
mean or instrument for that purpose. We take this to
be the view on which the Law Officers of Ireland propose
to found a prosecution against particular members of
the Association as separated and contradistinguished
from the body at large. This use of the proceedings of
the Association in the proposed mode as proof of the
particular conspiracy of the individuals who may be prosecuted, we think, in concurrence with the Law Officers
of Ireland, is without a precedent to be drawn from any
similar case, at least as far as we are aware. The argument before a jury to get rid of the effect of them when
brought to bear against the separate individuals would
be, that while the acts of the Catholic Association as
such were not made the subject of direct prosecution,
nor the parties assembling prosecuted for associating
and taking the measures which passed at each meeting,

as violators of the law, the same acts and proceedings ought not to be considered as sufficient proof of an individual charge, collaterally raised against a few members of the Association for a particular conspiracy of their own. In point of legal principle, however, we think that a conspiracy of the above nature may so exist, and that as far as the mere rules of evidence are concerned, these proceedings would be admissible on such a prosecution. Having thus stated the remarks which have occurred to us on the mode last suggested of prosecuting particular individuals for a conspiracy, we beg to say that we feel the disadvantage of that want of local information which might otherwise have enabled us to submit our judgment to you as to the expediency or prudence of instituting a prosecution of that nature, and which certainly leaves us much at a loss upon the delicate question of the probable success or failure of such an attempt.

"We have the honour to be, Sir,

"Your obedient humble servants,

"CHARLES WETHERELL.

"N. C. TINDAL."

Lord ANGLESEY to Mr. PEEL.

"Phœnix Park, December 18, 1828.

(Extract.)

"I have received your letter of the 14th.

"The Attorney and Solicitor-General have derived much satisfaction from the remarkable coincidence of opinion between them and their brethren of England upon points of such novelty and variety as those which have been respectively submitted to them."

I have thus brought down the confidential corre- spondence with the Lord-Lieutenant and Chief Secre- tary of Ireland to the close of the year 1828. It is perhaps desirable to insert one or two letters from per- sons not officially connected with Ireland, which show the state of public feeling among the Protestants of that country. The two following letters are from Mr. Vesey Fitzgerald and Mr. Leslie Foster, the one a supporter, the other an opponent of the Catholic claims. Both fall into the error so prevalent in Ireland, of imputing to the misconduct of men in authority evils which were in truth inseparable from a diseased state of society, and from that defective constitution of the Government which united public men differing in opinion on the most important of Irish questions in the administration of Irish affairs. The letter of Mr. Leslie Foster will show that in his opinion some decided change in the system on which the Irish Government had been conducted was absolutely necessary, and that it was his persuasion that no serious opposition would be offered even by the most vehement Protestants "to a settlement of the Catholic Question upon proper terms."

In the opinion expressed by Mr. Leslie Foster, that such settlement might be advantageously effected by concessions falling short of the establishment of civil equality, in his belief that the Roman Catholic Bar would be satisfied by their admission to professional, remaining excluded from political office and distinction, I could not participate.

Mr. VESEY FITZGERALD to Mr. PEEL.

" Sudbourne, October 2,* 1828.

" MY DEAR PEEL,

" I cannot receive the enclosed letter, one of eight that I have had this morning, all full of anxiety with respect to the state of the country, without wishing that you should see what never was meant to meet your eye, the impression on the mind of an Irish Protestant as to our situation in Ireland.

" I therefore enclose confidentially to you Foster's letter to me.

" The sentiment is universal of disgust, indignation, and alarm at the proceedings of Lord Anglesey's Government, and at the tone of his partisans and his press. Whether the collision will happen so soon as is contemplated, I know not—I rather think not. The Association is frightened ; and if the demonstrations of the South are interrupted, and that Mr. Lawless's progress in the West be not persevered in, it is possible, and it is to be hoped, that the hostile parties may not come to an effusion of blood. But can we read the reports of the meetings which are taking place, and expect that before

---

* Thus in the MS., but most probably a slip of the pen for a later month and day, since the enclosure is dated November 14.—(*Eds.*)

the winter is over, the gentry of the country, emancipators as well as Brunswickers, will not call on the Government to take a part, to have an opinion, and to save us from these horrors?

"I cannot object to your using Leslie's letter, if you wish to show it to the Duke, and I am quite ready to go over to Ireland, if you think that my report to you, or such information as I may be able to send you, may be of any use. What my correspondents complain of, and it is natural that it should be complained of in a country such as Ireland, is that no Protestant is consulted, no one trusted except those who are canvassing for a mob popularity, or ready to do whatever is asked or commanded by the Association.

"I suppose you get the Irish papers where you are; if not, you will be struck by an address of Mr. Winter's to the county of Meath. In your time in Ireland he was general of the Liberals. He has embodied my own feelings and experiences, and therefore it is perhaps that I am inclined to approve of his address.

"I dislike associations, or I could form such a one in the South; but besides that I object to them on principle, I fear our gentry have not capacity to direct them.

"I send you an 'Evening Post,' containing his address. The lines marked in Sheil's speech are Foster's, and are meant to point out to me the seditious and prosecutable passages.

"I know you will forgive my writing to you as I do; next to my deep anxiety about the state of my country, I cannot but feel a strong solicitude on your account, and on account of the character of the Government.

" If you think the Duke would take ill, however, what Foster says in his allusion to the Irish Government, it would not be kind to him to show it ; but to you, I know that I may in confidence communicate whatever he writes to me.

" Believe me, &c.,

" W. F. VESEY FITZGERALD."

Mr. L. FOSTER to Mr. VESEY FITZGERALD.

" Dublin, November 14, 1828.

" MY DEAR FITZGERALD,

" I was about to forward to you the 'Evening Mail' when your father carried it away. It contained just 20 columns of Brunswick Resolutions. The spirit is still unexhausted. Even in Limerick 500 new members have lately been added to the Club in one day. You must have been struck by the altered tones of the Catholics. They are astounded by the extent of the reaction, and now prove how easily a firm hand might have held them quiet during the years that have passed. If the Government are disposed to deal with the Irish question, what a power the Brunswickers afford them ! I see no danger, so far as the Irish Brunswickers are concerned, of their feelings becoming so strong as to embarrass the Government, even if considerable concession were in contemplation, always supposing that the suppression of the Association and the regulation of the franchise were to form a part of the intended

N

measures. I have not a doubt that a majority even of the Brunswickers are friendly to a settlement upon proper terms.

" The Protestants of Ireland may now be thus distributed :—almost all the peasantry, the farmers, and mechanics belong, or are on the eve of belonging, to the Brunswickers. The majority of the upper and middle ranks do not belong to them, but wish them all success. None but a few insulated individuals retain any real good feeling towards the Catholics. The northern peasantry are scarcely less warlike in their feelings than their ancestors who served in Cromwell's army, but they are manageable by the gentlemen who have placed themselves everywhere at their head.

" I wish I could foresee how Government would act, with the tenth part of the certainty that I should feel in predicting how the country would conform to any given course they might adopt. Depend upon it, let Parliament do what they may, the Catholics will not rebel. Their leaders are more deeply convinced than you are of the utter and immediate ruin that would be the result of any insurrectionary movement; and in every rank among them, down to the lowest, there is a due fear of the power of England, the facilities of a steam invasion, the character of the Duke, and not least, perhaps above all, the readiness of the Ulster Protestants for battle. It is further to be borne in mind, that at no period within our memory was the condition of the people so rapidly improving, or their employment so great as at the present moment, and there is a real substantial disinclination, in consequence, among all ranks above the mere rabble, to hazard any course that would involve the country in confusion.

" If the Government were able and willing to induce the House of Commons to consent to the abolition of *every species* of forty-shilling franchise, as a measure in itself, without reference to the Catholic Question, I am perfectly convinced that we should have no violence, except that of language, in this country ; and that, however keen might be the feelings of individuals, the peace of the country would soon be the result. I am even strongly of opinion that, in the scarcely supposable event of the forty-shilling franchise being preserved to Protestants and taken away from Catholics, we should neither have a rebellion nor a serious thought of it ; but I could not recommend such a course as this last, for it would place us in a position in which I think we should not long continue.

" It often occurs to me that the abolition of all forty-shilling franchises, the admission of Catholic lawyers to the Bench, and of the Catholics generally to all offices not political, continuing their exclusion from Parliament, and accompanying the whole with a really Protestant Government in Ireland, promoting Catholic merit where really to be found, but stern towards their misconduct, and incapable of courting their favour by the ways and means which we have witnessed, would be the soundest state that our distempered condition now admits of, and that it would even induce the same sort of quiet that has existed among the Catholics of England. I should expect marked results from silencing the Catholic Bar, which the opening professional hopes

would certainly effect. The subservience of their Bar-
risters while they have a hope of personal promotion is
as remarkable as the extent of popular influence which
they acquire when their hope is afterwards abandoned
—you would never have another O'Connell or Sheil.
Had the Bar been thus silenced a few years ago, what
agitation would ever have existed? No other profession
or calling has produced an agitator of any real influence.

" Some experiment must surely be tried different
from the system which has been adopted in Ireland.
Some are for unmitigated resistance to the claims—some
for more or less of concession; but there is no man in
Ireland who doubts that the present principle of government in this country is essentially bad, and mainly productive of the evils with which we are everywhere beset.

" Whatever may be now done, I have a strong feeling that the measures should have in them such a mix-
ture of austerity as will preclude all notion that they
have originated in fear.

" Ever, &c. &c.

" J. LESLIE FOSTER."

I now revert to the position of the Government in
relation to the Catholic Question, and to my communications with the Duke of Wellington on that subject.

I have already observed that I entirely confided to
the Duke of Wellington's judgment the selection of the
period at which the requisite communications should be
made to the King, to the members of the Government,
and to Peers of Parliament, lay and spiritual, with

whom it might be advisable to enter into preliminary explanations.

At the close of the year 1828 little, if any, progress had been made in removing the difficulties with which the Duke of Wellington had to contend.

Several events had occurred during the course of the year calculated to increase those difficulties.

In the month of May the secession of Mr. Huskisson and his friends who acted with him had taken place.

In the month of August the Duke of Clarence (the heir presumptive to the Throne) had been removed from the office of High Admiral.

The circumstances which led to that removal are explained in the following letter from the Duke of Wellington of the 13th of August :—

Duke of WELLINGTON to Mr. PEEL.

"August 13, 1828.

" MY DEAR PEEL,

"I return you your correspondence with the Duke of Clarence, and I send you mine in regard to his recent cruise, which has ended in his resignation of his office of Lord High Admiral.

"After writing to the King on the 1st instant, as we had settled in the Cabinet that I should write, I intended to take no more notice of what had passed, unless the Duke should by his conduct render some notice necessary upon his arrival in London.

"He came to London on the 7th, and behaved very rudely to Cockburn—in short, laid him aside altogether, sending his orders to the Council through Sir Edward

Owen.   I saw Cockburn and Croker on that afternoon
and next morning, and both agreed in stating that the
machine would no longer work.

"I therefore consulted the Cabinet on the 8th, and,
with their concurrence, wrote to the Duke the letter of
the 8th upon finding that he had left town before I
went to him.

"The correspondence will explain the rest.   I sent it
to the King as it passed, and I received on Sunday the
King's last letter, which I forwarded to the Duke at
Bushy, and he answered me immediately, and wrote to
the Lord Chancellor to tell him that a meeting which he
had fixed with his Lordship for to-morrow, the 14th,
would not take place, as he had resigned.

"It was quite obvious that the Duke had misunderstood the King's letter, which certainly held out an
alternative to obey the law or resign; and as I saw the
King yesterday, I suggested to His Majesty to explain
the meaning of his letter to the Duke.

"The King made this explanation in the presence of
the Lord Chancellor, and urged the Duke not to decide
that he would not obey the law.   The truth then came
out that His Royal Highness would not remain in office
unless Sir George Cockburn was removed.

"His Royal Highness repeated the same afterwards
to the Lord Chancellor.   He said that he would do
whatever was wished; that he had no reason to complain of me or of the King, but that of Sir George
Cockburn he did complain, and that he must be removed.

"I spoke to the King after dinner, and explained to
His Majesty that His Royal Highness had now put the

question upon its true footing ; but that I must tell His Majesty that it would not answer to remove from his office a gentleman who had performed his duty, for no reason excepting that he had remonstrated against a breach of the law by the Duke.

" His Royal Highness is therefore out of office. We must consider of the arrangement to be made in consequence, and this without loss of time.

" In my opinion we ought to put Lord Melville at the Admiralty, and Lord Ellenborough at the Board of Control. I should wish him still to hold the Privy Seal, intending to keep that office at the disposition of the Government till later in the year, for reasons into which I will enter in another letter.

" Ever, &c.,

" WELLINGTON."

The Duke of Wellington's intention with regard to the Privy Seal referred to in the concluding paragraph of the above letter, was to keep that appointment vacant in order that he might have it available in the event of my resignation of office. He thought it might facilitate the new arrangements of the Government which would then become necessary.

In writing to me on the 16th of August the Duke observed,—

Duke of WELLINGTON to Mr. PEEL.

" August 16, 1828.

" I quite agree with you that it is very unfortunate that the Duke of Clarence has resigned. I

did everything in my power to avoid that result—excepting give up Cockburn; and I was in hopes that
the King, who I knew wished that he would stay, would
have prevailed on him to take back his resignation."

Adverting in the same letter to the office of Lord
Privy Seal, the Duke observes:

" I propose to keep the office of Privy Seal vacant,
because I am under the necessity of looking forward to
future misfortunes.

" I consider you not pledged to anything; but I
cannot but look to the not impossible case of your finding
yourself obliged to leave us to ourselves.   In this case
I must have the command of all the means possible to
make an arrangement to carry on the King's service,
and I would keep other offices vacant if I could.

" Ever yours, &c.,
" WELLINGTON."

In addition to the secession of Mr. Huskisson and
his friends, and the termination of our official connection
with the Duke of Clarence, it became necessary at the
close of the year to intimate to Lord Anglesey that we
felt it to be our duty to advise the King to place the
Government of Ireland in other hands.

As the circumstances which in our opinion compelled
us to offer that advice are fully detailed in the speeches
delivered in the House of Lords by Lord Anglesey and
the Duke of Wellington on the 4th of May, 1829, and
as, in the course of the discussion which then took place,

the correspondence that had passed between the Duke and Lord Anglesey was read, and is placed upon record, I need make no further reference to that subject.

On the recall of Lord Anglesey, the Duke of Wellington proposed to Lord Bathurst, one of our colleagues, to undertake the Lieutenancy of Ireland.

The following letter from the Duke of Wellington announces the failure of that proposal, and shows the difficulty, in the divided state of men's opinions on the Catholic Question, of making satisfactory arrangements with respect to the Executive Government of Ireland. It shows also that at the close of the year 1828 nothing had been finally arranged with respect to the Catholic Question and the position of the Government in regard to it.

Duke of WELLINGTON to Mr. PEEL.

" December 30, 1828.

" MY DEAR PEEL,

" I have heard from Lord Bathurst in answer to my letter upon the Lieutenancy of Ireland. He positively declines.

" The whole question turns upon the Roman Catholic Question. If we are to concede, we may find one qualified; if we are not, I am afraid that it will be difficult to find one with whom Lord Francis would stay.

" Lord Bathurst thinks that Lord ——— would not do us much good.

" Believe me, &c.,

" WELLINGTON."

With regard to the necessity of relinquishing the
official services of so many eminent and distinguished
persons, I had in each case of separation entirely and
cordially concurred with the Duke of Wellington.

As, however, without a single exception, they would
all have zealously co-operated with us in the attempt to
effect a settlement of the Catholic Question, the loss of
their assistance at such a critical period was peculiarly
unfortunate.

The chief difficulty was with the King. At the commencement of the month of January, 1829, His Majesty
had not yet signified his consent that the whole subject
of Ireland, including the Catholic Question, should be
taken into consideration by his confidential servants.
In his interviews with the Duke of Wellington in the
course of the autumn, the King had manifested much
uneasiness and irritation, and had hitherto shown no
disposition to relax the opposition which (of late years
at least) he had manifested to the consideration by his
Government of the claims of the Roman Catholics.

In the ' Life of Lord Eldon,' by Mr. Twiss, are published the Memoranda of conversations between the King
and Lord Eldon in the months of March and April,
1829, in the course of which the King expresses himself
very strongly on this subject, declaring that it was with
the utmost pain and reluctance that he had acted upon
the advice which he received from his Ministers.

His Majesty is reported by Lord Eldon to have said
that " he was miserable and wretched, and that his
situation was dreadful,"—" that if he gave his assent to
the Roman Catholic Relief Bill, he would go to the

Baths abroad, and from them to Hanover; that he would return no more to England, and that his subjects might get a Catholic King in the Duke of Clarence."

Lord Eldon, in the report of his conversation with the King on the 28th of March, which lasted four hours, observes, " His Majesty employed a very considerable portion of his time in stating all that he represented to have passed when Mr. Canning was made Minister, and expressly stated that Mr. Canning would never, and that he engaged that he would never, allow him to be troubled about the Roman Catholic Question.   He blamed all the Ministers who had retired upon Canning's appointment, representing in substance that their retirement, and not he, had made Canning Minister."

There must, no doubt, have been some misapprehension on the King's mind as to the engagement or intentions of Mr. Canning with regard to the Catholic Question.   I feel very confident that Mr. Canning would not have accepted office, having entered into any engagement or given any assurances which would have the effect of placing his Government and himself in that relation to George the Fourth with respect to the Catholic Question in which preceding Ministers had stood to George the Third.

There was, however, a general belief that when the King appointed Mr. Canning to be his Chief Minister, His Majesty had personally given assurances to the Archbishop of Canterbury and other of the Bishops that his own opinions on the Catholic Question were the same with those of his father, and that it was his determination to resist to the uttermost the repeal of the disabling laws.

In all the communications which I had with His Majesty on this subject, his determination to maintain these laws was most strongly expressed.

In a letter which I received from His Majesty in 1824, he thus expresses himself.

The KING to Mr. PEEL.

(Extract.)

" November 19, 1824.

" The sentiments of the King upon Catholic Emancipation are those of his revered and excellent father; from these sentiments the King never can, and never will deviate."

All subsequent declarations of opinion on the part of the King were to the same effect, and the events which were passing in Ireland, the systematic agitation, the intemperate conduct of some of the Roman Catholic leaders, the violent and abusive speeches of others, the acts of the Association assuming the functions of Government, and as it appeared to the King the passiveness and want of energy in the Irish Executive, irritated His Majesty, and indisposed him the more to recede from his declared resolution to maintain inviolate the existing law.

In the early part of the month of January, 1829, the Duke of Wellington had an interview with the Archbishop of Canterbury, the Bishop of London, and the Bishop of Durham. He sought that interview for the

purpose of laying before them the state of affairs in
Ireland, and in the hope of convincing them that the
public interests, and those interests especially which
they must naturally regard with the greatest solicitude,
demanded the adjustment of the Catholic Question, and
the adoption of other legislative measures which without such adjustment it was hopeless to attempt. A
disposition on the part of such high ecclesiastical authorities favourably to consider this proposal, or even to
admit the necessity for grave deliberation by an united
Government on the whole condition of Ireland, would
no doubt have had great influence on the mind of the
King, and would probably have removed one of the
main obstacles to concession on the part of His Majesty.

At the interview, however, to which I have referred,
or at a second interview, immediately following the first,
the Archbishop of Canterbury and the Bishops of London and Durham informed the Duke of Wellington
that they could not lend their sanction to the proposed
course of proceeding, but must offer a decided opposition to the removal of Roman Catholic disabilities.

The following letter from the Bishop of Oxford was
written after a visit to the Archbishop of Canterbury :—

Bishop of OXFORD to Mr. PEEL.

(Private.)

" Thorpe Lee, January 1, 1829.

" MY DEAR PEEL,

" I have only time to say that I have just
returned from Addington, and find that the Duke

reported quite rightly the sentiments of the three Bishops.

" They are decidedly hostile to all concessions, and will not consent to them in any form. I consider that matter therefore as settled.

" We said very little of the political part of the question, and your individual position was not mentioned.

" Send to me if you desire to see me. I must in the mean time take some time to think.

" Yours,

" C. O."

I now feared that the difficulties were almost insuperable.

There was the declared opinion of the King—the declared opinion of the House of Lords—the declared opinion of the Church—unfavourable to the measures we were disposed to recommend.

What I chiefly apprehended was this—that the King, hearing the result of the Duke's conference with the Bishops, would make some public and formal declaration of his resolution to maintain, as a matter of conscience and religious obligation, the excluding laws; and would thus take a position in reference to the Catholic Question similar to that in which his father had stood, which it might be almost impossible for His Majesty, however urgent the necessity, hereafter to abandon.

Up to this period I had cherished the hope that the Duke of Wellington might be enabled to overcome the difficulties which were opposed to his undertaking, and that I might be allowed to retire from office, and in a private station to lend every assistance in my power during the progress of the contemplated measures through Parliament. I had proposed my retirement from office much more from a sincere belief that by the sacrifice of office my co-operation with the Duke of Wellington would be the more effectual, than from any other consideration. All that had passed since my letter to the Duke of the 11th of August, 1828, had confirmed the impression on my mind that the whole state of Ireland must be considered by the Cabinet—that the Catholic Question must be adjusted without further delay; and, above all, I felt convinced that any insuperable impediment suddenly interposed in the way of that adjustment—such, for instance, as a fixed and publicly-declared resolution of hostility on the part of the Sovereign—would be most injurious to the public welfare, and might preclude the hope of any future settlement—peaceful settlement at least—of the question at issue between Great Britain and Ireland. I could not but perceive, in the course of my constant intercourse with him, that the Duke of Wellington began to despair of success. It had been his constant desire to consult my wishes as to the retirement from office, and to avail himself of the offer of my zealous and cordial co-operation in a private capacity. He well knew that there would be nothing in the resignation of office half so painful to my feelings as the separation from him at a period of serious difficulty. From the moment of his appointment to the chief place in the Government not a

day had passed without the most unreserved communication personally or in writing—not a point had arisen
on which (as my correspondence with the Duke will
amply testify) there had not been the most complete and
cordial concurrence of opinion.

The period was at hand, on account of the near approach of the meeting of Parliament, when a formal
proposal must be made to the King in respect to the
position of his Government and the consideration of the
state of Ireland. I was firmly convinced that if the
Duke of Wellington should fail in procuring the King's
consent to the proposal so to be submitted to His
Majesty, no other public man could succeed in procuring that assent, and in prevailing over the opposition
to be encountered in the House of Lords. It may perhaps have been thought by some that the high and
established character of Earl Grey—his great abilities
and great political experience—would have enabled him
to surmount these various difficulties. In addition to
those high qualifications, Earl Grey had the advantage
of having been the strenuous and consistent advocate
of the Roman Catholic cause—the advantage also of
having stood aloof from the administrations of Mr.
Canning and Lord Ripon, and of having strong claims
on the esteem and respect of all parties, without being
fettered by the trammels of any. I had, however, the
strongest reasons for the conviction that Lord Grey
could not have succeeded in an undertaking which, in
the supposed case of his accession to power, would have
been abandoned as hopeless by the Duke of Wellington,

and abandoned on the ground that the Sovereign would not adopt the advice of his servants in respect of the consideration of the Catholic Question.

Being convinced that the Catholic Question must be settled, and without delay—being resolved that no act of mine should obstruct or retard its settlement—impressed with the strongest feelings of attachment to the Duke of Wellington—of admiration of his upright conduct and intentions as Prime Minister—of deep interest in the success of an undertaking on which he had entered from the purest motives and the highest sense of public duty—I determined not to insist upon retirement from office, but to make to the Duke the voluntary offer of that official co-operation, should he consider it indispensable, which he scrupled, from the influence of kind and considerate feelings, to require from me.

On the 12th of January, 1829, I addressed to the Duke the following letter:—on the blank leaf of that copy of the letter which I retain is this memorandum, made at the time:—" When I wrote this letter the Archbishop of Canterbury, the Bishop of London, and the Bishop of Durham had just previously had an interview with the Duke of Wellington on the subject of the proposed measures for the settlement of the Catholic Question, and had declared to him that they must give their decided opposition to the proposed plan of relief from disabilities."

Mr. PEEL to Duke of WELLINGTON.

(Private and confidential.)

" Whitehall, January 12, 1829.

" MY DEAR DUKE OF WELLINGTON,

" Notwithstanding the constant and unreserved intercourse which I have personally had with you in regard to the state of Ireland and the position of the Government with respect to the Catholic Question, I have thought it as well to commit to paper the general views which I have from time to time expressed upon those most important subjects.

" I still feel that the conclusion to which I have arrived in the accompanying Memorandum ought to be followed by my retirement from office.

" My retirement will not only be the single step which I can take that will be at all satisfactory to my own feelings, but followed, as it shall be, by the warmest support of any Government of which you are the head, and by an explicit declaration of the opinions which I have thus placed upon record, it certainly appears to me to be the step better calculated than any other which I can take to facilitate the settlement of the Catholic Question by an administration conducted by you.

" If I were to go out of office resisting the question, and encouraging resistance by others, I can well conceive, in the present excited state of the country, that my retirement might be productive of serious embarrassment; but I need not assure you that the course which I should take in a private capacity would be decidedly the opposite to that. I repeat therefore the proposal which I made to you in August last respecting my retirement.

" You will make allowance for my very peculiar situation—a situation in which no other individual stands. If I were to remain in office, I might have, and probably should have, to conduct through the House of Commons a measure to which I have been uniformly opposed.

" Putting all private considerations out of the question—should I stand in such a position, in reference either to those who have supported the question or those who have opposed it, as could make it advantageous that the conduct of any measure for the adjustment of the Catholic Question should be committed to me?

" I am bound to tell you that in my opinion I should not.

" But I will have no reserve with you. I know all the difficulties of your situation. I know how those difficulties have been recently increased, as well by the communications which have taken place with the Bishops, as by the necessary recall of Lord Anglesey.

" You will do justice to the motives of the declaration which I am about to make, and you will take no advantage of it unless it be absolutely necessary.

" If my retirement should prove, in your opinion, after the communications which you may have with the King, or with those whom it may be necessary for you to consult, an *insuperable obstacle* to the adoption of the course which upon the whole I believe to be the least open to objection under all the circumstances of the time—in that case you shall command every service that I can render in any capacity.

" Believe me, &c.

" ROBERT PEEL."

This letter was accompanied by a Memorandum which I sent to the Duke of Wellington for the purpose of formally placing my opinions upon record, and in the hope of aiding the Duke in his endeavour to induce the King to permit his confidential servants to take the whole condition of Ireland, without restriction or exception, into their immediate consideration.

Mr. PEEL'S MEMORANDUM, January 12, 1829.

" The time is come when, in my opinion, His Majesty's Government ought to be constituted in such a manner as may enable it to consider the state of Ireland and every matter connected with it, upon the same principles on which the Government can consider every other question of national policy.

" I think that the Roman Catholic Question can no longer remain what is called an open question, but that some definite course must be taken with respect to it by His Majesty's servants in their collective capacity.

" It is not consistent with the character of the Government—with the proper exercise of authority in Ireland—nor with the permanent interests of the Protestant Establishments—that the Roman Catholic Question should continue to be thrown loose upon the country— the King's Ministers maintaining neutrality, and expressing no opinion in common upon the subject.

" Experience must have convinced us that neither a divided Government in Ireland, nor a Government in that country united in opinion, but acting under a divided Government in this, can administer the law with that vigour and authority which are requisite in the present condition of Irish affairs.

" With respect to discussions in Parliament, I consider the present position of the administration untenable.

" Supposing it to maintain the same relation to the Catholic Question in which it has hitherto stood, it must pursue one or other of two courses at the meeting of Parliament.

" It must either remain inactive with respect to Irish affairs, or it must propose measures of restriction and control unaccompanied by the expectation of any measure of concession.

" To remain altogether inactive—to have no measures to propose—no opinion in common to pronounce in regard to the state of Ireland—is surely impossible.

" Can the other course be taken ?   Can restraints be imposed or additional power be exacted for the Government, with an avowal that nothing else is in contemplation ?

" I will not inquire whether the Government, constituted as it at present is, would consent to the adoption of this course, because I think little doubt can be entertained that, if adopted, it would fail, and that the result of failure would be mischievous in the extreme.

" It is needless to refer, in proof of the probability of its failure, to more than to one fact, namely, that in the last Session of Parliament the House of Commons decided by a majority of six votes that the Catholic Question ought to be taken into consideration with a view to its adjustment.

" Is it probable that mere measures of coercion would be carried through all their several stages, in the face of an actual majority that had decided in favour of another principle of proceeding ?

" It is true that in 1825 the House of Commons passed the Bill intended for the suppression of the Roman Catholic Association; but they followed up that Bill, in the course of the same Session, by another, which passed the House of Commons, for the complete removal of the disabilities of the Roman Catholics.

" I come therefore to my first conclusion—a conclusion to which I apprehend most other persons are come—that matters cannot remain as they are—that the position of the Government with respect to the Catholic Question and to Ireland must be altered.

" What course shall be adopted in lieu of that which it is proposed to abandon ?

" I answer, in the first place, that the Government must be so constituted as to be enabled to pronounce, in its collective capacity, an opinion of some kind or other in reference to Irish affairs and to every question connected with them. I say more, that I see no advantage in the formation of a Government which should offer an opposition to the Catholic claims merely on grounds of temporary expediency, or which should grant some few additional privileges to the Roman Catholics, without looking into other questions which connect themselves with the discussion of the main question. The more I consider the subject the more I am satisfied that a Government ought to make its choice between two courses of action, either to offer united and unqualified resistance to the grant of further privileges to the Roman Catholics, or to undertake to consider without delay the whole state of Ireland, and to attempt to make some satisfactory adjustment on the various points which are involved in what is called the Catholic Question.

" If it be admitted that such are the alternatives, it remains to be considered which of the two it is most practicable or most expedient to adopt.

" Can the first be adopted ?   Can a Government be formed on the principle of unqualified resistance, which shall be composed of persons of sufficient ability and experience in public life to fill with credit the high offices of the State, and which can command such a majority of the House of Commons as shall enable it to maintain the principle on which it is founded, and to transact the public business ?

" I think it must be granted that the failure of such a Government—either through its sudden dissolution or its inability to conduct public business on account of its weakness in the House of Commons—would have a prejudicial effect generally, and particularly in reference to the Catholic Question. It would surely render some settlement of the question in the way of concession unavoidable, and would in all probability materially diminish the chances of a safe and satisfactory settlement.

" No man can therefore honestly advise the formation

of an exclusive Protestant Government, unless he believes that it can maintain its ground, and can conduct with credit and success the general administration of the country.

" The present state of the House of Commons appears to me an insuperable obstacle, if there were no other, to the successful issue of this experiment.

" It may not be immaterial to look back to the proceedings of the House of Commons on the Catholic Question for some time past.

" Since the year 1807 there have been five Parliaments—a General Election having taken place in each of the following years:—1807, 1812, 1818, 1820, and 1826. In the course of each of those five Parliaments, with one exception, the House of Commons has come to a decision in favour of a consideration of the Catholic Question.

" The exception was in the case of the House of Commons elected in 1818; but that House negatived the consideration by a majority of only two voices, the numbers being—

> 243 against, and
> 241 for consideration.

" In the course of the period to which I have above referred there were no doubt various decisions adverse to consideration; but the fact is as I state it—that the House of Commons, in four out of the last five Parliaments, did on some occasion pronounce an opinion in favour of an attempt to settle the question.

" The House of Commons elected in 1820 (the one

preceding the present) twice sent up Bills to the Lords removing the disabilities of the Roman Catholics.

" The present House of Commons decided in the year 1827 against the question by a majority of four voices, the numbers being 276 to 272; but in the last Session of Parliament their decision was in favour of the question by a majority of 272 to 266. I am not aware that any changes have taken place calculated materially to affect the relative numbers of the present House of Commons; and I do not conceive it possible that a Government formed expressly upon a principle adverse to the opinion of 272 members of the House of Commons could conduct with vigour and advantage the public business.

" It may be said, ' Dissolve the Parliament '—but immediate Dissolution is impossible. The supplies of the year must be voted—and a trial of strength, and such a trial as would probably decide the fate of a Government, would be inevitable.

" Even, however, if immediate Dissolution could take place, the state of the representation in Ireland, and the effect of a General Election in that country, would demand serious attention.

" In the course of last Session 93 members for Ireland voted on the Catholic Question. The relative numbers were—

> 61 in favour of the question,
> 32 against it.

" Of the 64 members for Irish counties, 61 voted—

> 45 in favour of,
> 16 against the question.

o

" We may lament the existence of such a preponderance in the Irish representation, but in the case we are discussing, what would be our remedy? What would be the effect on that representation, supposing an exclusive Protestant Government to be formed, and a Dissolution of Parliament to take place, the constituent body in Ireland remaining the same?

" I assume that that body would remain the same, because I do not consider it possible that an alteration in the elective franchise of Ireland could be made previously to a Dissolution of Parliament in the case which I am now supposing—that of the formation of an exclusive Protestant Government.

" The effect, I apprehend, would be increased excitement in Ireland—a confirmation of the influence of the priesthood over the forty-shilling freeholders—the further exclusion of Members in the Protestant interest, and of moderate and reasonable advocates of the Roman Catholics, and the return of persons neither connected with nor representing the landed aristocracy or property of the country, but selected purely for their ultra-devotion to Roman Catholic interests.

" Now I cannot too strongly express my opinion that, supposing the effect of a Dissolution should be materially to strengthen the hands of a Protestant Government by the returns from Great Britain, that circumstance would not be a sufficient compensation for the evil of an Irish representative body such as I have supposed. You might on important occasions overbear that representation by a majority in Parliament, but depend upon it that intolerable evils would still remain.

" The local Government of Ireland would be weakened in a most material degree by having opposed to it a vast majority of the constituent and representative body of the country.

" The Parliamentary business would be impeded by the addition to the House of Commons of fifty or sixty members, whose only chance of maintaining their influence would be unremitting attendance in the House, and violent and vexatious opposition to the progress of public business.

" The very circumstance of severing altogether the connection between the constituent body of Ireland and the natural aristocracy of the country would be a great, perhaps an irreparable misfortune.

" For these reasons, and firmly believing that an attempt to form an exclusive Protestant Government on a principle which must at once compel the dissolution of the present Government, would be ultimately injurious, and injurious above all to the Protestant interest, I cannot advise it.

" I am thus conducted by the course of reasoning which I have pursued to the following conclusions :—

" That the time is come when the Catholic Question ought not longer to remain an open question.

" That the Government of this country, be it in whose hands it may, ought to take some definite and decisive course with respect to that question and to Irish affairs generally.

" That a Government has the choice of two courses of proceeding, either resistance to concession on permanent grounds, or a deliberate consideration of the whole state of Ireland—every question bearing upon the condition of this country being included in its view.

" I have assigned the reasons for which I consider the former of those courses unadvisable.

" I will not shrink therefore from expressing my opinion in favour of the course which appears to me, under the circumstances of the present time, to present the least of difficulty and danger.

" In this Memorandum I have hitherto chiefly dwelt upon the state of the House of Commons with reference to the Catholic Question, and the difficulties which it presents to the Government.

" I will not, however, deny that there are other considerations which incline me to think that the attempt to settle that question should be made.

" I pretend to no new lights upon the subject, and I attach their full weight to the powerful arguments which are opposed to concession. But the practical evils of the present state of things are very great, and I fear increasing—and increasing in a direction unfavourable to that interest which I wish to uphold.

" First—There is the evil of continued division between two branches of the Legislature on a great constitutional question.

" Secondly—The power of the Roman Catholics is unduly increased by the House of Commons repeatedly pronouncing an opinion in their favour. There are many points in regard to the Roman Catholic religion and Roman Catholic proceedings in Ireland, on which Protestant opinion would be united, or at least predo-

minant, if it were not for the difference which exists as
to the civil incapacities.

" Thirdly—In the course of the last autumn, out of a
regular infantry force in the United Kingdom, amount-
ing to about 30,000 men, 25,000 men were stationed
either in Ireland or on the west coast of England with
a view to the maintenance of tranquillity in Ireland—
this country being at peace with the whole world.

" Fourthly—Though I have not the slightest apprehension of the result of civil commotion—though I
believe it could be put down at once—yet I think the
necessity of being constantly prepared for it while the
Government is divided, and the two Houses of Parliament are divided, on the Catholic Question, is a much
worse evil than its actual occurrence.

" Fifthly—The state of political excitement in Ireland will soon render it almost impracticable to administer justice in cases in which political or religious
considerations are involved.   Trial by jury will not be
a just or a safe tribunal, and, above all, not just nor
safe in cases wherein the Government is a party.

" These are practical and growing evils, for which I
see no sufficient remedy if the present state of things is
to continue ; and the actual pressure is so great as fully
to warrant, in my opinion, a recourse to other measures.

" My advice therefore to His Majesty will be, not to
grant the Catholic claims, or any part of them, precipitately and unadvisedly, but in the first instance to
remove the barrier which prevents the consideration of
the Catholic Question by the Cabinet—to permit his
confidential servants to consider it in all its relations,

on the same principles on which they consider any other great question of public policy, in the hope that some plan of adjustment can be proposed, on the authority and responsibility of a Government likely to command the assent of Parliament, and to unite in its support a powerful weight of Protestant opinion, from a conviction that it is a settlement equitable towards the Roman Catholics, and safe as it concerns the Protestant Establishment.

" ROBERT PEEL."

The above paper was communicated by the Duke of Wellington to the King. On the 17th of January the Duke of Wellington called upon me in Whitehall Gardens, and placed in my hands the following letter:—

Duke of WELLINGTON to Mr. PEEL.

" London, January 17, 1829.

" MY DEAR PEEL,

" I entirely concur with the sentiments and opinions contained in the paper on the existing state of questions respecting Ireland, which, by your desire, I have given to the King; and I am equally of opinion with you, that the only chance that we have of getting the better of all the evils of the position in which the country is placed, is that we should consider in Cabinet the whole situation of Ireland, and propose to Parliament the measures which may be the result of that consideration.

" You have been informed of what has passed between the King and me, and certain of the Bishops and me, upon this subject, and you must see the difficulties with which we shall be surrounded in taking this course.

" I tell you fairly that I do not see the smallest chance of getting the better of these difficulties if you should not continue in office.   Even if I should be able to obtain the King's consent to enter upon the course which it will probably be found the wisest to adopt, which it is almost certain that I shall not if I should not have your assistance in office, the difficulties in Parliament will be augmented tenfold in consequence of your secession, while the means of getting the better of them will be diminished in the same proportion.

" I entreat you then to reconsider the subject, and to give us and the country the benefit of your advice and assistance in this most difficult and important crisis.

" Believe me, &c.

" WELLINGTON."

On this letter is a Memorandum made at the time, which I transcribe :—

" The Duke of Wellington brought this letter to me on the 17th of January.   I read it in his presence, and at once told him that I would not press my retirement from office, but would remain in office and would propose (with the King's consent) the measures contemplated by the Government for the settlement of the Catholic Question."—R. P.

Immediately after this decision was taken I attended a meeting of the Cabinet, and announced my determination to my colleagues.

From Lord Ellenborough and Lord Bathurst, who had hitherto differed on the Catholic Question, I received the following communications :—

Lord ELLENBOROUGH to Mr. PEEL.

(Private.)

" Connaught Place, January 19, 1829.
" MY DEAR MR. PEEL,

" I cannot resist telling you how much I admire your conduct to-day. You have adopted a line of conduct dictated, as far as I am capable of forming a judgment, by true statesmanlike wisdom; but I am quite sure you have acted nobly towards the Government, and in a manner which no member of it will forget.

" Believe me, &c.
" ELLENBOROUGH."

Lord Bathurst concludes a letter, dated the 20th of January, after some observations on the state of the elective franchise in Ireland, in this manner :—

Lord BATHURST to Mr. PEEL.

(Extract.)

" January 20, 1829.
" You must forgive me if I cannot conclude this letter without expressing what I sincerely feel with

regard to the course you have taken on this (to you) trying business. There is no occasion where an honest man's principles are put to so severe a test as when he may consult his ease, and obtain a popular cry in his favour, by quitting the field instead of standing stoutly up to the conscientious discharge of his duty.

" Yours very sincerely,

" BATHURST."

Attached to the paper enclosed in my letter to the Duke of Wellington of the 12th of January, previously inserted, is a Memorandum made at the time which I transcribe.

ENDORSEMENT on Mr. PEEL'S MEMORANDUM
of 12th January, 1829.

" The paper of which this is a copy was communicated to the King by the Duke of Wellington. The day after its receipt by His Majesty, those of his Ministers who had voted uniformly against the Catholic claims had each a separate interview with His Majesty, and expressed opinions in general conformity with those expressed in this paper.

" The Ministers were—

The Duke of WELLINGTON.	Mr. GOULBURN.
The CHANCELLOR.	Mr. HERRIES.
Lord BATHURST.	Mr. PEEL.

" The King, after this interview, intimated his consent that the Cabinet should consider the whole state of Ireland, and submit their views to His Majesty; His

Majesty being by such consent in no degree pledged to the adoption of the views of his Government, even if it should concur unanimously in the course to be pursued.

" ROBERT PEEL."

I fear from the accompanying note from Lord Bathurst, that His Majesty was not satisfied by the argument which I submitted for his consideration.

Lord BATHURST to Mr. PEEL.

" Council Office, January 17, 1829
" MY DEAR MR. PEEL,

" Many thanks for having been good enough to send me the paper which you had sent to the King, and the receipt of which he mentioned to me.

" It is certainly what the King seemed to admit it to be—a good statement; and I should say an argumentative one, if my gracious Master had not denied it to be one.

" Yours very sincerely,
" BATHURST."

We received from His Majesty the permission required to consider in Cabinet the whole state of Ireland, and to offer our advice to His Majesty with regard to it. No member of the Cabinet objected to the proposed alteration of the principle on which the Government had been constituted—the principle, I mean, of leaving the Catholic Question an open question.

It was now the 17th of January; Parliament was summoned for the 6th of February. It was absolutely necessary that the Speech from the Throne should contain a general indication of the intention of the King and his Government with regard to Ireland and the Irish questions. It was requisite therefore to devote the short interval that remained to the important objects that must be accomplished without delay: the preparation of the several measures for the suppression of the Roman Catholic Association, the repeal of the disabling laws, the regulation of the Elective Franchise.

Upon the details at least of all these measures, the collective opinion of the Government had yet to be taken; and the consent of the King to the actual proposal of the measures to Parliament, with the sanction of the Crown, had yet to be signified. The consent hitherto given had been strictly limited to the submitting of advice to the King by his Cabinet on all questions relating to Ireland, without any pledge as to the adoption of that advice by His Majesty.

As the duty would devolve upon me to submit to the House of Commons, as the organ of the Government, the several measures that were in contemplation, and to superintend their progress through that House of Parliament, with the sanction and by the desire of the Duke of Wellington I brought them under the consideration of the Cabinet in a Memorandum, treating separately of each.

The following is the Memorandum, which had reference to the subject generally, and especially to that branch of it which embraced the removal of civil incapacity :—

Mr. Peel's Memorandum, 17th January, 1829.

" The three leading considerations involved in what is called the Catholic Question are these :—

" 1st. The extent to which civil incapacities shall be removed, and the manner of removing them.

" 2nd. The regulation and restriction of the Elective Franchise.

" 3rd. The relation in which the Roman Catholic Religion shall stand in future towards the State.

" Under the last head I include all questions relating to intercourse with the See of Rome—the exercise of any spiritual authority—and the appointment to any spiritual office, either of prelacy or priesthood, or the control over such appointment.

" The object of this Memorandum is rather to suggest topics for the mature consideration of the Cabinet than to express any settled opinion on measures of detail. I may occasionally express an opinion, but it will be open in every case to reconsideration.

" This portion of the Memorandum shall be confined to the first of the three points : the degree to which the civil incapacities shall be removed, and the best mode of effecting their removal.

" It is of course notorious that the state of the Roman Catholics of England materially differs from that of the Irish Roman Catholics in respect to civil privileges; but I take for granted that whatever concessions are made to the Irish will in an equal degree be extended to the English—that they will be put on the same footing.

" The principle of the law in respect to the Roman
Catholics of Scotland differs from that of the laws
which apply to the English and Irish Catholics respectively.

" The latter are disqualified as a consequence of
their refusal to take certain oaths, and are disqualified
solely on that account. In Scotland the exclusion of
the Roman Catholic is, as to certain privileges at
least, direct. He is disqualified by name as a Roman
Catholic; and not consequentially, because he refuses
certain oaths.

" As to seats in Parliament, the exclusion of the
Scottish Roman Catholics is positive and direct; and
the exclusion forms part of the Act of Union between
England and Scotland.

" This part of the question, however, may be reserved for separate consideration. In my opinion, no
distinction ought to be made in the case of the Scotch
Roman Catholic. The Act of Union with Scotland
ought not to be a bar to his participation in whatever
privileges are granted to the Roman Catholics of other
parts of the Empire.

" As to the extent to which the civil incapacities
should be removed, my impression is that there is no
intermediate step between the line drawn by the Irish
Act of 1793, and the general repeal of civil incapacities.
I do not mean to say that there ought to be no single
office excepted, or no restrictions upon the exercise of
certain functions appertaining to certain offices: but I
think the broad principle to be maintained should be
equality of civil privilege; that that should be the rule,

and that the exceptions from it should rest on special grounds.

" The removal of incapacity will confer power, at least the eligibility to power, derived from two different, perhaps two opposite sources—the Crown on the one hand, and Constituent Bodies of the People on the other.

" Office in the service of the Crown must be derived chiefly from the Crown; but Corporate office and seats in the House of Commons are dependent, not upon the will of the Crown, but upon that of certain portions of the people.

" To exclude from Corporate office, or from Parliament, would, so far as Ireland is concerned, leave the adjustment of the question incomplete.

" If you remove those exclusions, and thus open every avenue to that description of power which is derived from the people, or from other authorities than the Crown, would it be expedient to limit the prerogative and the means of influence of the Crown by restricting the capacity of the Roman Catholic for that species of favour, distinction, or power which the Crown can confer?

" Would it not be dangerous to the State, if the Crown could neither employ nor influence those on whom popular favour had conferred real authority? Would it not invert constitutional relations to make the people the fountain of honour and of power, and the Crown the bar to them?

" It may, however, be expedient to except from the general rule of complete admissibility the offices which were excepted in the Bills brought in by Mr. Grattan, Mr. Plunket, and Sir Francis Burdett.

" The offices excepted were these :—

" All offices belonging to the Established Church.

" Offices in the Ecclesiastical Courts of Judicature.

" Offices in the Universities, or Schools of Ecclesiastical foundation.

" Offices of Lord Chancellor in England and Ireland, and of Lord Lieutenant of Ireland.

" Roman Catholics were not to have the right of presentation to Benefices; and if a Roman Catholic was appointed to an office which had the right of presentation to Ecclesiastical Benefices, the King might appoint a Protestant Commissioner to exercise *pro tempore* that right of presentation.

" With the above exceptions, or others resting on the same principle, the removal of civil incapacity ought in my opinion to be general and complete.

" Secondly. As to the mode of relieving the Roman Catholic from his present disabilities.

" The obstacle to the admission of the Roman Catholics in England and Ireland to Parliament and certain high civil offices is to be found in the Oath of Supremacy, and the Declaration against Transubstantiation.

" The Declaration against Transubstantiation ought, I think, to be absolutely repealed, excepting indeed that it must continue to be taken by the King or Queen previous to Coronation.

" It will be much better for every purpose positively to enact that certain offices shall not be held by Roman

Catholics than to retain the Declaration against Transubstantiation, with the view of excluding them through its instrumentality.

" The remaining obstacle is the Oath of Supremacy. I wish that oath could be retained in its present form, and that the Roman Catholic could be persuaded to take it in the sense in which I believe it to have been originally meant to be taken.

" In the Bill brought in by Mr. Plunket in 1821, it was originally proposed to retain without any alteration the present Oath of Supremacy, and to require the Roman Catholic to take that oath as a condition of his holding office ; there being inserted in the Bill a legislative interpretation of the oath, importing that those who might take the oath should be understood to declare nothing more than that they denied to any foreign Prince any jurisdiction, temporal or spiritual, that could conflict with their duty of full and undivided allegiance.

" The Bill was, however, afterwards altered in this respect ; and an oath was proposed for the Roman Catholics, differing from the present Oath of Supremacy.

" The legislative interpretation was abandoned, and the Roman Catholic was called on to take an oath which denied to any foreign Prince in express terms any superiority, ecclesiastical or spiritual, that could conflict with his allegiance to the King.

" I have already observed that I wish it were possible to retain the present Oath of Supremacy to be taken in common by Protestant and Roman Catholic ; at the same time I think even an alteration of the oath is preferable to a legislative interpretation of it.

" I doubt whether any other expedient will be found less open to objection than that which I am now about to suggest.

" Repeal the Declaration against Transubstantiation and the worship of the Virgin Mary.

" Leave the Oath of Supremacy, which is of great antiquity, to be taken in its present form by all Protestants, and by Roman Catholics who choose to take it.

" Retain the Oath of Allegiance, and (for the present at least) the Oath of Abjuration; to be taken by Protestant and Roman Catholic in common.

" It will remain to be considered what test of civil allegiance shall be administered to the Roman Catholic.

" I advise one which shall be a purely civil test, but by which the Roman Catholic shall be compelled to abjure any principles or opinions that are dangerous to the State."

NOTE upon the MEMORANDUM as above.

" The oath I suggested was compiled from the existing oaths taken by the Roman Catholics under the Acts of 1781, 1782, 1791, and 1793, and was that which is contained in the Roman Catholic Relief Bill.

" The last sheet of this Memorandum was taken by the Solicitor-General, in order to copy the form of oath from it, and was not returned to me; but it merely contained the form of oath for the Roman Catholic included in the Relief Bill."—R. P.

" March 31, 1829."

ENDORSEMENT upon the MEMORANDUM as above.

" I brought this Memorandum to the Cabinet Room
at the beginning of our discussions in the Cabinet on
the Roman Catholic Question, and read it to the
Cabinet as containing my opinion on the general principle of the measures that ought to be adopted for the
settlement of the Catholic Question."—R. P.

My advice to the Cabinet was not to risk the failure
of the two great measures, the relief from civil disabilities, and the regulation of the Elective Franchise,
by attempting too much, by uniting with them measures
for defining the relation of the Roman Catholic Religion to the State, or for making a pecuniary provision
for the ministers of that religion.

I was not insensible to the vast importance of these
latter measures. I entertained no objection to them in
point of principle; but there was, in my opinion, very
great danger that the whole attempt might fail, if the
opposition which we should have to encounter, on grounds
rather political than religious, were strengthened by an
opposition on purely religious grounds to the endowment of the Roman Catholic faith.

Any delay in the progress of the political measures
beyond that necessary for fair deliberation and discussion was greatly to be deprecated; but the appeal
for delay would have been irresistible if we had proposed
for simultaneous consideration a series of measures of
such vast importance (and, as it would have been contended in argument, so intimately connected and inter-

woven) as the suppression of the Association, the repeal
of civil disability, the regulation of the Elective Franchise, together with measures for endowing the Roman
Catholic clergy, for providing the pecuniary means of
that endowment, and defining the conditions on which
it should be holden.

Various opinions were of course expressed even
among those who concurred in the main object we had
in view, namely, the establishment of civil equality between Protestant and Roman Catholic, as to the mode
in which we effected that object, and as to our policy in
accompanying, or in omitting to accompany, the main
enactment with collateral measures.

Some thought the preliminary suppression of the
Association a needless parade of vigour; some blamed
us for dismissing from offices of trust and for prosecuting the agitators in Ireland, for declining any
sort of amicable concert and communication with the
Roman Catholic party, and for refusing to Mr. O'Connell
the benefit of his recent election for the county of Clare.

Others thought that the establishment of relations
with the Church of Rome, or at least the endowment of
the ministers of that Church, ought to have been proposed by us, if not as an essential condition, at least as
a concomitant, of Emancipation, to which the Government attached equal importance. It would be useless
now to discuss the validity of these several objections to
the course we pursued.

For any error of this kind, either of omission or of
commission, I must assume my full share of responsibility.
But before too severe a judgment is pronounced upon

such errors, the great difficulties with which we had to contend in accomplishing the main object ought not to be overlooked. We were about to forfeit the confidence, and encounter the hostility, of a very great portion of our own party. We had no claim upon the confidence or good will of the Roman Catholic party. The principle of concession had been affirmed by the House of Commons, on the last discussion, by the very smallest majority—276 to 272. It had been negatived in the House of Lords by a majority of 44. The King was hostile, the Church was hostile, a majority probably of the people of Great Britain was hostile, to concession. It was not, as was imputed, from paltry jealousy or personal pique, that we resolved not to permit Mr. O'Connell to take his seat for Clare on an election which had taken place previously to the passing of the Relief Act. It was not from insensibility to the importance of establishing some bond of connection between the Roman Catholic Clergy and the State, that a provision for their maintenance formed no part of our plan. The refusal in the one case, and the omission in the other, were deliberate acts, determined on in the sincere belief that in different degrees and for different reasons they were important to the ultimate success of our undertaking.

I revert to the narrative of events in the order in which they occurred.

The draft of the Speech from the Throne was prepared, and of course submitted to the King. That part of the Speech which had reference to Ireland and the Catholic Question was as follows :—

SPEECH from the THRONE, 1829.

(Extract.)

"The state of Ireland has been the object of His Majesty's continued solicitude.

"His Majesty laments that in that part of the United Kingdom an Association should still exist which is dangerous to the public peace and inconsistent with the spirit of the Constitution, which keeps alive discord and ill-will among His Majesty's subjects, and which must, if permitted to continue, effectually obstruct every effort permanently to improve the condition of Ireland.

"His Majesty confidently relies upon the wisdom and on the support of his Parliament; and His Majesty feels assured that you will commit to him such powers as may enable His Majesty to maintain his just authority.

"His Majesty recommends that, when this essential object shall have been accomplished, you should take into your deliberate consideration the whole condition of Ireland; and that you should review the laws which impose civil disabilities on His Majesty's Roman Catholic subjects.

"You will consider whether the removal of those disabilities can be effected consistently with the full and permanent security of our establishments in Church and State, with the maintenance of the Reformed Religion established by law, and of the rights and privileges of the Bishops and of the clergy of his realm, and of the churches committed to their charge

"These are institutions which must ever be held sacred in this Protestant kingdom, and which it is the duty and the determination of His Majesty to preserve inviolate.

"His Majesty most earnestly recommends to you to enter upon the consideration of a subject of such paramount importance, deeply interesting to the best feelings of his people, and involving the tranquillity and concord of the United Kingdom, with the temper and the moderation which will best ensure the successful issue of your deliberations."

The King gave a reluctant assent to this communication from the Throne to Parliament. Though worded, after the manner of Royal Speeches, with all due reserve and cautious qualifications, no one could doubt the import of the terms. They were justly construed to imply an intention on the part of the Government to make a decisive effort to adjust the Catholic Question.

When I resolved to advise and to promote to the utmost of my power the settlement of that question, I resolved at the same time to relinquish, not only my official station, but the representation of the University of Oxford.

I thought that such decisive proofs that I could have no object, political or personal, in taking a course different from that which I had previously taken, would add to my influence and authority, so far at least as the adjustment of the particular question at issue was concerned.

I have explained the reasons for which I consented to abandon my intention in respect to the resignation of office. They were not applicable to the seat for the University, which I determined to vacate the moment that I was at liberty publicly to announce my decision in regard to the Catholic Question. It was no doubt the fact that there had been indications, even before the events of the autumn of 1828, that the opposition to concession on the part of the University was gradually becoming less decided. In the accompanying letter, written in March 1828, the Bishop of Oxford speaks of the resistance offered by increasing numbers of the University to the Petition against concession.

Bishop of OXFORD to Mr. PEEL.

" Christ Church, March 13, 1828.
" MY DEAR PEEL,

"The signs of the times grow more and more manifest. To-day there was an opposition to the Roman Catholic Petition beyond any we have ever had. We carried it, however—Protestants, 63 ; Catholics, 32 ; but the advance of the opponents was not only remarkable from the number, but the opposition had always hitherto been confined to the Masters of Arts—to-day several of the Doctors and Heads of Houses were among the opponents."

Still I could not doubt that the feeling of the Academic body, speaking generally, was hostile to concession. I cannot deny that in vacating my seat

I was acting upon the impulse of private feelings, rather than upon a dispassionate consideration of the constitutional relation between a representative and his constituents.

I will not seek to defend the resolution to which I came by arguments drawn from the peculiar character of the Academic body, or from the special nature of the trust confided to its Members. Still less will I contend that my example ought to be followed by others to whom may be offered the same painful alternative of disregarding the dictates of their own consciences, or of acting in opposition to the opinions and disappointing the expectations of their constituents. I will say no more than that my position was a very peculiar one, that I had many painful sacrifices to make, and that it would have been a great aggravation of them if it could have been said with truth that I was exercising an authority derived from the confidence of the University to promote measures injurious, in her deliberate judgment, either to her own interests or to those of the Church.

Under the influence of such feelings, I addressed, on the day before the meeting of Parliament, the following letter to the Vice-Chancellor of Oxford.

Mr. PEEL to the Vice-Chancellor of OXFORD.

"Whitehall, February 4, 1829.

" MY DEAR SIR,

"I take the very first opportunity of which I am at liberty to avail myself, to make a communication to you which is most distressing to my feelings.

" I have considered it to be my duty, as one of the responsible advisers of the King, humbly to signify to His Majesty the opinion which I have formed in entire concurrence with all my colleagues in the Government, that the period is arrived when His Majesty's servants must take in their collective capacity some decisive line with regard to the state of Ireland, and to the various subjects affecting the tranquillity of that country which are involved in what is called the Catholic Question.

" After maturely weighing the present position of affairs, and the prospects of the future, adverting to the opinions repeatedly expressed by majorities in the House of Commons, to the difficulties which must arise in the present state of Ireland from continued division in the councils of His Majesty, and disunion between the two Houses of Parliament, it has appeared to His Majesty's Government that there is less of evil and less of danger, under the existing circumstances of the country, in the attempt to make some satisfactory adjustment of the Catholic Question, than in any other course which we can suggest.

" In the offer of my advice to His Majesty as one of his confidential and responsible servants, I have been compelled to exclude every consideration but that of the interests and necessities of the country.

" No sooner, however, had I fulfilled the obligations of my duty to His Majesty, than I began maturely to reflect on the relation in which I stand to the University of Oxford.

" I cannot doubt that the resistance which I have hitherto offered to the claims of the Roman Catholics

P

has been one of the main grounds upon which I have
been entitled to the confidence and support of a very
large body of my constituents ; and although I discontinue that resistance solely from the firm belief that
perseverance in it would be not only unavailing, but
would be injurious, to those interests which it is my
especial duty to uphold, yet I consider myself bound to
surrender to the University without delay the trust
which they have confided to me.

" I take the liberty of requesting that you will communicate this letter to those leading members of the
University with whom you may think it proper to
confer, and that you will consult with them as to the
period at which it will be most convenient to the
University that my seat in Parliament should be vacated.

" I will be guided by the suggestions with which
you may favour me in this respect in making my
application to the Crown for some nominal appointment
which may vacate my seat.

" By this painful sacrifice, by the forfeiture of that
high distinction which I have prized much more than
any other object of ambition, I shall at least give a decisive proof that I have not taken my present course
without the most mature deliberation, and that I have
not suffered myself to be influenced by any other motive
than that of an overpowering sense of public duty.

" My present relation to the University will be terminated ; but believe me that to the latest hour of my
existence I shall never be unmindful of the confidence
with which I have been honoured, and of the kindness
and indulgence which I have invariably experienced,

and that I shall study to maintain with unabated zeal
the privileges and interests of the University, and of the
Church of England, notwithstanding the dissolution of
those ties which have more immediately bound me to
their service.

"I have the honour to be, my dear Sir,
    "With every sentiment of respect and regard,
        "Your most faithful servant,
            "ROBERT PEEL."

I transmitted a copy of this letter to the Chancellor
of the University (Lord Grenville) and to the Dean of
Christ Church, the head of the college of which I was a
member.

I shall proceed to give the correspondence which took
place on this subject, and the communications which
subsequently passed, fully explaining the circumstances
under which, after vacating my seat, I was put in nomination as candidate for the representation of the University. I make no apology for adding these communications to others of greater public interest. I am not
writing a History: this Memoir partakes more of the
character of a personal narrative.

The motive for writing it is the hope of rescuing
hereafter my memory from unjust imputations when I
shall have no other means of repelling them than by
such an appeal as this to those original documents that
are the contemporary and faithful record, not only of
the conduct, but of the inmost thoughts of public men.

For a period of now forty years I have been in

public life, for a considerable portion of that time in
the service of the Crown. It is not for me to claim any
other credit than that due to industry and upright intentions. If even that be conceded to me, it is not too
much to ask in return (it is all that I do ask) that the
materials for forming a just judgment shall be dispassionately weighed before I am calumniated after my
death as I have been during my life. This is the ground
on which I hope to be pardoned if I incorporate with
this Memoir some communications which may appear to
refer rather to my personal relation to the University
of Oxford than to matters of national importance.

The following are the letters which I received from
the Vice-Chancellor, with my replies, and letters from
the Dean of Christ Church (Dr. Gaisford*), and Lord
Grenville, in answer to those which I had addressed to
them.

Vice-Chancellor of OXFORD to Mr. PEEL.

" Exeter College, February 5, 1829.

" MY DEAR SIR,

" I received the favour of your letter by this
morning's post; and from the general tenor of the communication I thought it highly expedient to lay it before
the Board of Heads of Houses and Proctors; by whom
it was agreed that the letter should be read in Convocation immediately after the sense of the House had been
taken on the subject of the petitions proposed this day

* Thus in the MS., but plainly a slip of the pen for Dr. S. Smith,
who preceded Dr. Gaisford as Dean.—(*Eds.*)

against any further concessions to the Roman Catholics.

" I trust that this course of proceeding will meet with
your approbation, as there seemed to be no doubt in
your mind respecting the resolution which you had
taken, and as the whole letter was such as could not
but enhance the value universally entertained of the
relation in which you have been so long connected
with us.

" I shall doubtless have occasion very soon to communicate to you our further sentiments on the point
which you are pleased to refer to our suggestion, respecting the particular time of your vacating your seat
in Parliament. This at all events cannot but affect us
with the deepest regret.

" The petitions were carried by a majority of 164 to
48, and I have forwarded them by a special messenger ;
the one to Lord Grenville, the other to yourself. I
confess that I have deeply felt the delicacy of addressing the latter to your patronage under all the circumstances of the case ; but I have reason to apprehend that
your colleague, Mr. Estcourt, is at present detained in
the country by a domestic affliction, which may possibly
prevent him from taking his seat at the opening of the
present Session.

" I have the honour, &c.,

" J. C. Jones, V. C."

Vice-Chancellor of OXFORD to Mr. PEEL.

" Exeter College, February 5, 1829.
" MY DEAR SIR,

" It is my official duty to transmit to you a petition to the House of Commons on the subject of the
Catholic claims, which was this day proposed and passed
in Convocation by a majority of 164 to 48.

" I make no apology for the liberty I take in placing
the petition in your hands under the present circumstances, as I have already adverted to it in my answer
to the favour of your communication by this morning's
post; which answer will, I doubt not, anticipate the
delivery of the document itself by the bearer, who is
charged with the conveyance to Lord Grenville of a
similar petition for the House of Lords.

" I have the honour, &c.,
" J. C. JONES, V. C."

Vice-Chancellor of OXFORD to Mr. PEEL.

" Exeter College, February 6, 1829.
" MY DEAR SIR,

" At the meeting yesterday of the Board of
Heads of Houses and Proctors (the only advisers to
whom I felt I could safely defer your communication
without the hazard of the most unpleasant imputations),
it was resolved that your letter should be read in the
Convocation then about to assemble, and that we should
this morning take into consideration the liberal offer
expressed by you to accede to any suggestions we might

have to make as to the period at which it would be most convenient to the University that your seat in Parliament should be vacated.

" On the part of the Board, I am now authorized to request you to use your own discretion on this point, and to express our earnest hope that you will only have the goodness to give due notice to the University of the particular time which you may think proper to fix for making the vacancy.

" I am on this occasion also desired to repeat the expression of our unfeigned and deep regret that any circumstances should have occurred to dictate the necessity or the propriety of such a determination, which, however injurious to our interest or our feelings, we cannot but regard as an honourable sacrifice to a high sense of duty, and as evincing a dignified spirit of independence.

" I have the honour, &c.,

" J. C. JONES, V. C."

Mr. PEEL to the Vice-Chancellor of OXFORD.

" Whitehall, February 7, 1829.

" MY DEAR SIR,

" It is a great consolation to me to receive your assurances that the motives of my recent determination are justly appreciated by those with whom you have conferred. The necessary surrender of the trust which the University committed to me is the greatest, though not the only sacrifice which I make to an imperative call of public duty.

" I hope to be enabled on Monday, or at any rate on

some early day of next week, to notify to you the period
at which I will apply for the Chiltern Hundreds for the
purpose of vacating my seat in Parliament; and I will
not fail to select a period which shall enable me to
comply with your wish to have due previous notice.

" I have, &c.,

" ROBERT PEEL."

Mr. PEEL to the Vice-Chancellor of OXFORD.

" Whitehall, February 7, 1829.

" MY DEAR SIR,

"I have had the honour of receiving the petition of the University on the subject of the Roman Catholic claims.

" I feel most sensibly the kind consideration which
has permitted this petition to be committed to my hands.
I will take the earliest opportunity of presenting it to
the House of Commons, and of doing all the justice in
my power to the views and sentiments of those from
whom it proceeds.

" I have, &c.,

" ROBERT PEEL."

Dean of CHRIST CHURCH to Mr. PEEL.

" Christ Church, February 5, 1829.

" MY DEAR SIR,

"I went to the Vice-Chancellor as soon as I
received your letter this morning. It seemed not proper
that he should confine himself to a smaller body of ad-

visers than the Heads of Houses, so he called a meeting
at noon, and read your letter to them.

" Much regret was expressed at your determination.
It was agreed that to-morrow it should be considered,
and an answer given to your question as to time, &c.

" I have been so hurried ever since the Convocation,
that I have hardly time to say more than that I should
entreat you not to resign till the measures which are to
be brought forward have been fully explained in Parliament : in truth your resignation at this moment would
be attended with the greatest inconvenience.

" Many persons declared that you should be elected
again.

" Your letter was read in Convocation, it having
been determined by the Heads of Houses that your
declaration could not be communicated to the body of
your constituents in a more convenient manner.   The
numbers on the petition were 164 to 48.

" The Vice-Chancellor will write to you again to-
morrow, and I will do so too, and I hope more at my
leisure than I do now.

" Believe me, &c.,

" S. SMITH."

Lord GRENVILLE to Mr. PEEL.

" Dropmore, February 6, 1829.

" DEAR SIR,

" I cannot but be highly sensible of the obliging
and flattering attention of your letter, which I have just
received, together with the papers to which it refers.
On the subject of that communication it would ill be-

come me to anticipate any decision of the University. The choice and continuance of its representatives in Parliament is a matter on which, above all others, it least belongs to me to express any opinion ; but there can be no impropriety in my assuring you, which I do with great sincerity, that any circumstance, whatever it might be, which could tend to deprive us of services in so many respects of the highest value to us, would, on that account at least, be considered by me as a cause of very great regret.

" I have the honour, &c.,

" GRENVILLE."

I have already stated that of all my friends in the University of Oxford the one with whom I had maintained the most unreserved intercourse after quitting the University was Charles Lloyd, the Bishop of Oxford. The correspondence with him and with other attached friends will explain the circumstances under which I became engaged in an unsuccessful contest for the representation of the University with Sir R. Inglis.

It was far from my wish to enter into that contest ; but if I had positively forbidden a perfectly unsuggested and independent appeal on my behalf to the judgment of the University, there might have been the appearance of doubt on my part as to the rectitude of the course I had pursued, and of some shrinking on the very threshold of the difficulties which I was about to encounter.

The accompanying letters will speak for themselves, and will require no observation on my part.

Bishop of OXFORD to Mr. PEEL.

"Pulteney Hotel, February 5, 1829.

" MY DEAR PEEL,

"I am this moment arrived from Oxford. I saw your letter before I left home. Nothing could be better; and the mode of proceeding perfect. I could be of no use at Oxford, not having a voice among the Heads of Houses; so I came away, for I am in as great a state of anxiety as you can be. I shall hear to-morrow an exact account of what has been done, both in regard to your letter and to our petition.

" Ever yours,

" C. O."

Bishop of OXFORD to Mr. PEEL.

" February 8, 1829.

" MY DEAR PEEL,

"The Dean, before my arrival here, had settled everything about your letter and the scrape that he had got into. He sent for the Censors on Friday morning, and told them that he was shocked to find among his papers a copy of your letter, which had evidently been forwarded by Wednesday's post. He told me that he was so distressed during the whole of Thursday, that he really did not know what he was doing.

"I have seen to-day Gaisford, Barnes, Marsham, and the Dean. Last night I saw Short. Short is

very decided and positive for re-election; but he is
of very ultra liberal principles. Marsham, however,
is equally decided that the University will be dis-
graced in case they do not re-elect you; and his
principles are sound and his judgment good. The
Provost of Worcester, Dr. Landon, the Head of an
old Tory College, said to the Dean, after the Convocation on Thursday, 'Well, Mr. Dean, I suppose
you will propose him again immediately.' Short and
Marsham both came to me separately for the same
object; namely, to know whether you had any objection
to be re-elected. To Short I spoke very cautiously,
and said that I could really not presume to say one
word about it. He asked me whether, if you were
re-elected, you would reject your election. I told him
I had no reason to suppose you would. To Marsham
I spoke more openly and confidentially: I told him
that my chief reason of doubt was the fear of the
smallest attack upon your character, in case you should
be re-elected, as we argued yesterday. He laughed
at this, and said it was hyper Quixotism; and that
if the voices of your constituents were fairly taken,
you were then clearly the fit member for the University. He says that he has no doubt that the whole
of the Law will come down for you. The Dean says that
if the Censors determine on you, he shall propose you.

"The Dean asked me to-day when I thought you
would vacate your seat. I told him I thought you
would do so within a fortnight. He seemed to think
that would do. You may write to the Vice-Chancellor,
by to-morrow's post, a short and very civil letter.

"Unless you say positively to me that you will not be re-elected, I shall allow your friends to take their course. I conceive that you would have to fight the battle with the Attorney-General. There is no doubt that some men here are thinking of him. If you were quite certain of being re-elected, I cannot help thinking that a decision of the University in your favour would be a great declaration for the line of policy you have chosen. But it is now exceedingly difficult for me to discover the real feelings of the University.

"Pray send me the securities as soon as possible,— even one by one, as you provide them. How will you carry into effect your provision that no one shall exercise Episcopal functions without the King's leave, in case they refuse to accept your Bill, as they did on the occasion of Grattan's Bill?

"Send me an account, also, of any accession in the House of Lords.

"I was told, yesterday morning, that the King had only given leave to mention the subject in the Speech, but did not consider himself bound not to put his Veto on the measure, even if the Bill passed both Houses. This is surely impossible.

"Send me word of anything that tends to alleviate your difficulties and mitigate your struggles.

"Ever, my dear Peel,

"Most affectionately yours,

"C. O."

Mr. PEEL to the Bishop of OXFORD.

"Whitehall, February 11, 1829.*

" MY DEAR LLOYD,

"You will have got my letter of yesterday. I determined, last night, to give a specimen of the state of Ireland; and I ask any honest man whether he believes that it is consistent with the interests of the Empire, and above all with the *interests of the Established Church in Ireland*, that such a state of things should continue, and no attempt be made at an effectual remedy, or at some change of some kind or other.

"Surely it would be much better for Christ Church to take a candidate whose election it could secure than to run any risk by proposing me.

"In very homely phrase I say to you (what I could not say to any one else) I care very little about the matter.

"I will do nothing whatever that could in the slightest degree be considered disrespectful to the University or to my most violent opponents, or rather enemies, in it.

"I can so arrange matters that I can disqualify myself for re-election. I can vacate on Friday, and be returned for some small borough on the following day, or on Monday, and then I should be ineligible for the University.

---

* On the 10th February I brought in the Bill for suppressing the Roman Catholic Association in Ireland.—(R. P.)

" For God's sake take no step, directly or indirectly, that could appear to intimate a wish on my part to be returned. I have no such wish, and I think a protracted contest, even if it ended successfully, would be very embarrassing and painful to me.

" I am against my nomination; but I am at the same time unwilling to say, for instance, ' I would refuse an election,' ' I would vacate again if elected,' or anything which would appear peevish and ill-humoured, or disrespectful.

" Let Christ Church take the course which will best ensure its own just influence in the University. The more I think of the subject, the more adverse I am personally to nomination, and decidedly to contest.

" Ever, &c.,

" ROBERT PEEL."

Mr. PEEL to the Bishop of OXFORD.

(Most private.)

" Whitehall, February 13, 1829.

" MY DEAR LLOYD,

" I cannot help thinking that by far the best course is to make no sort of declarations in reference to the proceedings of the University.

" I mean to resign absolutely. I have written to the Vice-Chancellor, stating that I propose to resign on Friday next, the 20th.

" His answer was that he had laid my letter

before the Convocation; that they acquiesced in my resignation on that day; but that they did not wish the new Writ to be moved for some time, in order that the Election might not be concurrent in point of time with the Assizes.

" With the motives for the new Writ I have nothing to do. I express no opinion on the subject, and can be no party whatever to anything respecting it.

" I mean, under any circumstances, to vacate on Friday morning next. The public business requires that I should, without delay, be returned to Parliament. I have taken measures for that purpose.

" Why should I do or say anything more? that I have either a wish to be re-elected, or that I would refuse, under any conceivable circumstances, to be re-elected ?

" Let the University take its own course, and I will take mine; remaining *bonâ fide* perfectly passive with respect to the University course, and doing nothing that can bear upon it, excepting that I must expedite my return for some other place. If returned, I am not eligible for the University.

" Enclosed is a letter for Marsham. Read it, and exercise your own discretion as to the delivering of it to him, for it is difficult to form a judgment at a distance, and when circumstances vary so much from day to day.

" Ever, &c.,

" ROBERT PEEL."

Bishop of OXFORD to Mr. PEEL.

"Christ Church, February 14, 1829.

" MY DEAR PEEL,

"I sent your letter to Marsham. He proposed
to the Committee to lay it before them. They (as I
understand) refused to hear it; saying that they acted
on their own responsibility, without any communication
with Mr. Peel, who could not be allowed to interfere in
an University election. I have not mentioned to anybody that I heard from you to-day; so I shall allow
them to follow their own devices, though, according to
your plan, I do not see how it can end, unless indeed
they should before next Friday have such a majority as
may enable them to announce to you that your election
is secure.

"I send you a letter from Mr. Lyall, Archdeacon of
Colchester, a very able man, and an exceedingly high
churchman. Read it with attention.

"There are, as far as we can find, 160 members of
the Convocation, and I suspect all that are against you,
signed the paper I sent last night; the rest are either
for you, or not against you.

"Ever yours,

"C. O."

Mr. PEEL to the Vice-Chancellor of OXFORD.

"Whitehall, February 10, 1829.

" MY DEAR SIR,

"I propose to apply for the Chiltern Hundreds
on Friday, the 20th of February, on which day the Writ

for the University can be moved in the House of Commons.

"I name rather a distant day for the purpose of being enabled to give you ample notice.

"If you should see any reason to prefer an earlier vacancy, I will at once comply with any suggestion which you may be good enough to convey to me.

"I have, &c.,

"ROBERT PEEL."

Vice-Chancellor of OXFORD to Mr. PEEL.

"Exeter College, February 11, 1829.

"MY DEAR SIR,

"The proposal contained in the honour of your letter by this morning's post was received by the Board of Heads of Houses, to whom I immediately communicated it, with the deference which was due to it.

"An earlier season for your acceptance of the Chiltern Hundreds was considered by no means desirable, and, as we apprehend that the motion for the new Writ is entirely a distinct measure, we are anxious that this should not be done under any hazard of the interference of the Election with our Assizes, which usually take place during the first week in March.

"I have the honour, &c.,

"J. C. JONES, V. C."

Warden of MERTON to Mr. PEEL.

"Merton College, February 12, 1829.

" MY DEAR PEEL,

"Several members of Convocation, including
five Heads of Houses and two of Halls, the Proctors,
and some other highly respectable individuals, have met
in Oxford to-day for the purpose of procuring your
re-election, and we propose to take steps for the attainment of that object. The measure originated out of
Christ Church, but we have asked and received a great
addition to our numbers from it.

" I write this merely to apprise you of the circumstance, with the privity of many of the conspirators, and
require no answer.

"Believe me, &c.,

" ROBERT MARSHAM."

Mr. PEEL to the Warden of MERTON.

"Whitehall, February 13, 1829.

" MY DEAR MARSHAM,

" I must disobey your injunction—if it be only
to assure you how deeply sensible I am of the kind and
generous feeling which has prompted your communication.

" The only answer I can give to your letter is ex-
plicitly to declare the course I have pursued, and to
which I must adhere.

" I have written to the Vice-Chancellor, proposing to
accept the Chiltern Hundreds on Friday next, the 20th.

He has replied that he sees no objection to my vacating on that day, but intimates a wish that the Writ should not be immediately moved for, in order that a new Election may not be concurrent in point of time with the Assizes.

" With this latter point my acceptance of the Chiltern Hundreds has no concern. On Friday morning I shall accept them; and I think it would not be right that any step should be taken with respect to the moving for the Writ at any time without communication with the Vice-Chancellor, and with his full consent.

" This is the only opinion which I shall presume to express in reference to the future.

" I cannot see the list of names of those who think I have done nothing to forfeit the esteem of the University without feeling proud of their good opinion. I cannot on the other hand hear of the objections to my return for it without admitting them to proceed from natural, justifiable, and honourable motives.

" One feeling predominates in my mind: I should deeply regret if I were to be the means of sowing dissension in the University—of placing one class of the constituent body in opposition to another.

" No defeat would be half so painful as any triumph embittered by such reflections.

" One course is open to me, and that a very plain one, which avoids either triumph or defeat. I must resign, in pursuance of my declared intention to the Vice-Chancellor, on Friday next; and it is absolutely necessary that I should resume my place in the House of Commons without delay.

" The convenience of the University forbids a contest during the Assizes. The public business requires that I should be forthwith returned.

" Let me, therefore, be elected for some other place, and let the Writ for the University be moved according to the express wishes of the Vice-Chancellor on other and sufficient grounds, at a period when I am out of the question by being ineligible.

" I am, &c.,

" ROBERT PEEL."

Mr. VERNON to Mr. PEEL.

" Grove, East Retford, February 12, 1829.

" MY DEAR SIR,

" As one of your constituents, I presume to trespass on your valuable time for the purpose of briefly but earnestly urging a suggestion, which, however it may have been anticipated by others, cannot be superfluously multiplied upon your consideration.

" I honour and approve your resignation of your seat ; I believe it to have been the sacrifice of what was most precious to you, except your honour ; and yet in its terms there was no coquetting—no longing, lingering look behind. You have done your duty to your constituents as well as to your country ; it remains for those who think so to do theirs to you.

" I know not how far etiquette may permit on the occasion of a vacancy your expression of your willingness to serve us again, but I, who have heretofore felt no alloy in the pride and satisfaction of having you as our

representative except such as sprung from your temperate, but as I felt, unfortunate opposition to the
settlement of the Catholic Question—*I* should esteem it
very unfair to be precluded from an opportunity of
electing a Member who would command my unqualified
admiration and suffrage.

" I have reason to believe that I speak the sentiments
of many, and I may be permitted to add that I believe
my position would give me considerable influence with
the clergy in this diocese. I cannot subscribe to the
doctrine that the resident members of the University are
entitled to meet in their cells and dictate in their dark-
ness to the collective body. I did not think that I
should ever have concerned myself with Oxford politics;
but, believing that her interests and those of the Church
Establishment cannot be taken out of your hands without detriment as well as dishonour to ourselves, I entreat
you to authorize your friends to *propose you again*, and
I proffer a zealous co-operation with their efforts. I
beg you will not trouble yourself to reply to this letter
unless you have occasion for my services.

" Whatever our Lord Lieutenant, instructed by the
incumbents of his livings, may say, I will aver that there
is a complete apathy on the subject of the Catholic
Question in this county.

" Yours ever faithfully,

" GRANVILLE V. VERNON."

Mr. PEEL to Mr. VERNON.

"Whitehall, February 13, 1829.

" MY DEAR SIR,

" I am very much gratified by your letter, and am compelled to send a very hasty reply to it.

" I have resolved to take no part whatever with reference to the future election for Oxford—to express no wish or opinion of any kind whatever in respect to it.

" I mean to vacate on Friday next, the 20th, and have secured my return for another place.

" What I am saying to you now is exactly what I have said to the Bishop of Oxford, which I am afraid you will reply is nothing at all.

" The fact is, I wish to leave it to the University to determine, uninfluenced by anything whatever said or done by me, what is the course which it is the most fitting for it to pursue.

" Ever, &c.,

" ROBERT PEEL."

Mr. BERENS to Mr. PEEL.

" 19, Queen Street, May Fair (Thursday night),
February 12, 1829.

" MY DEAR PEEL,

" I am sure you will excuse my troubling you at this moment ; but a report having been whispered about, which I hope is without foundation, that you would now have a personal objection to represent the University of Oxford, I am very anxious to have the best authority for contradicting it, hoping, too, at the same time, that you will allow your friends to exert themselves for your re-election. I feel very confident as to the result, but no time should be lost in making a start. I have, within the last two days, seen several members of Convocation in town, and they all, with one only exception, expressed themselves just as they ought to do. If you could send me an answer before two o'clock to-morrow, when I set off for Oxford, I should be glad.

" Yours very sincerely,

" R. BERENS."

Mr. PEEL to Mr. BERENS.

" Whitehall, February 13, 1829.

" MY DEAR BERENS,

" I will say to you exactly what I have said to Henley Eden, who has just been with me.

" My intention is absolutely to resign. I have intimated to the Vice-Chancellor the day on which I shall apply for the Chiltern Hundreds, namely, this day week. To that intention I must adhere, and I have taken the necessary steps for securing my re-election for another place.

" The Vice-Chancellor has informed me that it will not be convenient to the University to have a new election during the Assizes, and that he does not wish, therefore, that the new Writ for Oxford should be moved immediately upon my acceptance of the Chiltern Hundreds.

" I have told Eden that as to re-election for Oxford, I do not feel myself at liberty to say a word. My course is clear—to resign—to resign on the day which I have named to the Vice-Chancellor, namely, Friday next—and to provide on account of public business for my resuming my place in the House of Commons with as little delay as possible.

" Ever, &c.,

" ROBERT PEEL."

Lord BATHURST to Mr. PEEL.

" Cumberland Street, February 14, 1829.

" MY DEAR MR. PEEL,

" You must forgive my entreating you not to think of refusing to allow your name to be put in nomination for the University, if a proper application should come to that effect.

" Depend upon it your refusal would be misconstrued, and would arrest in its progress the warm interest which men of all parties are taking against the attacks which have been made against you.

" If an application should be made to you, your answer would probably be, however respectably signed the application might be, that unless your own College also expressed their wish for you to be re-elected, you must decline the invitation. This would show sufficiently that you were not too impatient to be re-elected, and would, I believe, be in conformity with University usage. But I am little anxious as to the manner in which the matter shall be conducted ; but do not act in any way to

Q

expose you to the charge of want of temper, or to the suspicion that you had a misgiving of your success.

"Yours very sincerely,

"BATHURST."

The contest terminated in favour of my opponent. The numbers polled were, for—

Sir ROBERT INGLIS 755

Mr. PEEL 609

Majority . . . 146

I find this paper, giving an account of the quality of the minority which supported me :—

"Mr. Peel polled 146 votes less than Sir Robert Inglis, and had twice as many First-class men, 14 out of 20 Professors, and 24 out of 28 Prizemen (the 24 Prizemen having gained 36 prizes!).

"Of Christ Church (the College of both candidates), Mr. Peel had 39 First-class men, his opponent only 8; he had also all the Noblemen who voted; 4 Deans out of 5, and 333 Clergymen, as an argument for the 'No Popery' and 'Church in danger' gentlemen!"

On being apprised of the probable result of the contest, I wrote the following letter to the Warden of Merton College, and received the accompanying reply.

Mr. Peel to the Warden of Merton.

"Whitehall, February 28, 1829.

" My dear Marsham,

"I have not heard of the close of the poll; but I am writing under the full impression that the election will be decided in favour of Sir Robert Inglis by a large majority.

"I beg to assure you with the utmost sincerity, that I do not in the slightest degree regret the course which has been taken.

"I have been gratified beyond measure by the generous enthusiasm and ardent exertions of my friends. I am proud of the support which I have received from so large a proportion of the eminent men of the University under circumstances of no ordinary difficulty, and of peculiar excitement; and I have a complete consolation for defeat in the unshaken conviction which I feel, that I owe that defeat to the discharge of a public duty, and to the preference which I have given to the real interests of the country, and of the Church, and of the University, over every private object and personal concern.

"I request you to express to the members of the Oxford Committee who have been acting with you my warmest acknowledgments, to assure them that I think they were entirely right in giving to such a minority as that which has voted for me the opportunity of recording their sentiments, and that my earnest wish is, that

Q 2

though I have lost them as constituents, I may be allowed to regard them as attached personal friends.

" Ever, &c.,

" ROBERT PEEL."

Warden of MERTON to Mr. PEEL.

" Merton College, March 2, 1829.

" MY DEAR PEEL,

" I have this morning communicated your letter to your friends on the Oxford Committee, and am requested to state that it has afforded universal satisfaction.

" It is perhaps superfluous for me to tell you, that our object in putting you in nomination was to uphold the character of the University, which we thought likely to suffer in the estimation of the world if your claims and services were to pass unregarded.

" Your assurance that you do not regret the course taken has removed the only doubt which occurred to us as to its propriety, and we share your exultation in the fact that so large a proportion of the eminent men of the University should have joined with us in the support of our undertaking. We rejoice that we embraced the opportunity of making this known, and that the effort of re-electing you has been made, though we sincerely lament that it has been ineffectual.

" Believe me, &c.,

" ROBERT MARSHAM."

The letter to Lord Granville Somerset, the chairman of my Election Committee, expressed my warm acknowledgments to him for the admirable manner in which he had discharged his duties in that capacity. It enclosed a draft for 99*l*., which (I mention it to the honour of the constituent body) defrayed the whole of the expenses incurred in the course of a very arduous contest which were allowed to fall upon the candidate.

Mr. PEEL to Lord GRANVILLE SOMERSET.

" Whitehall, March 30, 1829.

" MY DEAR LORD GRANVILLE,

" I enclose the amount of my pecuniary obligations on account of the Oxford election.

" The obligations for your zeal, friendship, and many personal sacrifices of time and comfort, I shall never be able to discharge.

" Ever, &c.,

" ROBERT PEEL."

As there was some delay after the meeting of Parliament in vacating the seat for the University (in consequence of the wish to that effect expressed by the Vice-Chancellor), I was enabled to take part in the debate on the Address, and to propose to Parliament, and to conduct through its several stages, the Bill for the Suppression of the Roman Catholic Association.

That Bill was read a third time on the 17th of February. On the 20th I accepted the Chiltern Hundreds, and ceased to be a Member of the House of Commons.

After my rejection by the University, there being a convenient vacancy at Westbury, I became a candidate (a very unpopular one I must admit) for that borough. The Protestant feeling was much excited, even among the quiet population of a small country town; and notwithstanding all the assistance which Sir Manasseh Lopez (the patron of the borough) could render me, my return was not effected without considerable difficulty.

Sir Manasseh himself suffered in his person from one of the many missiles with which the Town-hall was assailed during the ceremony of the election. It was fortunate for me that that ceremony was not unduly protracted. Very shortly after my return had been declared by the proper officer, the arrival of a Protestant candidate in a chaise and four from London was announced. If he had entered the town a few hours earlier, it is highly probable that I should have fared no better at Westbury than I had done at Oxford.

I took my seat on Tuesday the 3rd of March. We had continued our deliberations in Cabinet up to that time, and had agreed with perfect unanimity on the general outline, and indeed on the details, of the several measures to be proposed to Parliament. We acted under the impression that we had the sanction (the reluctant certainly, but still the complete sanction) of the King for our proceedings. Being anxious that there should not be a moment of unnecessary delay, I gave notice on the 3rd of March that I would on Thursday the 5th call the attention of the House of Commons to that part of the Speech from the Throne which related to the state of Ireland, and the removal of the civil disabilities under which the Roman Catholics laboured.

In the interim circumstances wholly unforeseen occurred, which appeared for a time to oppose an insuperable barrier to any further progress with the measures of which the actual notice had been thus given.

On the evening of Tuesday, the 3rd of March, the King commanded the Duke of Wellington, the Lord Chancellor, and myself to attend His Majesty at Windsor at an early hour on the following day. We went there accordingly, and on our arrival were ushered into the presence of the King, who received us with his usual kindness and cordiality.

He was grave, and apparently labouring under some anxiety and uneasiness.

His Majesty said that we must be fully aware that it had caused him the greatest pain to give his assent to the proposition made to him by his Cabinet that they should be at liberty to offer their collective advice on the Catholic Question, and still greater pain to feel that he had no alternative but to act upon the advice which he had received.

His Majesty then observed, that as the question was about to be brought forward in Parliament, he wished to have a previous personal conference with those of his Ministers whom he had summoned on this occasion to attend him, and whom he must regard as chiefly responsible for the advice tendered to him. He said that he desired to receive from us a more complete and detailed explanation of the manner in which we proposed to effect the object we had in view.

Upon this requisition from His Majesty, being probably most familiar with the details of the measure
which I had to submit to the House of Commons on the
following day, I proceeded to explain them to the King.
I observed to His Majesty that the chief impediment
to the enjoyment of complete civil privileges by his
Roman Catholic subjects was the obligation to make
the Declaration against Transubstantiation and to take
the Oath of Supremacy as qualifications for such privileges—that we proposed to repeal altogether the Declaration against Transubstantiation, and to modify in
the case of the Roman Catholics that part of the Oath
of Supremacy which relates to the spiritual and ecclesiastical jurisdiction and superiority of the Pope.

On this reference to the Oath of Supremacy, the
King seemed much surprised, and said rapidly and
earnestly, "What is this? you surely do not mean to
alter the ancient Oath of Supremacy!" He appealed to
each of his Ministers on this point. We explained to
His Majesty that we proposed that to all his subjects,
excepting the Roman Catholics, the Oath should be
administered in its present form, and that the Roman
Catholic should be required to declare on Oath his
belief that no foreign Prince or Prelate hath any temporal or civil jurisdiction, power, superiority, or pre-
eminence, directly or indirectly, within this realm.
We added, that if the Roman Catholic was still required,
before his admission to office or to Parliament, to declare
his belief that no foreign Prelate hath or ought to have
any spiritual or ecclesiastical jurisdiction, power, or pre-
eminence within the realm, the measure of relief would

be unavailing; that an effectual impediment to the enjoyment of civil privileges would remain unremoved.

The King observed, that be that as it might, he could not possibly consent to any alteration of the ancient Oath of Supremacy—that he was exceedingly sorry that there had been any misunderstanding on so essential a point—that he did not blame us on account of that misunderstanding—that he did not mean to imply that in the explanation which we had previously given to him in writing there had been any concealment or reserve on this point: still the undoubted fact was that he had given his sanction to our proceedings under misapprehension with regard to one particular point, and that a most important one, namely, the alteration of the Oath of Supremacy; and he felt assured that our opinions would be in concurrence with his own—that a sanction so given ought not to be binding upon the Sovereign, and that His Majesty had no alternative but to retract his consent, if the measure to which it had been given under an erroneous impression were *bonâ fide* disapproved of by his deliberate and conscientious judgment.

In answer to this appeal we expressed our deep concern that there had been any misunderstanding on so important a matter, but our entire acquiescence in the King's opinion that His Majesty ought not to be bound by a consent unwarily given to important public measures under a misapprehension of their real character and import. After a short lapse of time, His Majesty then said, " But after this explanation of my feelings what course do you propose to take as my Ministers?"

He observed that notice had been given of proceedings in the House of Commons for the following day; and addressing himself particularly to me, who had charge of those proceedings, said, " Now, Mr. Peel, tell me what course you propose to take to-morrow." I replied that with all deference and respect for His Majesty, I could not have a moment's hesitation as to my course— that the Speech from the Throne had justified the universal expectation that the Government intended to propose measures for the complete relief of the Roman Catholics from civil incapacities—that I had vacated the seat for Oxford on the assumption that such measures would be proposed—that the consent of the House of Commons had been given to the Bill for the Suppression of the Roman Catholic Association, if not on the express assurance, at least with the full understanding, that the measure of coercion would be immediately followed by the measure of relief—that I must therefore entreat His Majesty at once to accept my resignation of office, and to permit me on the following day to inform the House of Commons that unforeseen impediments, which would be hereafter explained, prevented the King's servants from proposing to Parliament the measures that had been announced—that I no longer held the seals of the Home Department, and that it was my painful duty to withdraw the notice which had been given in my name.

The King put a similar question to the Duke of Wellington, who replied that he desired to be permitted by His Majesty to retire from office, and to make to the House of Lords an announcement to the same effect with that which I wished to make to the House of Commons.

The Chancellor intimated his entire acquiescence in the course which the Duke of Wellington and I proposed to pursue.

His Majesty was pleased to express his deep regret that we could not remain in his service consistently with our sense of honour and public duty. His Majesty said moreover that he could not be surprised at our decision, or blame us for the conclusion at which we had arrived.

Our interview with His Majesty lasted for the long period of five hours: there was unintermitted conversation during the whole time, but nothing material passed excepting that the purport of which I have faithfully reported. At the close of the interview the King took leave of us with great composure and great kindness, gave to each of us a salute on each cheek, and accepted our resignation of office, frequently expressing his sincere regret at the necessity which compelled us to retire from his service.

The following passages, having reference to this interview, are extracted from the Memoranda left by Lord Eldon of the conversations which he had with His Majesty a few weeks subsequently to our conference with the King.

Lord Eldon saw the King on the 28th of March and on the 9th of April. In the account of the conversation of the first day is the following passage.

Lord ELDON'S MEMORANDA.

" The King complained that he had never seen the

Bills, &c., &c., that he was in the state of a person with a pistol presented to his breast, that he had nothing to fall back upon, that his Ministers had threatened (I think he said twice at the time of my seeing him) to resign if the measures were not proceeded in, and that he had said to them 'Go on,' when he knew not how to relieve himself from the state in which he was placed, and that in one of those meetings, when resignation was threatened, he was urged to the sort of consent he gave by what passed in the interview between him and his Ministers, till the interview and talk had brought him into such a state that he hardly knew what he was about when he, after several hours, said 'Go on.' "—See p. 510, vol. vii. *Campbell's Chancellors.*

In speaking of his interview with the King on the second day, Lord Eldon observes—

"This led to the King's mentioning again what he had to say as to his *assent.* In the former interview it had been represented that, after much conversation twice with his Ministers, or such as had come down, he had said 'Go on;' and upon the latter of these two occasions, after many hours' fatigue, and exhausted by the fatigue of conversation, he had said 'Go on.' He now produced two papers, which he represented as copies of what he had written to them, in which he assents to their proceedings and going on with the Bill, adding certainly in each, as he read them, very strong expressions of the pain and misery the proceedings gave him."—*Campbell's Chancellors,* vol. vii. p. 512.

Lord Eldon must have misunderstood the account

which he received from His Majesty of our interview
with the King.   In the first place there was only one
interview such as that to which I have referred—one
interview, I mean, between His Majesty and certain
of his Ministers, in which the offer of resignation was
made.   In the second place His Majesty did not give
us at the close of the interview permission to " Go on."
His Majesty accepted from each of us the tender of
resignation, and we returned to London under the full
persuasion that the Government was dissolved—at least
that we individually were no longer in the service of
the Crown.   On our return to London we joined our
colleagues, who were assembled at a Cabinet dinner (I
think at Lord Bathurst's), and announced, to their infinite astonishment, that we had ceased to be members of
the Government.

A sudden change, however, took place in the King's
intentions.   At a late hour on the evening of the 4th
of March the King wrote a letter to the Duke of
Wellington, informing him that His Majesty anticipated so much difficulty in the attempt to form another
administration, that he could not dispense with our
services; that he must therefore desire us to withdraw
our resignation, and that we were at liberty to proceed
with the measures of which notice had been given in
Parliament.

The Duke of Wellington sent immediately this letter
to me: I kept no copy of it, and am giving from
memory the purport of this and the following communications with the King on the same subject.

Either the Duke of Wellington observed in sending

this letter to me, or I suggested to the Duke in returning it, that after what had passed in the morning, the mere permission by His Majesty to proceed with the measures was not sufficient authority; and that we ought to make a further reference to the King for the purpose of ascertaining distinctly whether we were authorized to assure Parliament that the measures in contemplation were proposed by us with the entire consent and sanction of His Majesty.

Accordingly a reference to this effect was made to His Majesty in the course of the night, and an answer was received from the King, giving us full authority to proceed with the measures in question.

For the purpose of silencing all cavil on this subject, in opening those measures on the following day in the House of Commons I commenced my speech in this manner :—

" I rise as a Minister of the King, and sustained by the just authority which belongs to that character, to vindicate the advice given to His Majesty by an united Cabinet," &c., &c.

In relating the particulars of our interview with the King, I have confined myself to a narrative of facts. I have no information as to the circumstances which led to that interview, and know not whether it took place exclusively by the King's own desire, and for the satisfaction of His Majesty's own feelings, or at the suggestion of others. It is manifest from the published Life of Lord Eldon, that Lord Eldon was in confidential communication with the King on the measures of the Government before they had passed the House of

Lords; but there is, I believe, no reference to any such communication having taken place previously to our conference with the King on the 4th of March.

I need not dilate upon the enactments in detail which were contained in the several Bills for the suppression of the Roman Catholic Association, the removal of civil disabilities, and the regulation of the elective franchise in Ireland.

The original drafts submitted to the consideration of the Cabinet differ in no material degree from the Bills as they finally passed. There was an entire agreement among the members of the Government both as to the principle and the details of the several measures.

In preparing the drafts, I received the valuable assistance of the Solicitor-General (Sir Nicholas Tindal), Mr. Doherty (the Solicitor-General for Ireland), and Mr. Leslie Foster, afterwards a Baron of the Irish Exchequer.

The great difficulty was in devising any measures to accompany those of relief calculated to give satisfaction to the Protestant mind by taking precautions against the undue influence of the Roman Catholic religion or the abuse of the new power about to be conferred on the professors of that faith.

There was no disinclination on our part to propose such measures (" securities" as they were popularly called) if they could be devised: there was a strong impression indeed that by the proposal of them we should greatly diminish the force of the objections to the total removal of civil disqualifications. But the difficulty was inherent in the subject.

There were three different classes of "security" that might be suggested. The first and the chief security was in the abolition of those distinctions between Protestant and Roman Catholic which implied suspicion and distrust in the loyalty, and fidelity, and civil worth of the Roman Catholic, in the opening to him of all the avenues to honour and political power, in the consequent discouragement of hostile designs and irregular ambition, in the breaking up of those combinations dangerous to the State that were of perpetual recurrence in Ireland, and owed their origin and their strength to the sympathies awakened and confirmed by a common grievance.

This was a moral as distinguished from a legislative security. It was a security founded on a generous confidence in the loyalty of the Roman Catholic, and on the hope that he would have new motives for attachment to a Constitution from none of the privileges of which he was to be hereafter debarred.

It was possible no doubt to suggest other securities, securities enforced by law, against the abuse of power by the Roman Catholic; but there was necessity for great caution lest such securities, without being of any real value in themselves, should, by implying the continuance of suspicion and distrust, detract from the efficacy of the moral security to which I have referred.

The more I considered the subject, the more I was disposed to abandon all thought of legislative securities, of imposing restrictions for instance on the number of Roman Catholics admissible to Parliament, or of maintaining distinctions of any kind in respect to the capacity for power, or the exercise of power, legislative or official, between Protestant and Roman Catholic.

With respect to religious securities, as distinguished from those purely political, securities I mean which had reference to the exercise of the Roman Catholic religion, to the mode of appointing the priests or prelates of that Church, the regulation of the intercourse with the See of Rome, the inspection of Bulls, Rescripts, &c., it appeared to me that this question was decided when we decided not to propose, as an accompaniment to the measure of relief, any stipendiary provision for the ministers of the Roman Catholic Church.

Independently of this consideration, the experience of the past in respect to the devising of such religious securities was not very encouraging.

The Veto of the Crown on the appointment of Roman Catholic Bishops, the oath to be taken by persons in Holy Orders that they would not concur in the consecration of any Roman Catholic Bishop or Dean but such as they conscientiously deemed to be of loyal and peaceable conduct, the appointment of a Board of Commissioners for the inspection of Bulls, Dispensations, and other instruments received from the See of Rome; all these and similar securities had, when proposed, provoked fierce and endless controversy, had given great dissatisfaction to the Roman Catholics, and no countervailing contentment or confidence to the Protestants.

There has been lately published, in the Memoirs and

Correspondence of Lord Castlereagh, a Memorandum by Lord Castlereagh on the "securities" proposed by Mr. Grattan and Mr. Canning.

He refers, I presume, to those included in the Relief Bill of the year 1813. Of the oath to be taken by the priests, "that they will never consent to the appointment of any person to be a Bishop whom they do not judge loyal and peaceable, and that they will only correspond with the Pope on matters purely ecclesiastical," Lord Castlereagh speaks very irreverently. He says, "As to the regulation of the new oath, by way of security to our establishment, it is the greatest farce I ever read."

With respect to the Commissioners, who were to be entrusted with the inspection of Bulls, &c., and "to have an absolute power to negative the appointment of a Bishop for not being loyal or peaceable," Lord Castlereagh, while he expresses an opinion that "a Commission of Lay Catholics to communicate between Government and their Church would be a very good institution," urges many objections to the manner in which the particular Commission in the Bill of 1813 was to be appointed, and to the functions which it was intended to discharge.

He says that "the idea of a Lay Commission having power to set aside the election of a Bishop, and especially after the approval of the Pope, is fundamentally opposite to the principles of the Church of Rome."

Of the inquiry with regard to Papal Bulls, &c. &c., Lord Castlereagh says, "Why an oath of secrecy? Why is a copy of each Bull to be brought, and not the original? Why are such Bulls not to be examined which shall be sworn to be purely ecclesiastical? Such provisions arise from ignorance."

He says again, that all the regulations in the Bill imposing oaths as to the particular character of Papal Bulls, Rescripts, &c., &c., appear to him of no use, " for the titular Bishops can take no oath which is not subordinate to the oath they have taken to the Pope. But Mr. Canning's clause goes apparently to place the whole government of the Romish Church in these kingdoms beyond the possible cognizance of Government, and establishes by law as legal, and not to be examined into, the Pope's authority over the Catholic Church in England and Ireland in all matters purely ecclesiastical."

I quote these observations from a very high authority, from one decidedly favourable to a connection between the Roman Catholic religion and the State, for the purpose of proving the difficulty of devising such "securities" as were supposed to be afforded by giving to the State a control over ecclesiastical appointments in the Church of Rome, and by establishing restrictions on the intercourse with the Papal See.

If we had proposed any such securities in the year 1829, there can be little doubt that we should have had to encounter objections like those urged by Lord Castlereagh—objections from Roman Catholics on the one hand, from Protestants on the other; there would at any rate have been no hope of the speedy adjustment of a question of this nature, and yet we should have justly exposed ourselves to the charge of ill-faith if we

had postponed indefinitely the measures proffered as
"securities," and had urged at the same time the immediate adoption of the other measures, those which
conferred the unrestricted capacity for political power.

I am confident that the decision was a wise one, as
applicable to the position of affairs in 1829, and considering the urgency for an immediate settlement of the
political question, to encumber that question to as small
a degree as possible with extraneous matter, or with
matter which, if not extraneous, was so complicated and
difficult as to afford the ground for interminable controversy, and a just demand for delay.

On the 10th of April the Bills for the removal of the
civil incapacities of the Roman Catholics and for the
regulation of the elective franchise in Ireland were
each read a third time, and passed the House of Lords,
the latter without a division, the former by a majority,
including proxies, of 104 Peers.

The numbers were—

> Content, 213.
> Not Content, 109.

Thus terminated the Parliamentary conflict on these
important measures. I cannot advert to that conflict,
even after the interval of twenty years, without placing
on record my grateful acknowledgment of the cordial
support which we received in both Houses of Parliament, not only from all those with whom our official
connection had been then recently interrupted, but from
those also who had never had any political connection
with us, and might be considered, so far as the interests

and ties of party were concerned, our decided opponents.

It was not merely that they supported our measures, but they cautiously abstained from everything which might have thrown obstructions in our way, and in many instances forbore from pressing objections strongly felt to portions of the plan, in order that their general support of that plan as a whole might be cordial and effective.

As I must naturally have foreseen, the course which I felt it my duty to take in advising the adjustment of the Catholic Question, in standing forward as the proposer of the measures of the Government to Parliament, and the conductor of them to their final stage in the House of Commons, exposed me to the condemnation of those who remained unconvinced of the necessity or policy of these measures.

Such condemnation assumed every form and varied in every degree from friendly expostulation and the temperate expression of conscientious dissent to the most violent abuse, and the imputation of the basest motives.

Opponents who would listen to argument, I sought to mollify by respectful explanation. I let pass without notice the calumnies which were prompted by a zeal too fervent to be accessible to reason, and too uncharitable to believe in the possibility of an honest intention.

As an example of the class of opponents first referred to, I will give the correspondence which passed with a most worthy and respected Prelate, Dr. Jebb, the Bishop of Limerick. My letter, in reply to the first of the Bishop's letters, necessarily recapitulates arguments which have appeared in preceding documents; but the Bishop's second letter would be hardly intelligible without the insertion of that to which it is a rejoinder. It will be seen not only that I failed in my attempt to convince the Bishop of Limerick, but that the reasons on which I relied as conclusive in favour of the necessity for an altered course had the unfortunate result of increasing, if possible, the conviction in the mind of the Bishop that there was infinitely more danger in concession than in uncompromising resistance.

Bishop of Limerick to Mr. Peel.

" 5, York Terrace, Regent's Park,
February 7, 1829.

" My dear Sir,

" Since the memorable winter of 1821-2, I have had the honour at various times, with the assistance of a near friend, to make communications to a part of His Majesty's Government, which I have understood were taken in good part, at which, I am certain, dissatisfaction was never expressed to me.

" In the present state of things it seems to me a matter of duty to declare that my political opinions are wholly unchanged. Towards my Roman Catholic fellow-subjects I have ever felt and acted with kindness and good-will; but my conviction is unalterable, that the worst consequences, civil and ecclesiastical, to England and to Ireland, must arise from admitting, under any modifications, the Roman Catholic body or any part of it to political power.

"It is my sober, settled persuasion, that however it may suspend for a time, concession will remove none of the existing evils, but will greatly aggravate them all; that it may possibly purchase the chance of a temporary calm, but with a certainty of growing and permanent troubles, involving consequences beyond human calculation or control, the melancholy commencement of which may not improbably be witnessed by the present generation.

"As an Irish Bishop, not privileged during the present Session to state my sentiments in Parliament, I trust you will excuse my thus discharging my conscience. Former communications, from a sense of delicacy, I studiously avoided addressing directly to you or to any of your colleagues, and used, therefore, the kind and prudent intervention of my friend Sir Robert Inglis. On the present occasion similar motives induce me to write directly; relinquishing, for obvious reasons, the advantage of previous communication with him.

"I cannot conclude without returning, as I beg leave most cordially to do, my grateful acknowledgments for all your personal kindness, especially for that shown and felt during my trying indisposition: at such times we can, perhaps, form the best judgment whether a man's heart be in the right place.

"I have the honour to be, &c.,

"John Limerick."

Mr. PEEL to the Bishop of LIMERICK.

"Whitehall, February 8, 1829.

"MY DEAR LORD,

"I beg to assure you with perfect sincerity, that no opinions that you can express to me, and no course of public conduct that you may feel yourself called on to take, can diminish the gratification that I shall have in hearing your sentiments, and still less my unaffected respect for your unblemished name and great acquirements.

"I am the last person to express surprise that you should apprehend danger from concession to the Roman Catholics; but I entreat you dispassionately to consider the facts I am about to recall to your notice, the prospect which there is of being enabled to maintain permanent resistance to concession, and the danger that concession may be forced upon us under circumstances much more unfavourable than the present.

"In the first place there has been a division between the House of Lords and the House of Commons on this subject that has now endured sixteen years.

"Secondly, It has been found necessary, in carrying on the Government of this country for the last twenty-five years, not to exclude from the councils of the King such men as Mr. Pitt, the late Lord Melville, Lord Castlereagh, and Mr. Canning. Their exclusion from the Government in times of pressing difficulty was impossible. Their admission into it produced disunion in the Cabinet, and tended to advance Roman Catholic interests. Their inability immediately to carry their views into effect made them probably more decided in their language as to the necessity of ultimately adopting those views.

" Thirdly, The opinions of the young men who are now entering into public life, and who are likely to distinguish themselves, are, with scarcely an exception, if with one, in favour of an adjustment of the question.

" Fourthly, In the course of the last six months, England, being at peace with the whole world, has had five-sixths of the infantry force of the United Kingdom occupied in maintaining the peace and in police duties in Ireland.   I consider the state of things which requires such an application of military force much worse than open rebellion.

" Fifthly, There has been established an intimate union between the Roman Catholic laity and the Roman Catholic priesthood : in consequence of that union the representation of the counties of Waterford, Monaghan, Clare, and Louth has been wrested from the hands of the natural aristocracy of those counties ; and if the present state of things is to continue, if parties in Parliament are to remain so nicely balanced that each can paralyse the other, that one can prevent concession, the other can prevent restraint and control, we must make up our minds to see sixty or seventy Radicals sent from Ireland when a General Election shall take place.

" Sixthly, The state of society in Ireland will soon become perfectly incompatible with trial by jury in any political cases.   The Roman Catholics have discovered their strength in respect to the elective franchise.   Let us beware that we do not teach them how easy it will be to paralyse the Government and the law, unless we are prepared to substitute some other system of criminal jurisprudence for the present system.

"If this be the state of things at present, let me implore you to consider what would be the condition of England in the event of war.

"Would an English Parliament tolerate for one moment a state of things in Ireland which would compel the appropriation of half her military force to protect or rather to control that exposed part of the Empire?

"Can we forget, in reviewing the history of Ireland, what happened in 1782, what happened in 1793? It is easy to blame the concessions that were then made, but they were not made without an intimate conviction of their absolute necessity in order to prevent greater dangers.

"My firm impression is that, unless an united Government takes the whole condition of Ireland into its consideration, and attempts to settle the Catholic Question, we must be prepared for the necessity of settling it at some future period in a manner neither safe to Protestant establishments, nor consistent with the dignity of the Crown of England.

"Remove the differences as to civil disabilities, and I think the Protestant mind will be united against Popery in a ten times greater degree than it is at present.

"Excuse the haste in which I am obliged to write on a subject of such vast importance.

"Believe me, &c.,

"ROBERT PEEL."

Bishop of LIMERICK to Mr. PEEL.

" February 11, 1829.

" MY DEAR SIR,

"I have reconsidered (for they were not new to me) all the arguments in your letter with the utmost calmness and deliberation in my power. The result has been an increased conviction, if possible, that infinitely more difficulties and dangers will attach to concession than to uncompromising resistance.

"That our state is most awful I cannot, if I would, conceal from myself. The Papists of Ireland indeed know their strength; but their chief strength lies, and they know that too, in the weakness of our Government. After a long period of misrule, with an appalling military force in the country, no substantive measure has been taken within the last six months of total anarchy against the agitators and against treason worse than open rebellion. On the contrary, the friends of the Constitution have been discountenanced almost as enemies,—its enemies encouraged altogether as friends; and, humanly speaking, under such a system nothing can save us.

" But my ultimate reliance is placed, where it cannot be shaken, in Divine Providence. I trust that all will yet be right; but, in the mean time, in defence of all that is dear to British Protestants, I am cheerfully prepared, if necessary, as others of my Order have formerly done, to lay down life itself.

" With every feeling of personal kindness,

" I have, &c.,

" JOHN LIMERICK."

Of opponents of another class equally determined with the Bishop to resist the measure of relief, but less charitably disposed towards its author, there were abundant examples among the constituent body whose confidence I had the misfortune to forfeit.

If it had been alleged against me that the sudden adoption of a different policy had proved the want of early sagacity and foresight on my part—if the charge had been that I had adhered with too much pertinacity to a hopeless cause—that I had permitted for too long a period the engagements of party or undue deference to the wishes of constituents to outweigh the accumulating evidence of an approaching necessity—if this had been the accusation against me, I might find it more difficult to give it a complete and decisive refutation.

But the charge preferred by those whose favour and goodwill I had forfeited was the opposite of this: it was that I had without any sufficient reason, nay that I had from pusillanimous and unworthy motives, counselled the abandonment of resistance, which it would have been easy, as well as wise, to continue unabated.

I must leave it to others to determine, after weighing the evidence which I have adduced, and that additional evidence to which the lapse of time will no doubt give access, whether, at the period that concession was determined on, the reasons in favour of concession as opposed to continued and uncompromising resistance did or did not preponderate.

Of my own motives and intentions I may be allowed to speak.

Pusillanimity—the want of moral courage—would

have prompted a very different course from that which I pursued. If I had been swayed by any unworthy fears— the fear of obloquy—the fear of responsibility—the fear of Parliamentary conflict—I might have concealed my real opinion—might have sheltered myself under the dishonest plea of a false consistency, and have gained the hollow applause which is lavished upon those who inflexibly adhere to an opinion once pronounced, though altered circumstances may justify and demand the modification or abandonment of it.

If I had been stimulated by personal ambition—that sort of ambition, I mean, which is content with the lead of a political party, and the possession of official power— I might have encouraged and deferred to the scruples of the Sovereign, and might have appealed to the religious feelings of the country to rally round the Throne for the maintenance of the Protestant religion, and the protection of the Royal conscience.

From the imputation of other motives still more unworthy, the documents I now produce will, I trust, suffice to protect my memory. I can with truth affirm, as I do solemnly affirm in the presence of Almighty God, " to whom all hearts be open, all desires known, and from whom no secrets are hid," that in advising and promoting the measures of 1829 I was swayed by no fear except the fear of public calamity, and that I acted throughout on a deep conviction that those measures were not only conducive to the general welfare, but that they had become imperatively necessary in order to avert from interests which had a special claim upon my support—the interests of the Church and of institutions

R 3

connected with the Church—an imminent and increasing danger.

It may be that I was unconsciously influenced by motives less perfectly pure and disinterested—by the secret satisfaction of being,

> " ——— when the waves went high,
> A daring pilot in extremity."

But at any rate it was no ignoble ambition which prompted me to bear the brunt of a desperate conflict, and at the same time to submit to the sacrifice of everything dear to a public man, excepting the approval of his own conscience, and the hope of ultimate justice.

ROBERT PEEL.

LONDON: PRINTED BY WILLIAM CLOWES AND SONS, STAMFORD STREET,
AND CHARING CROSS.

LaVergne, TN USA
09 December 2010
208043LV00004B/124/P